John Mountford

INSIGHT INTO ENGLISH SPELLING

Hodder & Stoughton
A MEMBER OF THE HODDER HEADLINE GROUP

Order queries: please contact Bookpoint Ltd, 39 Milton Park, Abingdon, Oxon OX14 4TD.
Telephone: (44) 01235 400414, Fax: (44) 01235 400454. Lines are open from 9.00–6.00, Monday to Saturday,
with a 24 hour message answering service. Email address: orders@bookpoint.co.uk

British Library Cataloguing in Publication Data
A catalogue record for this title is available from The British Library

ISBN 0340 63094 9

First published 1998
Impression number 10 9 8 7 6 5 4 3 2 1
Year   2003 2002 2001 2000 1999 1998

Typeset by Wearset, Boldon, Tyne and Wear.
Printed in Great Britain for Hodder & Stoughton Educational, a division of Hodder Headline Plc, 338
Euston Road, London NW1 3BH by Redwood Books, Trowbridge, Wiltshire.

Contents

To the Reader (and Writer)

Expertise
The expertise that this book is concerned with is expertise about the spelling system – knowing the structure of the spelling system and how it works. This expertise has its part to play in two other forms of expertise expected of teachers – expertise in spelling and expertise in teaching. Professionalism in the teaching of spelling requires all three. *An Insight into English Spelling* concentrates on the first, on the structure of the spelling system, as this is an area of expertise in which teachers have for a long time been seriously let down.

Insight
It's not a textbook. In it I am trying to stimulate insight into the spelling system. For most of us, good spellers and bad spellers alike, the spelling system is a very familiar thing, in use all day long as we read the English that's in front of us (books, newspapers, forms . . .) and the English that's around us (signs, advertisements, notices . . .), as well as in the English we write. That is insight no. 1: the spelling system is familiar and we use it both in reading and in writing. Insight no. 2 is that it is analysable.

Spelling analysis
Analysing words into letters yields no insight. It is analysis into morphemes and symbols that yields insight. Copying words, learning spellings by rote, covering and checking, looking up in the dictionary – these may all have some value, but they are all essentially non-analytic. In our spelling system, between the highest unit, the word, and the lowest unit, the letter, are the two 'hidden' units, the morpheme and the symbol. These enable us to analyse word-spellings and to build up a picture of the spelling system as a system.

Spelling improvement
Many able people, in all walks of life, are uncertain about their spelling. Confident spellers are often unaware how shaky their colleagues are, even about words like 'tomorrow' and 'across', let alone 'existence' or 'commitment' (see below). This is not a happy state of affairs. It starts in school – weak spellers self-protective, shy or on the defensive, strong spellers oblivious, helpless, or (worst of all) scornful. We can change it, if we begin, as a society, to *talk* about spelling.

Computers as a substitute for learning spelling are an educational nightmare; computers as an aid to learning spelling are an educational dream. But not without *talk*. Reading *Insight* will, I hope, help you towards an understanding of our spelling system; but – confident and unconfident alike – do *talk* as well. It is high time good spellers learned how to help weak spellers: *the spelling of a word is not just a sequence of letters*.

Structure of the book

Part One 'Junctions' (12 chapters) is about words and morphemes, with sounds very much in the background.
Part Two 'Symbols' (12 chapters) is about sound/symbol relations, with plenty of reference to individual sounds by means of a fairly homely notation for stating correspondences.
Part Three 'SOE' (6 chapters) is about the Standard Orthography of English (the world's most widely used writing-system), about two kinds of spelling error in SOE, and about the role of SOE throughout education and beyond.

This structure is best seen from the Contents pages, where the three Parts are set out by chapters, and the chapters are set out by sections. Most of the thirty chapters are quite short. I have included cross-references and repetitions so that readers can, within reason, enter at any chapter that catches their eye. The following list offers a foretaste of the book as a whole, and some possible points of entry into it.

Some Terms, Concepts, Instances and Ideas

Note Words in bold type refer to entries in this list. Sections in the book are referred to always by chapter-and-section numbers.

ACROSS   or, in notation, °across *accross: see 28.2.

ALPHABET   A hugely important concept in our **writing-system** (Chapters 26–7). I've made great use of alphabetical order because it's so helpful to readers.

CATEGORIES   I've used 'categories' especially in connection with the fundamental categories of **consonant** and **vowel**, which are applicable to **sounds, letters**, and **symbols** (14.1), and to **correspondences** (Chapters 23 and 24). (It can also be applied usefully to other fundamental binary or twofold classifications, such as **Content Words** and **Function Words**, or to plus-**junctions** and change-**junctions** – though there's nothing binary about the term 'category'.)

CIRCLET   A distinctive name for ° (raised circle or degree sign) which I've used to indicate **letters** as opposed to **sounds**. More generally, it indicates focus on spelling (see 2.3, 11.3). See also **Notations**.

CLASSIFICATION   I've printed 'structured classifications' at various points (3.4, 4.3) because genus and species, type and subtype, superordinate class and subordinate class are such important concepts in analysis, and they lend themselves to diagrams. (They are not the only such concepts. Whole and part or 'composition' is as important as classification (26.3). 'Constituency', drawing on one-member sets in set theory, is important in understanding language structure in general and the spelling system in particular (25.2). And counting (7.1, 13.3) is important!)

COMMITMENT or, in notation, °commitment *committment; see 28.3.

CONSONANT   See **categories**. Consonant entities are much more manageable than **vowel** entities (see 15.3, 20.4).

CONTENT WORDS   Nouns, verbs, adjectives, and (typical) adverbs. Sometimes called lexical words, full words, dictionary words. Contrast **Function Words**. See 16.2.

CORRESPONDENCES   I've expressed sound/symbol relationships in terms of correspondences (Ch. 15), always going from the **symbol**, which is a unit in the spelling, to the **sound**, which is a unit in the pronunciation. 'Hard C' and 'Soft C' are the names of two correspondences (15.3, 28.5), but there are plenty more (Chapters 23–24).

DICTIONARIES   Ordinary dictionaries are dictionaries of meanings. They give other information as well, including spellings. To use 'the dictionary' only for spellings is to throw away the grain in favour of the chaff. Words have senses, many of them many senses, which are detailed and described by our dictionaries. But the ordinary dictionary does not analyse spelling. Nor does a **reverse dictionary**.

EXISTENCE or, in notation, °existence *existance; see 29.1.

FUNCTION WORDS   Noun determiners, verb auxiliaries, pronouns, prepositions, conjunctions, particles. Sometimes called syntactic words, empty words, grammar words. Contrast **Content Words**. See 16.2.

GRAMMAR   I've treated the spelling system as part of the grammar of Standard English (Ch. 12). Words and morphemes are simultaneously grammatical units and spelling units; symbols and letters are purely spelling units. Together these four units offer an obvious point of entry, from below, into the grammar, complementary to entry 'from the top' (text analysis). The grammar of the spoken language can be entered by this route too – a route which became blocked in traditional grammar.

JUNCTIONS   °cats contains a plus-junction; °catty contains a change-junction. 'Junction' is just a superordinate term for a very simple classification of a basic feature of our spelling system. See 4.2 – or the whole of Part I from 2.4 on.

LETTERS   There are 26 letters in our spelling system. That is all I have dealt with. Capitalisation, apostrophes, hyphens must all be included in a wider view of the spelling system; they are certainly an important part of the total **writing-system** (see 27.4), as are acronyms and abbreviations. But I have concentrated on the spelling system constituted by the 26 letters, and on the core of that – a large enough topic. Part One can be read without radically adjusting your concept of 'letter' (see 5.1). In Part Two, be prepared for letters to be treated as the constituents of symbols: Single T in °cat is a symbol, Double T in °catty is a symbol; both symbols correspond to the sound /t/. This adjustment amounts to a reconceptualisation of 'letter' and of its role in the spelling system (see Chapters 13 and 25). It also enables us to think much more clearly about 'sound/symbol relations'. See **symbol**.

MORPHEMES   Analysing words into morphemes is the nettle that has to be grasped. Don't be intimidated by the term 'morpheme' (see 4.3–5, 19.3–4, 23.2). Morphemes are there for all to see: 'cat' is one morpheme, 'cats' is two. Dictionaries tend to make us think of 'cat' and 'cats' as "the same word", and rightly so from the dictionary point of view. But grammar can use 'word' in a different, more specific sense: it says firmly 'cat' is singular, 'cats' is plural – two different words sharing the morpheme 'cat' but distinguished by the morpheme '-s'. Every word consists of one or more morphemes. In extending this simple insight to all the words in the language, there are snags enough to deter the faint-hearted. But don't be [de[terr]ed]!

NOTATIONS   I've used two notations in this book. The first is a notation for units in the spelling system: it is signalled by **circlet** (see 2.3). The second is a notation for units in the **pronunciation** system: it is signalled by slant brackets or **obliques** (see 11.3).

OBLIQUES   Slant brackets /.../. These are a standard device for signalling phonemic notation and they ought to be much more widely known and used than at present. I've used them for **sounds** (phonemes, 14.2) and for syllables (units of rhythm, 14.4) – that is to say, for units in the phonology.

OUTLINES and PROFILES   These are notational devices for classifying and for generalising about words (and other units); so, for instance, [—] can stand for all words of one **morpheme**, and /–/ can stand for all words of one syllable (see 7.4). Profiles are enhanced outlines (see 14.3–4).

PRONUNCIATION   See 15.1 for the 'reference pronunciation' ('RefP') I've used; see 20.3 and 20.5 for the **notation**. Variety of pronunciation (the living word!) lies outside the scope of this book.

REVERSE DICTIONARY   An invaluable aid to exploring the **spelling system**. See 3.5 and 4.1 on *Walker's*.

SHWA and SHWI   These relate to two of the commonest vowel sounds in the pronunciation of English. See subsection on the minimal vowel in 20.6.

SOE   Short for the Standard Orthography of English, a name for our **writing-system**. See Chapter 27 and Part III generally.

SOUNDS   I've used 'sound' as a technical term instead of phoneme (see 14.1). For the sounds that I've used and for their **notations**, see 18.2 (brief) and Chapter 20 (very long).

SPELLING SYSTEM   Many people expect a book about the spelling system to be about the history of the system. This is an interesting topic in its own right, but this book has no historical axis. It's about the system which learners have to learn in becoming literate in English; that's not the history of the system, but the system itself. Another vital distinction is the distinction between the spelling system and the total **writing-system** of which it is part (see 26.3).

SYMBOLS   These are letters or groups of letters in the spelling that correspond to a sound in the pronunciation: °cat contains three symbols, so does °chat, so does °cheat. See Chapter 13 and Part II generally. (More technically, these are 'graphophonemic symbols, simple and complex', but I have not used these terms.) See also **letters**.

TOMORROW or, in notation, °tomorrow: see Chapter 2 and Section 28.2.

VOWEL   See **categories**. (See 20.4 for '**consonants** first' advice.)

WRITING-SYSTEM   Children learn figures as well as letters; they read them and they write them. We all do. They are part of our overall writing-system, along with punctuation and, of course, the spelling system (see 26.3). **SOE** is a name for our writing-system in its totality (see Chapter 27).

Acknowledgments

First and foremost my thanks go to Brenda and James at home, and then to Anna Clark and Lisa Hyde at Hodder and Stoughton, and to my editor Helen Skelton and to John Harris. Many other friends have helped in the course of the writing of this book; I think they will all take delight in my dedicating it to David Mackay, identified with *Breakthrough to Literacy* (see Chapter 30).

John Mountford
January 1998

Visiting Fellow
Centre for Language in Education
University of Southampton

PART

I

Junctions

CHAPTERS

1 Coming running

1.1 °coming or *comming?

Rather than start with 'cat', I will start with two longer words, prompted by a girl who pulled a long face at the mention of spelling. When I asked about her own spelling she told me that it was all right, but she did sometimes have trouble over 'double M's and things'. Further inquiry elicited a couple of examples of the trouble: words like 'coming' and 'running'.

The first thing to do is to put the two responses together. The only letter M that is a candidate for doubling is the one in 'coming'; 'running' is cited (I had no doubt) as an example of consonant-doubling. The problem lurking in the student's mind is 'Does "coming" go like "running"? Is it "comming"?'

Whether I've reconstructed this particular case rightly is immaterial. This student was having trouble with a very basic part of the spelling system, with a feature which recurs again and again in any text in English, including elementary texts. I asked her what she did about the problem, and she told me that when she found the right spelling for problem words, she made a note of it.

Now the problem of words like 'coming' and 'running' can be dealt with in a few sentences. Note that the student's technical description is confined to one feature, 'double M's' – a reference to consonant-doubling – whereas the examples she cites exemplify two features: consonant-doubling in 'running' and deletion of letter E in 'coming'. Both these features are basic to the spelling system: they both occur with common monosyllabic roots that are at the core of our vocabulary. They both occur when the very commonest suffixes are added to these roots, suffixes like '-ing'. Both features are rule-governed: in both cases the rule operates only when the suffix begins with a vowel-letter, as '-ing' does.

Consonant-doubling operates on roots like 'run' – for example, 'pad' 'step' 'slip' 'trot' 'strut'. The consonant/vowel distinction is at work inside these roots too, as well as in the suffix. I will give the details later, as well as the details regarding E-deletion (see Chapter 6).

For the moment, all I need say about E-deletion is that it operates only on final letter E. Obvious as that is, it's well worth stating. It means that E-deletion and consonant-doubling are mutually exclusive. These two features simply preclude each other. If you know how to spell 'come' and how to spell 'run' (and I think my student did), then the two spelling rules tell you, without fear of confusion, how to spell the derived forms. And the same applies to a host of other cases to which these two rules apply.

My talk with the student, however, was not an occasion for teaching linguistic facts about English, about its spelling system or any other aspect of its structure. It was rather one for gleaning linguistic facts of a different nature – psycholinguistic facts, for example about this girl's control of English spelling and her conception of the spelling system and how it is learnt. I asked her, accordingly, whether making a note of correct spellings did any good (I wondered how many times she'd made a note of 'coming'). I wasn't surprised when she pulled her long face again, and said 'No, not really'.

Now, I want to get on to the mundane linguistic facts which lie behind 'coming running', but I've related this episode because it is so revealing. E-deletion is by far the most active rule (save one) in English spelling. It applies to words used at the very beginning of literacy, and it never ceases to apply to new words entering our vocabulary at advanced stages of literacy: the same regularity is found in 'indicate/indicating' and in 'supererogate/supererogating' as is found in 'hate/hating', 'love/loving' or 'come/coming'. It is the most general rule (save one – see Section 3.4) that we have. If this rule eludes the learner, it is fairly safe to say that other rules will prove more elusive still. It needs to be learnt early to pave the way for other patterns of regularity. It is not surprising that it has traditionally formed part of what is taught in the Infant School.

The girl I was talking to had passed not merely through Infant School, but through Junior School, Secondary School and Sixth Form without learning it, *and* through one and a half years of a teacher-training course. In another year and a half, she would herself be teaching full-time. The level at which she would be teaching is immaterial, because it is evident from her story alone that, at all levels, children will be found who need to be taught the E-deletion rule. She, after all, was one of the ones who'd made the grade: she was in higher education; she was training to be a teacher. Yet she had not learnt a basic regularity about English spelling which belongs, with certain other basic regularities, to the curriculum of the Infant School – a regularity which concerns the same final letter E that Infant teachers introduce under the (quite suitable) guises of 'magic E', 'fairy E' and so on. She was, in fact, training to be an Infant teacher.

I have moved, in the last paragraph, from psycholinguistic facts about a particular individual to sociolinguistic facts about a system of education which has allowed certain aspects of the language of the curriculum (i.e. the language in which the curriculum is taught, and learnt) to be curiously neglected. But *An Insight into English Spelling* is not about psycho- or socio- aspects of

English spelling – it's about how the English spelling system works – '*centro*linguistic facts' (to coin a phrase) about how the spelling system works. And my point of entry into the spelling system is the fact that E-deletion and consonant-doubling are mutually exclusive.

1.2   About this book

'E-deletion and consonant-doubling are mutually exclusive.' This sounds rather like a theorem about English spelling. There is no harm in that, if it sets people thinking about how it might be proved or disproved – and the younger these people are, the better. I shall come back to it later on, by which time readers will be more familiar with the notion of 'spelling junctions'.

Before moving on, however, let me explain one or two things which have already cropped up. Section 1 of this chapter was headed:

°coming or *comming?

The circlet (°) flags a standard spelling; the asterisk (*) flags a non-standard spelling or a misspelling. I shall say more about these devices as we go on, especially about the circlet.

Circlet is the positive signal. It is the first step in a notation designed to make systematic exploration of English spelling a possibility for all learners, whether at school, out of school or beyond school – even well beyond.

'Systematic exploration' does not mean learning words in a certain order – quite the opposite. It means gradually making sense of the words you encounter and being ready to encounter as many as possible, perhaps for their own sake (because any aspect of language can be a realm of exploration in its own right), but first and foremost as a means of exploring the innumerable realms of human activity which compose our world.

And human activity is conducted paramountly (does that adverb exist?) in *talk*. The girl in the 'coming running' episode can't have talked about spelling (except perhaps to grieve) over all those years – fifteen long years. She used to 'make a note' of right spellings; she didn't *talk* about them or about her problems.

I doubt if that was her fault. In the first place there is a taboo about bad spelling which shuts people up. Good spellers in English are as much to blame for this as bad spellers – in fact, more so. In the second place the technical language most people have for talking about English spelling is not really technical at all. 'Double M's and things' is hardly a caricature of this language. Poor girl! Such unhappiness, such vagueness about the phenomena of E-deletion and consonant-doubling which are in front of her eyes every day of her life – ubiquitous, accessible and comprehensible.

But this book is not about social attitudes (encroaching on sociolinguistics) or about learners' difficulties (encroaching on psycholinguistics). As I said, its subject is centrolinguistic ('centrolinguistics' is more properly known as 'descriptive linguistics'): it offers a description of, or rather a way of talking about, and gaining insight into, the English spelling system.

You are using that spelling system now, as you read. If you weren't familiar with it, you wouldn't be able to read this book. This is a conceptual approach, one which needs thinking about. Thinking about spelling can begin very early if it is encouraged by *talk* – talk with teachers, talk with parents, talk with peers, with fellow-learners.

How old do you have to be to explain the deletion of °e in °coming – or why E-deletion and consonant-doubling are mutually exclusive?

2

°*tomorrow*
*(or *tommorrow and*
**tommorow and*
**tomorow)*

2.1   Spelling °tomorrow

Suppose the teacher meets the spelling *tommorrow. There's a letter too many, and he or she marks the mistake with an expulsion stroke through the first °m (='letter M'). What kind of experimentation – language exploration – can the pupil indulge in, if all he's got to do is drop the °m and write °tomorrow?

Well, what led him to make the mistake? And what is going to prevent him making it again? The simple memory of the correct spelling? The answer must go deeper than simple memory, for if mere exposure to standard spellings could do the trick there would have been no problem in the first place. The answer, for the pupil, lies in exploring the structure of the word °tomorrow; and for us it lies in studying his (or her) exploration.

Teacher: Do you know any words like 'tomorrow'?
Pupil: How do you mean 'like "tomorrow" '?
T: Well, words related to it – similar to it?
P: Do you mean rhyming?
T: No. Er – have you got a dictionary? No? Well, you'll find one in the library. Use a small one, and look up words beginning with the letters TO. Make a list of the ones which strike you as similar to 'tomorrow', and note those which seem to be like 'tomorrow' but which aren't. See what you can make of them.

P returns with a list consisting of:

today   tomato
together
tomorrow
towards

T: What's different about 'tomato'?
P: You can't split it up; it's all one piece.
T: Aren't the others all one piece? They're written as one piece.
P: But you can split off 'to-' at the beginning.
T: What, in all of them?
P: Yes. Well, I think so.
T: What do you mean – 'split off'? I can split off 'to-' in 'tomato', if I
        want to.
P: Yes, I know. But you're not left with anything. I mean, 'mato'
        doesn't mean anything on its own.
T: And 'day' does?
P: Yes, of course it does.
T: What about 'morrow', then?
P: Well . . .
T: How can you show me that 'today' consists of 'to' plus 'day'?
P: Well, 'day' is 'day', isn't it? I mean, it means 'day' like in 'today'.
        And 'to' . . . I don't know what 'to' means.
T: Do you know the word 'morrow'?
P: *(Uncertain)* Um . . .
T: Ever heard the expression 'Good morrow', like 'Good morning'? or
        'on the morrow', meaning 'next day'? 'On the morrow we took
        ship . . .'?
P: 'Gentlemen, I bid you good morrow!' That sort of thing?
T: That's it. You may not use it, but I bet you've heard it. You may
        even have sung it.
P: So 'tomorrow' is just like 'today' really?
T: Yes. And you didn't need me to prove it to you. What comes in
        between 'today' and 'tomorrow'?
P: Between 'today' and 'tomorrow'. . . ? Oh! Between 'today' and
        'tomorrow'! 'Tonight'!
T: I don't know how you missed that in your dictionary, but you did.
        Anyway, notice that you didn't really need your dictionary to think
        of it. Just use what's in your head already. What about '-wards' in
        'towards'? Can you throw any light on that?
P: Well, there's hospital wards . . .
T: Any connection?
P: No, I don't think so. What about westwards and eastwards?

T: Northwards and southwards. Excellent! Go on from there.

P: Downwards and upwards? Sidewards? No!

T: That's the way. Any more?

P: Outwards, inwards. Afterwards, beforewards – no! But 'afterwards', yes!

T: Yes. All these – 'out, in, down, up, after' – can replace 'to' in front of '-wards'. And there are others: what about 'backwards'?

P: And 'forwards'.

T: And 'London-wards'. No? Never heard it? No matter. There are various things to say about the pronunciation, and about the spelling; but you've got the idea. Now back to your list. Can you make anything of '-gether'?

P: *(Blank)*

T: What's it remind you of?

P: 'Gather'.

T: Any connection?

P: Not really.

T: Not really. Well, let's see. What's it mean, if you gather things? What do you do?

P: You bring them together – oh! *(Spots it for himself)*

T: See what I mean? Use the knowledge in your head. After all, it *is* yours. Make the most of it! Here's another example. Would you ever spell 'today' *(spelling it out)* T-O-D-D-A-Y?

P: *(Writing it up on the board)* No!

T: Why not?

P: Well, it's . . . it's . . . You just can't.

T: Why not? It's important to ask, because there's no more reason for spelling 'today' with two Ds than there is for spelling 'tomorrow' with two Ms. If, as you say, you can't double the D in 'today', then you can't double the M in 'tomorrow'. So you must ask yourself what prevents you from doubling the D. The answer's quite simple – so simple that people overlook it: we don't have doubled letters at the beginning of words in English.

    There's a hypothesis for you to go and test! You'll soon find counter-examples. But you can soon amend your hypothesis to take account of them. Right then! Plenty of doubled letters in English, but they don't occur at random. So when do they occur? Check on word-beginnings for a start. All you need is a dictionary. Or maybe just the knowledge in your head.

P: *(Turning back in the doorway)* But the D in 'today' wasn't at the beginning of the word.

T: No – you're right. Well, perhaps 'word' isn't quite the word we want. But it'll do for the present.

2.2   The role of talk

As I said in Chapter 1, we do not talk enough about English spelling.

I was prompted into 'Spelling °tomorrow' by a teaching episode I barely remember now except that the real participants were not school teacher and school pupil but myself and a college student, a girl training, like the student in 'Coming running' (Chapter 1), to be a teacher. The one thing I do remember vividly is that as she said 'You bring them together' she made a gathering motion with her arms. It was that involuntary gesture which clinched for her the identity of 'gather' and '-gether'.

Her awareness was gained in *talk* – gesture is one of the ingredients of talk which language has to do without in writing. Nevertheless, writing has resources of its own which make it the remarkable tool of mental advancement that it has proved to be down through human history. One of these resources is notation.

2.3   Notation

You might think of all writing as a form of notation, but I am using the term in a narrower sense to refer to special notations which are supplementary to ordinary orthography. Linguists, for example, use phonetic notation; this is something I shall avoid because this is not a book about how we speak but a book about the spelling system of English. I shall use notation, including a notation for sounds, but I shall keep it as simple as possible. The start I made with a notation in Chapter 1 was certainly simple, and I've used it in exactly the same way in the heading to this chapter.

circlet (°)	**asterisk (*)**
=standard spelling	=non-standard spelling or misspelling
°tomorrow	*tommorrow *tommorow *tomorow

In the teacher/pupil text itself, the circlet, which is simply the degree sign put to a new purpose, would have been very useful in order to cite words *with a focus on their spelling* (°tomato), to cite letter sequences (°to . . .) and to cite individual letters (°t °o).

In talking about language (whether in speech or in writing) we are constantly citing or quoting words. The first two lines of the dialogue illustrate this in a concentrated form. The teacher cites the word 'tomorrow' and the pupil then quotes the teacher's words: 'What do you mean – "like 'tomorrow' "?' But it's not this nesting of quote-marks within quote-marks that concerns me now so much as the variety of reasons for which we cite individual words. The pupil's question points to one aspect of that variety: 'Words like "tomorrow"?' In what way like 'tomorrow'? In sound, in rhythm, in number of syllables? In grammar, in meaning, in structure? In origin, in overtones, in everydayness?

This many-sidedness of words is one reason why it is good, in writing, to have a notation which signals 'focus on spelling'. It leaves quote-marks available for all those other purposes, and it 'specialises' spelling. Spelling is important enough, and interesting enough, to warrant its own notation.

Another reason is that individual words are not the only units we have to cite in talking or writing about spelling: we have to cite individual letters too. And the same device, the circlet, as you can see, comes in handy for this: read °m as 'letter M', °d as 'letter D', and so on. It's important to have a positive notation for the letters which is easy to do (especially on blackboards, OHPs and so on) and which is always the same whether in handwriting or in print. The full rationale for the circlet will emerge when we come to contrast letters and sounds (Section 11.3) and in dealing with other units of spelling besides words and letters.

So much, for the present, for notation – except that words and letters cited 'with focus on spelling' will always be in lower-case, never in upper-case (capitals). This is as much part of the notation as circlet itself and asterisk. I will permit myself the occasional capitalisation, for instance, for proper names: it helps identify them. And though proper names (despite the huge role they play in our lives) are not essential to this book, I shall not be able to resist °John and °Johnny, two words with unique spelling features (Section 15.5).

2.4   Learning from °tomorrow

What can we learn from 'Spelling °tomorrow'?

1   That °to and °morrow simply *join* to form °tomorrow. We can represent such a joining like this:

$$°to + morrow \rightarrow °tomorrow$$

We'll call this kind of joining a **plus-junction**.

2   That, whether you accept °morrow as a word in its own right or not, °tomorrow is analysable into °to- and °morrow. We know this from the existence of °today where there's no question about the status of °day (to say nothing of °tonight).

3   That °to- in °tomorrow is a **prefix**: it precedes the main portion of the word. It doesn't have a clear meaning of its own as a prefix, but it has a clear function, which is the same in °today, °tonight and °tomorrow. That function is to produce adverbs of time ('See you tonight' **adverb**; but also convertible to a **noun**, 'Tonight is OK' – but not an ordinary noun, because there's no plural 'tonights', though there is a possessive in 'tonight's schedule', 'today's news', 'tomorrow's leaders'). Note that the use of circlet can be stretched, for sheer convenience, where we are on the edge of spelling, and where quote-marks would be fiddly, as with °today, °tonight and °tomorrow in this paragraph.

4   That the misspelling *tommorrow is analysable as a **junction error**. It's turned a simple plus-junction into something more complicated by doubling the °m.

5   That from a spelling junction point of view, *tommorrow is the same kind of error as *todday or *tonnight. There is a regularity in the English spelling system which forbids all three.

2.5   Two kinds of spelling error

There are other things you can take up (creatively or critically) in the teacher/pupil piece itself, but let me revert to this chapter's subtitle. The second misspelling is *tommorow. This contains two errors: the first is a junction error, the second is not. There is no junction in °morrow, so there can be no junction error, any more than there can be one in °day or °night – or in °tomato which likewise contains no junction.

In a future chapter (Chapter 28) we shall see what this misspelling, *tommorow, has in common with the well-known misspellings *beggining and *dissapear, and also how it differs from these junctionally – that is, in the details of the junctions involved in °beginning and °disappear.

Finally, *tomorow: this contains only one error, and, in the light of the other two misspellings, we can see how credit is due to the speller for getting the plus-junction right!

3 °definitely

3.1 Ask the speller

The standard spelling is °definitely. The standard misspelling – if I may call it that – is *definately. Anyone can see what the mistake is: the letter before °t should be °i, not °a. It's a very simple matter, and can hardly give rise to a whole chapter. We shall see.

Ask the speller (in this case the misspeller) 'What's wrong with *definately?' – and be prepared for any of a wide range of answers:

from   'I shouldn't've put an E there, should I?' (*definatly)
or   'Is the E in the wrong place?' (*definatley)
to   'Oo, should it be double F?' (*deffinately).

Only by *talk* do we discover the individual learner's conceptions about spelling, and they are often as rudimentary and uncertain as these responses reveal.

This applies in Primary School – where 'coming' 'tomorrow' and 'definitely' first find their way from speech into writing – and it applies all the way up through education: remember that with all three words I am drawing on experiences at teacher-training level. Of the three words, °definitely has the richest structure and is the richest in the misconceptions it can reveal. That is why I have chosen it for close attention.

Of course, at the beginning of literacy, learners' conceptions about spelling are necessarily amorphous. They are going to be shaped into existence by a great deal of talk, with teachers especially, but also with parents, grandparents and other grown-ups and, one hopes, with other children. Five years later, ten years later, fifteen years later, we might expect education to have given all learners some common conceptual grip on such a key component of the curriculum.

This is not what we find. Ask the spellers, good or bad. The talk has died away.

Asking the speller is really a psycholinguistic inquiry, a probing of their spelling control, spelling conception, spelling history. This book is not about spellers (I'm sorry – they are much more interesting!), but about the spelling system – straight-down-the-middle 'centrolinguistics' of English. (On the opposite side, we would be veering into sociolinguistics – why, for instance, highly literate societies have highly standardised spelling systems.) It is time, then, to look closely at °definitely.

3.2   Plus-junctions in °definitely

The word 'definitely' is an **adverb**, formed in the regular way from the **adjective** 'definite'. The regular way is by means of the **suffix** '-ly'.

So much for the grammar, now for the spelling. Between °definite and °-ly there is a **plus-junction** (see Section 2.4): °definite does not change; °-ly does not change. They just join:

$$°definite + ly \rightarrow °definitely$$

There is nothing abstruse about this phenomenon. In fact, it is so plain and simple that it has been taken for granted in the past and gone unnamed. I call it a 'plus-junction' because it is purely additive: the letters on the left are joined to the letters on the right without any change on either side. What is more, the plus sign provides a convenient notation. We met it before in:

$$°to + morrow \rightarrow °tomorrow$$

I shall call such a statement, one with circlet, plus sign and arrow, a junction formula – a spelling junction formula. I shan't over-use this term, but I do want to emphasise that its purpose is to explicate, to unfold, the *spelling* of words, not their grammatical construction, even though we are always dealing with grammatical components such as prefixes and suffixes.

Here is another junction formula, this time involving a prefix:

$$°de + finitely \rightarrow °definitely$$

What this tells us is that at this particular junction no change takes place in the spelling on either side of the junction. We can combine it with the earlier formula involving the adverb suffix:

$$°de + finite + ly \rightarrow °definitely$$

I shall not make much use of such combined junction formulas, but this one serves a clear purpose: it brings out three components of the word °definitely, and it shows how simple the spelling phenomena are at the prefix boundary between °de- and °finite and at the suffix boundary between °finite and °-ly. They are both plus-junctions, the simplest kind of junction you could possibly have.

3.3   A change-junction in °definitely

From the point of view of grammar, we don't take the word °finitely and put the prefix °de- in front of it to produce °definitely: that would be, as linguists like to say, counter-intuitive. But there is nothing counter-intuitive about taking the word °definite and putting the suffix °-ly on the end of it to produce °definitely: that, as I said earlier, is a normal process of producing adverbs from adjectives.

With the adjective °definite in front of us it is easy to see another boundary between components, between the verb °define and the adjective suffix °-ite. There is the same verb/adjective relationship in °define/definite as there is in °compose/composite, °oppose/opposite. What we have established is a grammatical boundary within the word °definite, a second grammatical boundary:

°de | fin | ite

At each of these internal boundaries there is, in the written form of the word (which is what we are talking about, hence the rather liberal use of the circlet), a spelling junction.

At the first junction there's no change on either side; it is, as we have seen, a plus-junction:

°de + finite → °definite

At the second junction, there *is* change: °e is lost at the end of °define:

°define × ite → °definite

This is a **change-junction**. The change in the letters is exactly the same, before the same suffix, in:

°compose × ite → °composite
°oppose × ite → °opposite

and exactly the same, with a different suffix, as the change junction we met in Chapter 1:

$$°come \times ing \rightarrow °coming$$

E-Deletion, as I shall call it from now on (with a capital D), is by far the commonest form of change-junction in English. There will be much more to say about it as we go on. Back in Chapter 1, I coupled °come/coming with °run/running: the first is an example of E-Deletion, the second is an example of Consonant-Doubling (again note the capitalisation: this is now a technical term for us with a specialised meaning). Both are change-junctions, and we can notate them, as I have done, by a cross sign ($\times$) in contrast to the plus sign ($+$) of plus-junctions:

$$°come \times ing \rightarrow °coming \quad \text{(E-Deletion)}$$
$$°run \times ing \rightarrow °running \quad \text{(Consonant-Doubling)}$$

Our language and notation for talking about spelling are beginning to take shape.

3.4   The junction analysis of °definitely

The combined junction formula for °definitely would look like this:

$$°de + fine \times ite + ly \rightarrow °definitely$$

I am not fond of combined junction formulas (I'm not convinced that 'formula' is the best word, even for the very useful single junction formulas that I shall deploy throughout the next few chapters). But this one, which locates and classifies all three junctions in °definitely, is opportune at this point for two reasons.

In the first place, it displays the two kinds of spelling junction – plus and change. If all junctions in English were plus-junctions, I suppose we wouldn't need the concept of 'spelling junction'. But as it is, at every internal boundary created by the grammar there are, logically, two possibilities in the spelling system – *no* change in the letters on either side of the boundary, or *some* change; therefore the spelling junction is something distinct from the boundary. One can imagine a spelling system in which all junctions were plus-junctions; one can imagine, less easily, a spelling system in which all junctions were change-junctions. English has a spelling system with both kinds:

In the second place, °definitely happens to display two plus-junctions and one change-junction, and this can symbolise for us the preponderance of plus-junctions over change-junctions in our spelling system. In Chapter 1, I said that E-Deletion is the most general rule (save one) that we have. That reservation, 'save one', referred to plus-junctions. E-Deletion is easily the most common change-junction, but it is outnumbered – change-junctions as a whole are outnumbered – by plus-junctions.

Which is what one might expect: plus-junctions are the simplest possible junction and they predominate.

3.5   Adverbs

In terms of word-formation there are two kinds of adverbs in English: those that end in °-ly and those that don't.

Most of the ones that don't are simple, without either prefix or suffix, like 'soon' and 'fast' (there's no word 'fastly'). In Chapter 2, however, we came across a small group of adverbs of time which shared 'to-' as a prefix. There were only three of them ('together' makes a fourth adverb, but it's not an adverb of time); yet that was enough to establish 'to-' as a prefix.

In Section 3.3, I made a parallel between °define/definite, °compose/composite and °oppose/opposite. In fact, that's all the pairings there are which have exactly this pattern – but that's enough to establish it as a pattern.

Returning to adverbs – how many adverbs are there in English with the ending °-ly? Three? Thirty? Three hundred? No – the answer is between three and four *thousand*. You can count them for yourself in *Walker's Rhyming Dictionary*, which was also my source for the adjectives ending in °-ite (most of the words with °-ite as a suffix are names of explosives, like °dynamite).

The pupil in Chapter 2 was able to go away and look up words beginning with °to- in an ordinary dictionary; and that is fine for exploring prefixes. But in English, suffixes play a much larger role than prefixes: there are more of them and they form longer strings. Multiple suffixes are a feature of the grammatical structure of English words, for example:

$$1 \quad 2 \quad 3 \quad 4$$
educ | at | ion | al | ly

But how do you go about finding all the words which end in the same suffix, for example in °-ly? In an ordinary dictionary they are scattered throughout from °abdominally to °zymotically, each word being scanned, for alphabetisation, from left to right. Logically, then, all you need is a list of words scanned for alphabetisation from right to left:

°zymotically

°abdominally

°educationally

That's what *Walker's* gives you. It's a reverse dictionary: for adverbs ending in °-ly you can turn to all the words ending in °...y, and then, within those, still in alphabetical order, you find those ending in °...ly – some 4000 of them (but be warned – not all of them are adverbs).

You cannot explore English spelling systematically unless you are able to study words *en masse* as easily from the right-hand end, where most of the action is, as from the left-hand end. And yet, over many years, I have met only two teachers who knew of *Walker's Rhyming Dictionary*.

More about adverbs in a later chapter (Section 8.2); more about *Walker's* in the next chapter.

4 *De | fin | ite | ly*

4.1   *Walker's*: an appetiser

Of the two teachers of English mentioned in Chapter 3 who knew of *Walker's Rhyming Dictionary*, neither had ever used it in connection with their teaching in school. They are hardly to be blamed for this. They won't have found a copy in their classroom or in the school library; it won't have been mentioned in their teacher-training; they won't have been introduced to it when they were themselves at school.

Yet *Walker's* has been around for 200 years, probably never out of print, not unduly expensive – and quite fascinating. This is what it used to say on the dust-jacket:

WALKER'S RHYMING DICTIONARY OF THE ENGLISH LANGUAGE
The whole language arranged according to its terminations
For Poets • Songwriters • Crossword Enthusiasts

No mention of teachers.

That in itself is significant, at two levels. On the surface, you might expect teachers to be there at least on a par with the others, if not up front in larger type since there must be many more teachers than either poets or songwriters, or even crossword enthusiasts. But the significance at a deeper level is this. As I have said, if you are to study English spelling seriously, word-terminations must be as accessible to you as the word-beginnings which you can access through the normal forward dictionary. For decades *Walker's* has been the only reverse dictionary easily available, *but it hasn't been used by teachers*. If such an essential tool has not been used, then the question frames itself: Has the spelling system been systematically studied within the teaching profession? Have teachers been trained to teach it professionally?

Of course, in the 1990s, *Walker's*, always delightfully dated in content, now looks even more quaint beside computers and electronically created resources.

Don't let that stop you acquiring a copy of this historic book. Teachers should have been using it all along; and until handier means are available for studying, for example, all the regular adverbs in English, then *Walker's* rules! Where else will you find listed:

150 adverbs in °-ably	*e.g.* °suitably	°imperturbably
50 adverbs in °-ibly	terribly	ostensibly
50 adverbs in °-edly	hurriedly	contentedly
30 adverbs in °-idly	rapidly	pellucidly
20 adverbs in °-somely	handsomely	venturesomely
150 adverbs in °-ively	positively	corrosively
150 adverbs in °-ingly	seemingly	tantalisingly
50 adverbs in °-ishly	childishly	waspishly

and so on?

To explore the word-hoard of English at school, learners have always needed a dictionary. Enlightenment has added a thesaurus – traditionally it was Roget's. (But how many children get that far, when so many children do not get very far with the dictionary?) I would add a third basic aid – a reverse dictionary. And these three are only *aids* to exploration: they are not the exploration itself.

The three together are lexical aids to the exploration of the lexis, the word-hoard, or English. Part of that exploration (but only part) proceeds by way of mastery of the spelling system; and after this appetiser about *Walker's*, I must return to that central topic.

4.2   Prefixes, suffixes, and nuclei

In the last chapter (Chapter 3), which was all about the spelling of the word °definitely, we saw analysis at work. It took two forms:

1   Analysis, by breaking down the word into four grammatical components:

$$de \mid fin \mid ite \mid ly$$

2   Analysis, by classification of the three spelling junctions, one at each of the internal boundaries:

$$°de + fine \times ite + ly.$$

The technical terms I used in the analysis, apart from **word** and **letter**, were:

Grammar	**Spelling**
Adjective	Spelling junction
Adverb	Plus-junction
Prefix	Change-junction
Suffix	E-Deletion

We need to round these out.

On the spelling side, we already have a structured classification:

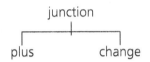

'(Spelling) junction' is the superordinate term. There are two subclasses of junction: every junction must be either plus or change. Next we need structured classifications on the grammar side.

'Adjective' and 'adverb' are traditionally subsumed under 'parts of speech', but there are other parts of speech, especially nouns and verbs, which I shall leave until later (Chapter 16).

As for 'prefix' and 'suffix', they are (names for) parts of words, and the superordinate term which embraces them both is 'affix':

'Prefix' is widely familiar as a grammatical term, but you meet it also in such diverse contexts as dog-shows and telephone numbers. Note that a *pre*fix *pre*cedes the main body of a word. 'Suffix' is less well-known. A *suf*fix *suc*ceeds the main body of a word – it 'comes after' as in 'successive wins', 'next in succession', 'succeeded to the throne'. 'Suffix' is not as transparent as 'prefix'; it is less used outside language study (though pedigree dogs can boast suffixes!) and within language, suffixes themselves lack the prominence that initial position in the word gives to prefixes. This is no excuse for overlooking them.

Still less must we overlook what I have been calling the 'main body' to which affixes are affixed, for example:

'sure' *in* unsure	*or*	'secure' *in* insecure
surely		securely
unsurely		insecurely

I shall call this main body a **nucleus**. A nucleus can, typically (but not always), exist on its own as a word, like 'sure' and 'secure'; affixes can't – they must be attached to a nucleus. The number of nuclei in English is enormous; the number of affixes is, in comparison, small. The lexis of English, the vast bulk of the words in the dictionary, is made up of nuclei either on their own or with affixes attached in the form of prefixes and suffixes.

Neither a normal forward dictionary nor a reverse dictionary assembles and arranges words by their nuclei. A nuclear dictionary might be a welcome fourth aid to lexical exploration. 'Nuclear power' with a difference!

4.3   Morphemes

We need a more general word still which will embrace all three constituent elements of 'unsurely' or of 'insecurely'. Both of these words consist of a prefix, a nucleus, and a suffix. The traditional term in linguistics for this more general concept is **morpheme**. The study of the morphemic make-up of words, as a branch of grammar, is called morphology. This term is used in other fields such as human morphology and geomorphology. Morphemes, however, are purely linguistic.

We now have a three-tiered structured classification for the constituent elements of words:

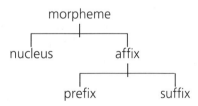

Every word in English is made up of morphemes. There may be only one morpheme, in which case it will be a nucleus without affixes. If there is more than one morpheme, it will be, typically, a single nucleus with one or more affixes: but there may be two nuclei as in words like 'football', often known as 'compound words'.

What has all this grammar got to do with spelling? Well, you can see straight away that the spelling junction in °football is a plus-junction. This regularity in English spelling is largely overlooked. Compound words are so common in English today that the plus-junctions they present are a good starting-point for the exploration of spelling. °football, °bedrock, °blackboard, °backside, °touchline – these five compound words all come from a very short article on coaching and each can be analysed into two morphemes and a plus-junction:

$$°\text{foot} + \text{ball} \quad \rightarrow °\text{football}$$
$$°\text{bed} + \text{rock} \quad \rightarrow °\text{bedrock}$$
$$°\text{black} + \text{board} \rightarrow °\text{blackboard}$$
$$°\text{back} + \text{side} \quad \rightarrow °\text{backside}$$
$$°\text{touch} + \text{line} \quad \rightarrow °\text{touchline}$$

The ten nuclear morphemes that result can take us a step further, into the spelling of plurals.

4.4   Plurals

Notice that all ten nuclear morphemes in those five words can be used as nouns, and note how many have what we can call 'plus-junction plurals':

$$°\text{bed} \quad + s \rightarrow °\text{beds}$$
$$°\text{black} \quad + s \rightarrow °\text{blacks}$$
$$°\text{back} \quad + s \rightarrow °\text{backs}$$
$$°\text{ball} \quad + s \rightarrow °\text{balls}$$
$$°\text{rock} \quad + s \rightarrow °\text{rocks}$$
$$°\text{board} + s \rightarrow °\text{boards}$$
$$°\text{side} \quad + s \rightarrow °\text{sides}$$
$$°\text{line} \quad + s \rightarrow °\text{lines}$$

Now have a look in a dictionary (an ordinary one) and, on some sample pages, see how many words listed are nouns – that is to say, the proportion of nouns to other parts of speech – and then note how many of those nouns take a plus-junction plural.

The great majority do. Of the minority that don't, most will take the S-morpheme but it will involve a change-junction, a change from °-s to °-es, as °touch does:

$$°\text{touch} \times s \rightarrow °\text{touches}$$

There's nothing irregular about this plural. The spelling system is accommodating the fact that the plural of 'touch' (one syllable) is 'touches' (two syllables); if you read over the eight plus-junction plurals in the list above you'll realise that both the singulars and the plurals are one syllable. Plurals like 'touches' are in a minority, but they are regular and rule-governed.

The plural of 'foot', on the other hand, is 'feet'. Plurals like this are irregular. The pattern 'foot/feet' is not unique (think of 'teeth' and 'geese'), but plurals without the S-morpheme number about a dozen in English, whereas plurals with the S-morpheme (°-s or °-es) run into tens of thousands.

Finally, some singular nouns do not have a plural – 'bedrock' doesn't seem to me to have a plural – though it may have for other people – but this is not a problem for the spelling system.

Nor is 'feet' a problem for the spelling system. From the point of view of grammar 'feet' can be analysed into two morphemes, 'foot' and 'PLURAL'. But the spelling system accommodates the fact that in the word 'feet' 'Plural' is not manifested as an affix but as a vowel change (we *could* write 'foots' and pronounce it 'feet'!). There is no *sequence* of morphemes in 'feet' and from the spelling point of view we can treat it as a single morpheme – a morpheme in the spelling structure. For the vast bulk of the language, morphemes in the spelling structure match the morphemes of grammar one-to-one; in irregular nouns like 'foot/feet' or (more numerous) irregular verbs like 'see/saw', 'sing/sang', 'speak/spoke', they do not – they match to the phonology (the pronunciation).

Before you put your dictionary away, take note that it does not treat 'bed' and 'beds' as separate words with separate entries: it treats them in one entry as two forms of the same word 'bed'. *They cannot be 'the same word' for us*: a word of two morphemes cannot be the same as a word of one morpheme. In spelling °beds we have to spell both morphemes.

4.5   Morphemic segmentation

Let's return to the adverb 'definitely'. What is its nucleus?

If every word consists of one or more morphemes, it must be possible to segment every word into morphemes. I have done this already for 'definitely':

$$\text{de} \mid \text{fin} \mid \text{ite} \mid \text{ly}$$

We can now add numbering (simple sequential numbering) and classification (classification into nucleus (N) and affixes (P = prefix, S = suffix)):

morpheme segmentation:	de	fin	ite	ly
morpheme numbering:	1	2	3	4
morpheme classification:	P	N	S	S

The question 'What is the nucleus of "definitely"?' seems to have been answered in advance: it is morpheme number 2.

From a grammatical point of view, that suffices. But our concern is with the spelling of that morpheme. There's no problem over the affixes: we can write or cite them as follows.

> No. 1   °de-   (the right-hand hyphen indicating a prefix)
> No. 3   °-ite   (the left-hand hyphen indicating a suffix)
> No. 4   °-ly   (the left-hand hyphen indicating a suffix)

How do we write or cite number 2? Do we write °fin or °fin- (as in °definite) or do we write °fine or perhaps °-fine (as in °define)?

Initially I shall opt for °fine. But I do not think that this morpheme, found in °define/definite/definition and °finite/infinite, is the same morpheme as °fine in °fine/finer/finest (of weather, goals and novels) or °fine in °fine/fines/fined (for motoring offences and overdue library books). Unlike these other two nuclear morphemes which happen to have the same spelling shape, I shall regard the morpheme °fine in °definitely as a nucleus that is not found as a word. So I shall put a hyphen on both sides of it and cite it as °-fine-.

A single hyphen to the left or right would make it look like an affix; but it is not an affix, it is a nucleus. It is, in fact, a 'lame' nucleus – it cannot stand on its own. Our language has quite a few such nuclei: think of °-mit- in °commitment, °-fess- in °profession, °-ceive- in °receive. In the lexis of English, however, lameness of this sort is no handicap: lame nuclei are often rich in the variety of affixes they take (see Section 9.3).

In the meantime the moral of this section is: don't be put off by doubts and details. The spelling of words is given you on the page. Every word can be analysed into morphemes. There may be only one morpheme – that makes it easy. Or there may be more than one. Segment as far as you can, then stop. Don't forget to *talk* – other people may segment differently!

In Chapter 1 we segmented °coming, and it is now time to return to that starting-point.

°*hoping and* °*hopping*

5.1   The importance of letters

Emma's difficulties described in Chapter 1 (I will call her Emma because of 'double M's and things') must have dated from her childhood. I wasn't able to delve into her spelling history, so I don't know to what extent it resembled that of another student (I will call her Pippa) who had also had trouble, as a child, with the word °coming. Her father had a friend called Mr Cummings. This did not help matters. She had to leave the whole matter conceptually unsorted until adult life, although, unlike Emma, she did master the standard spelling of °coming. This was after a tussle with °hoping.

The tussle ran something like this. 'If I take the E off "hope", I'm left with "hop-". Should I then double the P and write "hopping"? No, because that's what I would get if I started from "hop" itself. So I must write "hoping".' In some misty way the same thing applied to °come and produced °coming.

Notice first that Pippa carried on this form of argumentation with herself; like Emma, she didn't talk about spelling with other people.

Notice secondly that, though she may have been bothered by the sounds, she thinks only in terms of the letters. And as it happens, she was quite right to do so, because spelling junctions are a matter of letters, not of sounds. Let me explain.

In a verb like °hop, °p is doubled in the ING-form because it is a single consonant letter preceded by a single vowel letter:

$$°hop \times ing \rightarrow °hopping \qquad \text{(change-junction)}$$
$$°\text{CVC}$$

The same applies to the verb °skip:

$$°skip \times ing \rightarrow °skipping \qquad \text{(change-junction)}$$
$$°\text{CCVC}$$

But it does not apply to °jump:

°jump + ing → °jumping   (plus-junction)
°CV C C

nor to °leap:

°leap + ing → °leaping   (plus-junction)
°CVVC

The notation underneath °hop, °skip, °jump and °leap should be self-explanatory: °C (capital/upper-case) stands for consonant letter, and °V (capital/upper-case) stands for vowel letter. The resulting sequences of upper-case Cs and Vs give us **letter profiles** of the four words. It is the last three places in the profile that matter for Consonant-Doubling: they must be °CVC.

Later in this book (Chapter 12) we shall compare letter profiles with sound profiles, and the notation I am using is preparing the way for that: °C and °V (with circlet) indicating consonant letters and vowel letters, will contrast with /C/ and /V/ (with obliques) indicating consonant sounds and vowel sounds.

Notice that **letter** is taking on a more technical meaning: we can now see it as the superordinate term in a structured classification:

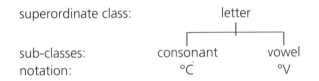

The classification and the notation make the meaning of 'consonant' and 'vowel' clear in this diagram, but in ordinary talk we have to be 100% sure that we know what 'consonant,' and 'vowel' refer to – to letters or to sounds. It is therefore best to use the full expressions, 'consonant letter' 'vowel letter' and 'consonant sound' 'vowel sound', whenever there can be the slightest doubt. In writing, we have the benefit of notation, which is at one and the same time economical and unequivocal.

I shall have more to say, in due course, about this classification of the letters (Section 18.6); like most apparently clear-cut divisions, it will need refining. But at this point we must concentrate on letter profiles.

5.2   The importance of letter profiles

Letter profiles underlie spelling junctions. We don't need the letter profile of the whole word, only of the bit near the boundary, that is the morpheme boundary between nucleus and suffix, as in:

$$°\text{rip} \times \text{ing} \rightarrow °\text{ripping}$$
$$°\text{trip} \times \text{ing} \rightarrow °\text{tripping}$$
$$°\text{strip} \times \text{ing} \rightarrow °\text{stripping}$$
$$°\text{CVC}$$

What matters is the °CVC at the end of all three nuclei. We can notate this ending as °...CVC, the dots indicating that other letters may come in front.

Consonant-Doubling, while it applies with great regularity, is a highly restricted change-junction: it only applies to nuclei, and it only applies to nuclei of one syllable, which are usually free-standing nuclei like °hop °skip and °run. This makes it sound so hedged about as to be worthless, but English is famous for its 'monosyllables' and these words ending in °...CVC are among the most typical 'monosyllables'. The significance of the dots in the generalised profile °...CVC is that Consonant-Doubling is not confined to words of three letters like °rip and °hop. We can make the generalised profile more informative by writing it with two optional consonant places indicated by round brackets: °(C)(C)CVC (a cluster of three consonant letters is as many as you will ever find at the beginning of such words). This allows just three possible profiles:

$$°\text{CVC} \qquad °\text{CCVC} \qquad °\text{CCCVC}$$

and 'monosyllables' (monosyllabic nuclei) ending in °...CVC can all be classified by letter profile under these three headings.

They will be outnumbered, however, by the no less typical monosyllabic nuclei ending in °...VCC (like °jump in Section 5.1) and °...VVC (like °leap in Section 5.1). These will include three-letter words like °end and °eat, four-letter words like °bend and °beat, five-letter words like °blend and °bleat, and six-letter words like °sprint °spring and °scream °shriek. (Remember, these are *letter* profiles.) All these words, if they take the suffix °-ing, will take it with a plus-junction.

°...VCC	°...VVC
°end + ing → °ending	°eat + ing → °eating
°bend + ing → °bending	°beat + ing → °beating
°blend + ing → °blending	°bleat + ing → °bleating
°sprint + ing → °sprinting	°scream + ing → °screaming
°spring + ing → °springing	°shriek + ing → °shrieking

(For those who don't like loose ends, let me add that the column on the left could be headed just °...CC, as that is all that is required to block the doubling of the final consonant; the third letter back can then be °V, as in the column, or

°C, as in °lunch, °flinch, °branch. In the column on the right, of course, the third letter back *is* required: it must be °V, or we would have °. . .CVC and a change-junction.)

5.3   The importance of the letter categories °C and °V

With **consonant letter** (°C) and **vowel letter** (°V) in place, our terminology and notation have reached an important point: we are properly equipped to talk about spelling junctions. Sound/symbol relations are still out of range, but we are moving towards them (we will reach them in Part II).

There is a sense in which we have been able to talk about spelling junctions ever since Chapter 1. Right back in Section 1.1 I used the argument that E-Deletion and Consonant-Doubling are mutually exclusive. We do not need the details about these two change-junctions in order to be convinced of this. All we need as an explicit argument is something along the following lines.

'Consonant-Doubling operates only on a final consonant-letter, while E-Deletion operates only on a final °e. °e is a vowel letter. If the final letter of a word is a consonant letter, it cannot be °e; if the final letter of a word is °e, it cannot be a consonant letter. E-Deletion and Consonant-Doubling are mutually exclusive. QED.'

In Section 1.1 I described both features, or change-junctions as I can now call them, as rule-governed and I promised to give details about how the consonant/vowel distinction operated in the two cases. In the last section (5.2) I gave details about the letter profile to which a final consonant must belong if it is to undergo doubling. It involves the preceding letter, which must be °V (a vowel letter), and the letter preceding that, which must be °C (a consonant letter). In short, the profile must be °. . .CVC, if the final consonant is to be liable to doubling.

E-Deletion is simpler. Only one letter, the immediately preceding letter, is involved: it must be °C. We can state the profile as °. . .Ce, where the upper-case character stands for the class of consonant letters, and the lower-case character stands for the specific vowel letter. In words ending in this profile, °e is liable to deletion.

I have been careful to say 'liable to doubling' and 'liable to deletion'. There is a parallelism about these two change-junctions, which I referred to in Section 1.1 when I said: 'Both features are rule-governed: in both cases the rule operates only when the suffix begins with a vowel-letter, as "-ing" does.'

What this means is that, in addition to the letter profile on the left-hand side of the junction, the letter profile on the right-hand side has to be taken into account. If the suffix begins with a vowel-letter, then the change-junction is triggered:

$$°hope × ing → °hoping \qquad (change\text{-}junction)$$
$$°cvce \quad °vcc$$

$$°hop × ing → °hopping \qquad (change\text{-}junction)$$
$$°cvc \quad °vcc$$

If it begins with a consonant-letter, however, no change takes place. Hence:

$$°hope + s → °hopes \qquad (plus\text{-}junction)$$
$$°cvce \quad °c$$

$$°hope + ful → °hopeful \qquad (plus\text{-}junction)$$
$$°cvce \quad °cvc$$

$$°hop + s → °hops \qquad (plus\text{-}junction)$$
$$°cvc \quad °c$$

$$°come + s → °comes \qquad (plus\text{-}junction)$$
$$°cvce \quad °c$$

There are no such words as 'hopful' or 'comeful'. This points to an underlying difference between suffixes such as °-s and °-ing on the one hand, and suffixes such as °-ful on the other (see Section 8.2). But it is not a difference which affects the spelling junctions: on the right-hand side of the junction it is simply the **letter category**, °C or °V, of the first letter, that matters. That letter, the right-hand letter, may constitute the whole of the suffix: °-s is a **consonant suffix**, just like °-ful. And in °shine/shining °shine/shiny, °-y is just as much a **vowel suffix** as °-ing (see Section 11.5).

But before we look more closely at suffixes and the right-hand side of junctions, we have to complete the picture of what happens on the left-hand side. The left-hand side is much the more important of the two. It is the site of the three core change-junctions (which will occupy us until Chapter 9): they all affect the left-hand letter. Two of these three changes are already familiar – E-Deletion and Consonant-Doubling. The third is called Y-Replacement. It concerns °y as a vowel letter.

If °y as a vowel suffix took you by surprise just now, was it because it was a suffix all on its own (a single-letter suffix, like °-s), or was it because it was a vowel letter? Or both?

6 *Two core change-junctions*

6.1   °drop/dropping/dropped

' "Dropped",,' he asked, 'Is it D-R-O-P-P-E-D, or is it D-R-O-P-E-D? I've put D-R-O-P-P-E-D; that's what I've written, look; but I think it may be D-R-O-P-E-D.'

He was spelling the word out loud and was genuinely anxious, but at least he was consulting someone. The teacher looked and ticked °dropped. Anxiety subsided. Writing continued.

Spelling out the letters twice over is not the best way of checking on alternative spellings, though it's one we often resort to (perhaps we learnt it in school). The 'problem point' has to be located by the difference between the two alternatives (which can be highlighted by the voice). But in this case I think there was a tacit understanding between teacher and taught that the trouble would be at the point where °drop (no problem) and °-ed (no problem) met.

An older learner might ask: 'Is it double P in "dropped"?' To which a teacher (or another learner) might reply: 'Well, how do you spell "dropping"?' And the chances are that there would be no difficulty over °dropping; °p would be doubled without a second thought.

We have now reached the point where we can state Consonant-Doubling as a rule (given the restriction to 'monosyllables'):

> **Consonant-Doubling** affects a **Terminal Consonant** by doubling it before V-suffixes but not before C-suffixes.

'Terminal Consonant' is another technical term: it's a quick way of referring to the final consonant of words that end with the letter-profile °...CVC, as discussed in Chapter 5. In a moment I shall handle 'Terminal-E' in the same way, since E-Deletion and Consonant-Doubling are closely parallel to each other.

But first let's look at the smaller-scale parallel between °dropping and °dropped:

°drop × ing → °dropping   (Consonant-Doubling)
°drop × ed → °dropped   (Consonant-Doubling)

Both °-ing and °-ed are V-suffixes (suffixes beginning with a vowel letter); therefore °p will be doubled in both cases.

As I said in Section 5.2, letter profiles underlie spelling junctions: if °dropping, then °dropped. Both suffixes begin with a vowel letter, and this, given the profile °...CVC in the nucleus, will trigger the change-junction. So why is it that, for some spellers, °dropped is a problem while °dropping isn't?

Pippa had the right idea in Section 5.1: 'spelling junctions are a matter of letters not of sounds'. The word 'drop' is one syllable; the word 'dropping' is two syllables – which is what you would expect since the suffix '-ing' is also a syllable. We can notate this with the help of 'rhythmic outlines':

Word	Rhythmic outline
drop	/–/
dropping	/– –/

All this does is to display in notation the number of syllables in the two words. The notation, as you can see, is very simple. The slant brackets are the same as those used for notating sounds (for instance, /p/ is the sound of °p in °drop, and of °pp in °dropping). They are used here because rhythm is part of the sound structure, and syllables are the basic units of rhythm.

Now contrast 'drop/dropping' with 'drop/dropped':

Word	Rhythmic outline
drop	/–/
dropped	/–/

While the letter process has been exactly the same, the sound process is at odds with it. There is no second syllable, even though '-ed' would seem to be as much a syllable as '-ing' is. The suffixed form is a 'monosyllable'. Not only that: the suffixed form, which consists of two morphemes (the nucleus 'drop', and the suffix '-ed') rhymes with 'opt', which is a simple nucleus. What has happened to '-ed'?

Its pronunciation has been reduced from a syllable to a single sound or phoneme: /t/. This is rule-governed, too, and we shall look at the pronunciation phenomena relating to '-ed' in Section 17.3. At present it is the rules governing the spelling which concern us, and they are much simpler. The boy who asks the question about 'dropped' has been drawn into uncertainty by the pronunciation – not the pronunciation of the nucleus 'drop' but of the suffix '-ed'. I shall call him Eddie: for it is important to note that, despite the pronunciation, he has no uncertainty about the spelling of '-ed': in both alternatives he gives it as °-ed ('letters ED'). He has the same intuitions as Pippa.

'-ed' and '-ing' are not merely parallel in being suffixes that begin with a vowel letter: they are both **verb inflections**. And that is our starting point for the three core change-junctions, of which the first two are E-Deletion and Consonant-Doubling.

6.2 E-Deletion and Consonant-Doubling

Inflections are a small subset of the suffixes of English which have a special role in the grammar in connection with the three main word classes (parts of speech) – nouns, verbs and adjectives. The verb has four forms – a base form (uninflected) and three inflected forms (each of these is a distinct word, see Sections 16.3 and also 4.4). I will revert to the verb 'to hop', and revert also to the circlet, now that spelling is fully in focus:

Uninflected:	°hop	Base form
	°hops	S-form
Inflected:	°hopping	ING-form
	°hopped	ED-form

In accordance with the rule stated in Section 6.1, we find a plus-junction in the S-form (since °s is a consonant letter, and the suffix °-s is therefore a C-suffix), and change-junctions in the ING-form and the ED-form.

The E-Deletion rule is exactly parallel to the Consonant-Doubling rule:

E-Deletion affects **Terminal-E** by deleting it before V-suffixes but not before C-suffixes.

'Terminal-E' is a technical term: it is a quick way of referring to a final °e which is immediately preceded by a consonant letter (or, using the notation developed for Consonant-Doubling: a final °e in a letter profile ending in °...Ce). For example:

°hope + s	→ °hopes	°site + s → °sites
°hope × ing	→ °hoping	°site × ing → °siting
°hope × ed	→ °hoped	°site × ed → °sited
°home + s	→ °homes	°side + s → °sides
°home × ing	→ °homing	°side × ing → °siding
°home × ed	→ °homed	°side × ed → °sided

The spelling phenomena, in terms of junctions, require no comment. But let me explain my choice of examples. °hope/hoped is like°drop/dropped in rhythm (see Section 6.1):

°hope	/–/		°drop	/–/
°hoped	/–/		°dropped	/–/

The final sound is the same, too: /t/. °home/homed is similar:

°home	/–/
°homed	/–/

Both the base-form and the ED-form are one syllable, but the final sound is /d/, not /t/ (note the association between these two sounds). °site and °side are different:

°site	/–/		°side	/–/
°sited	/– –/		°sided	/– –/

In these two examples the °-ed suffix is pronounced (as you might expect it always to be pronounced) as a syllable. This is because of the /t/ already in °site and the /d/ already in °side: you cannot pronounce either °sited or °sided as a single syllable. (Again the association between the sounds /t/ and /d/ should be noted. Table 20.4 is relevant.) In the case of °hoped and °homed you can happily pronounce them as one syllable, so you do. And you do the same with all the other consonant sounds at the ends of verbs, except /t/ and /d/.

All this is to do with the sounds. The spelling processes are unaffected. They are unaffected, too, by the difference in pronunciation between °home (same vowel sound as in °hope) and °come (same vowel sound as in °hum).

°home + s	→ °homes		°come + s	→ °comes
°home × ing	→ °homing		°come × ing	→ °coming
°home × ed	→ °homed		(°come & PAST	→ °came)

The letter profiles – the letter categories of consonant and vowel and the configurations of those categories – are all that counts. Here, to end with, is a regular verb that, for its vowel, has the same sound/symbol features as °come:

°love + s	→ °loves		°come + s	→ °comes
°love × ing	→ °loving		°come × ing	→ °coming
°love × ed	→ °loved		(°come & PAST	→ °came)

While the forms of 'come' are in front of us, it is worth pointing out that irregular verbs in English (of which there are about 200) are irregular in respect of the 'past' form (see °came); all verbs, regular and irregular alike, take the S-form and the ING-form in the same uniform way. (Like most statements about language, this will have to be modified as more detail is added, but it's a good generalisation to start with. There are, incidentally, some 10,000 regular verbs, in case you are wondering.)

We will now look at nouns and adjectives.

6.3   Further evidence

Verbs have three inflected forms, and the three inflections happen to include one beginning with a consonant letter (a C-suffix) and two beginning with vowel letters (V-suffixes). This enabled us to see the role of the right-hand letter at the junction, triggering or not triggering change.

Before we go on to nouns and adjectives, it is wise to remember that the general pattern at spelling junctions is no-change. Plus-junctions predominate. We are dealing now only with two terminal profiles: °...Ce (Terminal-E) and °...CVC (Terminal-Consonant). And so far we only have evidence on these two cases from monosyllabic verbs.

Nouns and adjectives together provide confirmation of the picture derived from verbs. Nouns have only one inflection, the plural S-inflection as in °cat/cats (I am ignoring the possessive inflection with its apostrophe). This is a C-suffix. Adjectives have two inflections, the comparative ER-inflection and the superlative EST-inflection as in black/blacker/blackest. These are V-suffixes. The spelling junctions that result are in accordance with the E-Deletion rule and the Consonant-Doubling rule formulated earlier in this chapter. For example:

	Terminal-E	Terminal-Consonant	Junction type
Noun pl.	°crime + s → °crimes	°shot + s → °shots	+
Adj. comp.	°crude × er → °cruder	°hot × er → °hotter	×
Adj. sup.	°crude × est → °crudest	°hot × est → °hottest	×

I have chosen (or tried to choose, for it's not easy with English monosyllabic nuclei) two nouns which can't be adjectives and two adjectives which can't be nouns. There's no need to, of course. Hundreds of 'monosyllables' can be substituted for these four, and some will be found to take verb inflections as well – for instance:

	Terminal-E	Terminal-Consonant	Junction type
Noun pl.	°fine + s → °fines	°fit + s → °fits	+
Adj. comp.	°fine × er → °finer	°fit × er → °fitter	×
Adj. sup.	°fine × est → °finest	°fit × est → °fittest	×
Vb -s	°fine + s → °fines	°fit + s → °fits	+
Vb -ing	°fine × ing→ °fining	°fit × ing→ °fitting	×
Vb -ed	°fine × ed → °fined	°fit × ed → °fitted	×

You may protest that, whereas 'fit' can be regarded as the same nuclear morpheme throughout, 'fine' is two (the noun/verb versus the adjective). I would accept this, and invite you to hunt for another word to fill the bill. But what difference does it make to the patterning of the spelling junctions? None.

In the next chapter we gain more evidence of the role of letters, from the third, and last, of the core change-junctions.

7 The third core change-junction

7.1 The 'arithmetic' of change-junctions

Eddie's trouble was a passing uncertainty over the Consonant-Doubling in °dropped; he had the right spelling but he couldn't have said why (he was nine years old at the time). Pippa also had the right spelling for °hoping and °hopping, but she had learnt them the hard way, by some kind of rote. Emma's trouble went deeper: she was still at sea with °coming – and she was nineteen. All three may have passed through a phase, which must afflict some children, when two aspects of early literacy, each with its own demands, are in conflict.

Letters are very countable things. Yet we don't make a special effort to encourage children to count letters in words. This reluctance may not be to their advantage in the long term. Certainly, in the short term, one instructive way of exploring short words is to keep the letter counts constant and to vary profiles against it, especially letter-category profiles (C/V profiles), as in Lewis Carroll's game of word-chains.

One reason why we don't encourage the counting of letters could be that they don't always add up: change-junctions, as it were, spoil the arithmetic. They don't, of course, contravene it; they just make one application of it more complicated at what may be a crucial moment in a child's engagement with literacy and numeracy.

Plus-junctions are purely additive:

$$\begin{array}{ccccc} 1234 & & 123 & & 1234567 \\ \text{°jump} & + & \text{ing} & \to & \text{°jumping} \\ 4 & + & 3 & = & 7 \end{array}$$

But the two change-junctions that we have looked at so far are, on the surface, very odd, not to say perverse:

```
1234    123     123456              123    123    1234567
°hope × ing → °hoping              °hop × ing → °hopping
   4  &  3  →    6                   3  &  3  →     7
```

Four letters and three letters 'make' six letters; three letters and three letters 'make' seven letters. That is, if you don't look at them as change-junctions, in which E-Deletion entails the subtraction of one letter, and Doubling entails the addition of one letter. And these curiosities may be encountered at a time when horizontal sums, of the $4 + 3 = 7$ sort, are also being mastered.

Whether or not confusion occurs in this way, we mustn't overlook the fact that the figures and operators of mathematics are black marks that we read and write, and that we read and write them, like the letters, from left to right, not from right to left, and down the page, not up. Figures and letters both belong to one writing-system, and children meet them simultaneously.

7.2   Y-Replacement in monosyllables

But what concerns us now is not the writing-system as a whole (which embraces not only figures but also punctuation and other black marks – see Chapter 27), but the spelling system, that enables us to get *words* on and off the page. Words have grammatical structure. As we saw in Chapter 4, they may be one morpheme long (°cat), or more than one morpheme long (°cats); and where they are more than one morpheme long we have one or more spelling junctions, one at each internal morpheme-boundary (or, algebraically: for n morphemes, there are $n - 1$ junctions).

We must never forget that the majority of spelling junctions are plus-junctions – the simplest possible kind of junction. Plus-junctions are additive and they leave unchanged the number of letters in the morphemes that are joined.

The third core change-junction, which completes the change-junctions operating before inflections, also leaves the number of letters unchanged – the number, but not the identity. It affects Terminal-Y (°...Cy – final °y following a consonant). It does not decrease the number of letters by removing one letter, as E-Deletion does; it does not increase the number of letters by insertion of one letter, as Consonant-Doubling does. What it does is to remove one letter and insert another letter in its place. It replaces °y by °i:

```
°cry × ed → °cried          °dry × ed  → °dried
°try × ed → °tried          °dry × er  → °drier
°ply × ed → °plied          °dry × est → °driest
```

In these examples we see Y-Replacement operating before the three vowel-inflections which begin with °e – four verbs taking °-ed, and one adjective taking °-er and °-est. Y-Replacement also operates before the S-inflection, but the S-inflection itself also changes, from a Consonant-suffix (°-s) into a Vowel-suffix (°-es), so the number of letters changes too:

$$
\begin{array}{ccc}
123 & 1 & 12345 \\
°cr\,y & \times\ s & \rightarrow °cr\,i\,e\,s \\
3 & \&\,1\rightarrow & 5
\end{array}
$$

Y-Replacement doesn't operate before °-ing: a plus-junction avoids adjacent °i's:

$$°cry + ing \rightarrow °crying$$

With this and earlier counter-examples, is the evidence for this third core change-junction getting a bit thin? After all, there are very few verbs like °cry (monosyllabic and ending in °. . .Cy – I can't include °fly, as it's irregular), and there are even fewer adjectives like °dry – and they often show plus-junctions anyway (in the alternative spellings °shyer °shyest °spryer °spryest, even °dryer °dryest)!

In fact, there is overwhelming evidence for this change-junction but we need to go beyond 'monosyllables' to find it in full strength.

7.3   Terminal-Y: First extension

°y is a much misunderstood letter.

An ordinary dictionary will list about 125 words beginning with °y. The list of words *ending* in °y in *Walker's Rhyming Dictionary* (see Section 4.1) occupies 80 pages. That's one-seventh of the whole dictionary – about 8000 words. You can guess which letter exceeds this: it's °e, with over 11,000 words, which is approaching one-fifth of the total. Between them, these two final letters account for one-third of the 54,000 words in the reverse dictionary.

In this section I only want to take a small step towards an understanding of the unique role and behaviour of °y.

There are very few monosyllables with °y as final letter following a consonant, or Terminal-Y as I called it in the last section. But if we move to words of two syllables we find plenty of support for the pattern of Y-Replacement before inflections beginning with °e.

To begin with verbs, here's a small sample:

	Rhythmic outline
°carry × ed → °carried	/– –/
°copy × ed → °copied	/– –/
°rally × ed → °rallied	/– –/
°tidy × ed → °tidied	/– –/
°weary × ed → °wearied	/– –/

Before I go on to two-syllable adjectives, note how tightly controlled the verb examples are, in two distinct ways.

First of all, they conform not only to the rhythmic *outline* of two syllables /– –/, but also to the rhythmic *profile* of two syllables with stress on the first syllable, notated as follows:

	Rhythmic profile
°carry × ed → °carried	/⁄ –/
°copy × ed → °copied	/⁄ –/
°rally × ed → °rallied	/⁄ –/
°tidy × ed → °tidied	/⁄ –/
°weary × ed → °wearied	/⁄ –/

You will come across a few verbs with the complementary rhythmic profile /– ⁄/, like °deny °rely: they also show Y-Replacement. But the typical pattern, as we shall see, is one in which the final syllable is unstressed. This is a *phonological* feature of these words – that is to say, it is to do with their sound structure and pronunciation.

The second control is a *grammatical* one, to do with their structure in terms of morphemes. Each of the words, though it contains two *syllables*, contains only one *morpheme* (the converse of °dropped in Section 6.1: one syllable, two morphemes). This point will become clearer in the light of the adjective examples which follow.

These adjectives (a small sample of six: °happy, °busy, °clumsy, °pretty, °tidy, °weary) are all two-syllable/one-morpheme adjectives ('disyllabic monomorphemes' in more jargonistic terminology). Our interest in them in this section is primarily that they show Y-Replacement in the comparative and the superlative:

Comparative	**Superlative**
°happy × er → °happier	°happy × est → °happiest
°busy × er → °busier	°busy × est → °busiest
°clumsy × er → °clumsier	°clumsy × est → °clumsiest
°pretty × er → °prettier	°pretty × est → °prettiest
°tidy × er → °tidier	°tidy × est → °tidiest
°weary × er → °wearier	°weary × est → °weariest

For these disyllabic adjectives there are no alternative plus-junction forms (*happyer *happyest) as there are in the case of the monosyllabic adjectives like °dry.

7.4 'Monosyllables'

I called the last section 'Terminal-Y: First extension', because there is another extension to come in Chapter 8. I said that °y is much misunderstood letter; perhaps I ought to say that it is a much underrated letter. We shall see.

Now is the right moment to pause over the term 'monosyllable'. I have tended to use it with quote-marks round it. Why? Because it is of fundamental importance to distinguish between syllables and morphemes (see Chapter 19).

To people in general, syllables are familiar, morphemes aren't. The simplest way of contrasting them is to give examples with a distinctive notation for each.

Word	Syllable structure		Morpheme structure	
°cat	/–/	1 syllable	[cat]	1 morpheme
°cats	/–/	1 syllable	[cat]s]	2 morphemes
°happy	/– –/	2 syllables	[happy]	1 morpheme
°catty	/– –/	2 syllables	[catt]y]	2 morphemes

On this simple basis, and with this simple notation, we can launch ourselves into the ocean of longer words that awaits us – and remain afloat!

'Monosyllables', by contrast, is a leaky term. By itself, it says nothing about morphemic structure, so it fails to distinguish between pairs of monosyllables like °lens (1 morpheme) and °pens (2 morphemes), or, more dramatically, °lend and °penned – or even more convincingly, °band and °banned. We need a more watertight terminology than that.

Here is notation again, to bring this simple truth home:

Word	Syllable structure		Morpheme structure	
°lens	/–/	1 syllable	[lens]	1 morpheme
°pens	/–/	1 syllable	[pen]s]	2 morphemes
°lend	/–/	1 syllable	[lend]	1 morpheme
°penned	/–/	1 syllable	[penn]ed]	2 morphemes

| °band | /–/ | 1 syllable | [band] | 1 morpheme |
| °banned | /–/ | 1 syllable | [bann]ed] | 2 morphemes |

We are now ready, almost, for 'Terminal-Y: Second extension' (Section 8.3).

8.1 'Most words in English are monosyllables'

To continue, for a moment, the theme of Section 7.4, I remember hearing 'Most words in English are monosyllables' asserted from the platform at a conference, and wondering whether this particular simplifying generalisation (and we cannot do without such generalisations) was a useful one, either at the research level from which it came or at the teaching level to which it was addressed.

Most words in English are not monosyllables, as a child looking in an ordinary dictionary (or *Walker's*!) can easily confirm. So what lies behind this assertion, which was certainly well-intentioned?

One factor of paramount importance is the difference between a **list** and a **text**. Contrasted in this way, both these words have a specialised meaning. A typical **list**, in this context, is a dictionary, which is, in essence, a list of head-words, so ordered that each head-word appears only once in the alphabetical arrangement. A typical **text** is what you're reading now. It's language in sentences – language in ordinary use in speech or writing. Linguists sometimes refer to this as 'discourse'.

Texts in English show a high proportion of monosyllables. If you want to know what is meant by 'high', count the monosyllables in this section (or just in this sentence). The disparity between dictionary list and discourse text as regards monosyllables is tied in with the difference between **content words** (nouns, verbs, adjectives and adverbs) and **function words** (the 'little words' – pronouns, prepositions, and the like (see Section 16.2). Text versus List and Content Words versus Function Words will occupy us increasingly as we gain insight into the spelling system (see Chapter 16).

For the present, it is enough if I repeat the warning given at the end of Chapter 7, that a one-syllable word may consist of two morphemes. (Conversely, a two-syllable word may consist of only one morpheme –

Section 7.3.) Here again are some of the examples in notation from the very end of 7.4:

Word	Syllable structure		Morpheme structure	
°lens	/–/	1 syllable	[lens]	1 morpheme
°pens	/–/	1 syllable	[pen]s]	2 morphemes
°lend	/–/	1 syllable	[lend]	1 morpheme
°penned	/–/	1 syllable	[penn]ed]	2 morphemes

This distinction between syllables and morphemes is as crucial as the distinction between sounds and letters (see Section 5.1). Insight into the spelling system begins with these distinctions.

8.2   Adverbs again

I have gone to *Walker's Rhyming Dictionary* twice so far to get some idea of quantities: once for an idea of the number of regular adverbs in English (>650, Section 4.1) and once for an idea of the number of words ending in °y (about 8000, Section 7.3). The former, of course, are a subset of the latter, as the regular adverb suffix is °-ly. This suffix forms adverbs from adjectives.

Among the suffixes of English, adverbial °-ly serves as a sort of halfway house between the half-dozen *inflectional suffixes* (°-s, °-ed, °-ing, °-er, °-est) and the hundred or more *derivational suffixes* (for example, °-ness, °-ful, °-ise, °-ate, °-al, °-ous). Like an inflection, it is universal: it applies, in principle, to all adjectives. But unlike an inflection, it changes the word-class (the 'part of speech'): adverbs are *derived* from adjectives by means of the suffix °-ly.

°-ly is unique in forming, to a very large extent, a word-class, namely adverbs, and adverbs are unique in being, to the same extent, a derived word-class. Here, then, is a small sample of short, regular adverbs, classified by the spelling terminal of the nucleus. A 'stable' terminal is one which never changes at all; a 'non-stable' terminal is one which is *liable* to change (it doesn't always change – see Section 5.3):

Stable terminals

I	II	III	IV (morphemes)	V (syllables)
°...CC				
°bold + ly → °boldly			[— —]	/– –/
°fond + ly → °fondly			[— —]	/– –/
°last + ly → °lastly			[— —]	/– –/

°limp + ly → °limply	[— —]	/– –/
°rich + ly → °richly	[— —]	/– –/
°faint + ly → °faintly	[— —]	/– –/
°staunch + ly → °staunchly	[— —]	/– –/

°...VVC

°vain + ly → °vainly	[— —]	/– –/
°taut + ly → °tautly	[— —]	/– –/
°mean + ly → °meanly	[— —]	/– –/
°deep + ly → °deeply	[— —]	/– –/
°cool + ly → °coolly	[— —]	/– –/
°broad + ly → °broadly	[— —]	/– –/
°proud + ly → °proudly	[— —]	/– –/

Non-stable terminals

°...Ce (Terminal-E)

°nice + ly → °nicely	[— —]	/– –/
°brave + ly → °bravely	[— —]	/– –/
°dense + ly → °densely	[— —]	/– –/
°loose + ly → °loosely	[— —]	/– –/
°sole + ly → °solely	[— —]	/– –/
°huge + ly → °hugely	[— —]	/– –/

°...CVC (Terminal-Consonant)

°mad + ly → °madly	[— —]	/– –/
°wet + ly → °wetly	[— —]	/– –/
°prim + ly → °primly	[— —]	/– –/
°hot + ly → °hotly	[— —]	/– –/
°glum + ly → °glumly	[— —]	/– –/

°...Cy (Terminal-Y)

°happy × ly → °happily	[— —]	/– – –/
°busy × ly → °busily	[— —]	/– – –/
°clumsy × ly → °clumsily	[— —]	/– – –/
°pretty × ly → °prettily	[— —]	/– – –/
°tidy × ly → °tidily	[— —]	/– – –/
°weary × ly → °wearily	[— —]	/– – –/

(If you are not convinced by °wetly as an adverb, how about °redly? *Collins English Dictionary* gives both!)

   The 31 junction formulas in this list are suggestive of the preponderance of plus-junctions over change-junctions, which, because most of our attention goes on the change-junctions, needs to be emphasised and re-emphasised. But the main point of the list is morphemic.

The list is made up of 32 different morphemes: 31 nuclear morphemes in Column I and one repeated suffix morpheme in Column 2. Of the 31 nuclears, the first 25 are one-syllable morphemes, and the last six – those with Terminal-Y – are two-syllable morphemes. One result of this is that the syllable outline of the first 25 adverbs is /– –/ (two syllables), and the syllable outline of the last six is /– – –/ (three syllables); whereas the morpheme outline in Column IV for all 31 is the same: [— —] (two morphemes).

You will recognise the last six nuclears as the adjectives from the end of Section 7.3 – six 'disyllabic monomorphemes' ending in Terminal-Y, introduced there because monosyllabic monomorphemes with Terminal-Y are thin on the ground. You can muster a handful of adjectives like °dry, °shy, °sly, °spry, but they are not typical of the set of all adjectives in English ending in Terminal-Y, and their compliance with the Y-Replacement rule fluctuates (as we saw, in Section 7.2, °dry and °shy comply better when they are verbs). The typical members of this set are two-syllables long (or longer) and the final syllable, to which the °y belongs, is an unstressed syllable in speech (see Section 12.4). These typical members obey the Y-Replacement rule consistently, which amounts to hundreds of adjectives rather than a handful.

8.3   Terminal-Y: Second extension

As I said earlier, °y is a much misunderstood, indeed underrated, letter.

We know already that 8000 or so words end in °y (second only to final °e). Often that final °y is part of a longer morpheme, and Section 7.3 'Terminal-Y: First extension' extended the treatment of °y from words like °dry to words like °happy. But sometimes a final °y is a morpheme *on its own*. Consider the contrast between the adjectives in Column I and the adjectives in Column II (morpheme-notated in Columns Ia and IIa):

I	Ia	II	IIa
°happy	[happy]	°jumpy	[jump]y]
°busy	[busy]	°fussy	[fuss]y]
°clumsy	[clumsy]	°lusty	[lust]y]
°pretty	[pretty]	°stuffy	[stuff]y]
°tidy	[tidy]	°beady	[bead]y]
°weary	[weary]	°beery	[beer]y]

There are no spelling junctions in the words in Column I. In Column II there is the same kind of spelling junction in each word – a plus-junction following a stable terminal in the nuclear:

Terminal °...CC: °jump + y → °jumpy
                          °fuss + y → °fussy
                          °lust + y → °lusty
                          °stuff + y → °stuffy
Terminal °...VVC: °bead + y → °beady
                          °beer + y → °beery

What about non-stable terminals in the nuclear? Here °y, as we expect of a vowel letter, triggers change-junctions (see Section 6.1):

Terminal-E: °stone × y → °stony
                         °noise × y → °noisy
Consonant-Doubling: °snap × y → °snappy
                         °skin × y → °skinny

We have now assembled six one-morpheme adjectives and ten two-morpheme adjectives, all sixteen ending in Terminal-Y. Terminal-Y is defined as a final °y following a consonant letter: so whether it is the last letter of a longer morpheme or constitutes a morpheme on its own, it is a non-stable terminal.

How non-stable is it? We saw in Chapter 7 what happens to Terminal-Y before V-suffixes – more specifically, before inflections beginning with a vowel: it is replaced by °i. We shall now see that the same replacement takes place before a C-suffix, in this case the derivational suffix °-ly, turning the adjectives into adverbs:

°happy × ly → °happily
°busy × ly → °busily
°clumsy × ly → °clumsily
°pretty × ly → °prettily
°tidy × ly → °tidily

°jumpy × ly → °jumpily
°fussy × ly → °fussily
°lusty × ly → °lustily
°stuffy × ly → °stuffily

°weary × ly → °wearily
°beady × ly → °beadily
°beery × ly → °beerily

°stony × ly → °stonily
°noisy × ly → °noisily

°snappy × ly → °snappily
°skinny × ly → °skinnily

Many more examples could be given. But enough has been said to show that Y-Replacement takes place before both C-suffixes and V-suffixes.

8.4   More suffixes to come

In this chapter, the adverb suffix °-ly, which has such a distinctive role in English word-formation, has acted as representative both of C-suffixes (a spelling classification) and derivational suffixes (a grammatical classification). In Chapter 9, we will look more widely at suffixes. V-suffixes outnumber C-suffixes: derivational suffixes tend to begin with a vowel letter rather than a consonant letter; as to inflectional suffixes, the only one beginning with a consonant-letter is the S-suffix.

The pattern of plus-junctions and change-junctions discovered so far will be confirmed.

9 *The three core change-junctions*

9.1 E-Deletion, Consonant-Doubling and Y-Replacement

The names may be new, but the phenomena they refer to are not new at all. The phenomena have been familiar for as long as English spelling has been standardised (that's 200 to 300 years), and rules respecting them have been formulated many times over and have been taught in all sorts of ways by generations of teachers to generations of children.

It always surprises me when I find teachers do not treat these three – E-Deletion, Consonant-Doubling and Y-Replacement – as a trio, a trio which it is appropriate to call the 'core change-junctions'. They belong together to the *grammatical core* of English and they belong together to the *lexical core* of English.

Grammatically, they relate to the inflections of nouns, verbs and adjectives and to the grammatical categories associated with these three word classes (particularly singular/plural, present/past, comparative/superlative).

Lexically, these inflections are first learnt in speech in association with the core vocabulary of the language, in which 'monosyllables' really do predominate – the homeliest part of the vocabulary or lexis of English (°mum °dad °face °hand °cat °dog °eat °drink °bed °sleep °hot °cold °red °green ° walk °run °fall °see °look °house and °home itself).

The names I've selected – E-Deletion, Consonant-Doubling and Y-Replacement – are not individually new, but grouping the three things together and doing so in a systematic framework gives them an air of novelty. I shall explore this further in Section 9.6.

9.2 The General Pattern: Plus-junctions

The backdrop to all this talk about change-junctions is the fact that, in English spelling, plus-junctions are the norm. The backdrop is 'plus-junctional' in several ways.

First, if we were to think of the boundaries between words (in a phrase or a sentence) in terms of junctions, they would all be plus-junctions, with the sole exception of the choice between °a and °an (see Section 11.2). But we would never do so, because words are not joined together into phrases with the same grammatical glue that joins morphemes together into words.

Secondly, words like °football (or °backdrop), which contain two nuclear morphemes, always have a plus-junction at their internal boundaries (exceptions to this, outside recent coinages, are very rare, for example °neck × kerchief → °neckerchief). In short, compound words are plus-junctional.

Thirdly, words with affixes (see Section 4.2) are the only words in which change-junctions occur, and where the nucleus/suffix boundary is concerned, a majority of nuclear morphemes have stable terminals, especially °...CC and °...VVC, which are not subject to change.

Fourthly, where nuclear morphemes do have non-stable terminals, change is not always triggered: consonant suffixes do not trigger change in Terminal-E or in Terminal-Consonants.

It is against this backdrop that the rest of this chapter must be seen. In the three sections which follow, the three core change-junction rules are dealt with in succession.

- E-Deletion comes first (Section 9.3): it operates extensively both in 'monosyllables' and in longer words

- Consonant-Doubling comes next (Section 9.4): it operates extensively in 'monosyllables', but not in longer words, and its operation is parallel to that of E-Deletion, as I have just mentioned.

- Y-Replacement comes last (Section 9.5): it does not operate extensively in 'monosyllables', but it does in longer words (perhaps more so than E-Deletion) and its 'mechanical' operation is not parallel to that of the other two, as change is triggered by C-suffixes as well as by V-suffixes.

9.3 The E-Deletion rule

As formulated in Section 6.2 (where Terminal-E is defined as a final °e following a consonant letter):

E-Deletion affects **Terminal-E** by deleting it before V-suffixes but not before C-suffixes.

This is the most extensive of the three core rules as it operates both on nuclear morphemes, of one or more syllables, and on suffix morphemes. Examples can be accommodated in a two-by-two matrix. Each box exemplifies a Terminal-E which undergoes deletion. In Boxes 1 and 2 (Column I), the Terminal-E belongs to a nuclear morpheme; in Boxes 3 and 4 (Column II) it belongs to a suffixal morpheme.

	I Acting on nuclears	II Acting on suffixals
Inflectionals	1 slave/slaving/slaved	3 moderate/moderating/moderated
Derivationals	2 slave/slavish/slavery	4 moderate/moderation/moderator

In the top row (Boxes 1 and 3), the suffixes triggering deletion are inflectional suffixes. In the bottom row (Boxes 2 and 4), they are derivational suffixes.

Each case may be expressed in full by means of a junction formula:

			(morphemes)	(syllables)
1	(inflect.)	°slave × ing → °slaving	[—]—]	/– –/
	(inflect.)	°slave × ed → °slaved	[—]—]	/–/
2	(deriv.)	°slave × ish → °slavish	[—]—]	/– –/
	(deriv.)	°slave × ery → °slavery	[—]—]	/– – –/
3	(inflect.)	°moderate × ing → °moderating	[—]—]—]	/– – – –/
	(inflect.)	°moderate × ed → °moderated	[—]—]—]	/– – – –/
4	(deriv.)	°moderate × ion → °moderation	[—]—]—]	/– – – –/
	(deriv.)	°moderate × or → °moderator	[—]—]—]	/– – – –/

A long commentary could follow, but the essence of the two-by-two matrix is as follows.

Boxes 1 and 2 will accommodate all cases of E-Deletion acting on a nuclear morpheme (all suffixes triggering deletion begin with a vowel letter):

Box 1 Large numbers of nuclear morphemes ending in Terminal-E could take the place of °slave in Box 1: most of them verbs with V-inflectionals °-ing and °-ed; some of them adjectives with V-inflectionals

°-er and °-est; none of them nouns as such, because their only inflection is °-s. Some nuclears will be more than one-syllable long.

Box 2   Some of the nuclears from Box 1 will also appear in Box 2, and some won't (°spate, for instance, is unlikely). Like inflectional suffixes, derivational suffixes tend to begin with a vowel letter. Unlike inflectionals, there is a great variety of them and different derivationals attach to different nuclears of the same word class in a thoroughly patchy way, but the total numbers of nouns, verbs and adjectives formed are large.

Boxes 3 and 4 will accommodate all cases of E-Deletion acting on a suffix morpheme. The nuclear morpheme in these boxes does not have to be one ending in Terminal-E: °moder- has been chosen as an example of a two-syllable morpheme to reinforce the distinction between morpheme (a unit of grammar) and syllable (a unit of rhythm) – see Section 7.4.

Box 3   A number of derivational suffixes (for example °-ate, °-ise forming verbs, °-ate, °-ive forming adjectives) themselves end in Terminal-E, which will be deleted before V-inflections. All of the verbs which qualify will appear in Box 3, duly inflected, but none of the adjectives which qualify will appear, since the grammar determines that we say 'more active, most active', for example, and not 'activer, activest'.

Box 4   In this box °activist, with °-ist, would be fine (even though it sounds the same as 'activest'). Strings of derivational suffixes are a feature of English word-formation, so from °active we form the noun °activist and the verb °activate. (From which verb another noun, °activator, can be formed with a second E-Deletion, and this can be pluralised with the S-inflection: °activators.)

A further variable, not illustrated so far, is the presence or absence of prefixes. Very often a nuclear with a prefix accepts a derivational suffix which the simple nuclear doesn't accept. Take °pulse for example:

No prefix:	pulse	———	———	———	pulsate
Prefix °in-:	impulse	impulsive	impulsion	———	———
Prefix °con-:	———	compulsive	compulsion	compulsory	———
Prefix °ex-:	———	expulsive	expulsion	———	———

This prefixal/suffixal eccentricity is even more marked with lame nuclears (Section 4.5) like °-moder-; such nuclears form an important part of the more sophisticated vocabulary of English.

°pulsate, incidentally, like most verbs in °-ate, takes the noun suffix °-ion, thus embodying two E-Deletions:

$$°pulse \times ate \times ion \rightarrow °pulsation$$

9.4 The Consonant-Doubling rule

This rule is parallel to the E-Deletion rule and was formulated in Section 6.1 as follows:

Consonant-Doubling affects a **Terminal Consonant** by doubling it before V-suffixes but not before C-suffixes.

'Terminal Consonant' was defined as the final letter in a terminal profile °...CVC – that is, a final consonant which follows a vowel which in turn follows a consonant (you see how labour-saving a notation is!).

Like E-Deletion, this change is confined to the 'left-hand letter' at the spelling junction, but the letter category (namely consonant as opposed to vowel) and the letter process (the nature of the change – doubling as opposed to deletion) are different. The parallelism lies in the conditions on the right of the junction: as with E-Deletion, the 'right-hand letter' must be a vowel letter; if it is a consonant letter, the junction is a plus-junction.

There is another kind of difference between E-Deletion and Consonant-Doubling. E-Deletion, as we have just seen in Section 9.3, takes place both in nuclear morphemes (such as °rise/rising) and in suffixal morphemes (such as °nationalise/nationalising). Consonant-Doubling is confined to nuclear morphemes (for example, °l is not doubled in °nationalise). As a result, Column II of the matrix used in Section 9.3 is empty:

	I Acting on nuclears	II Acting on suffixals
Inflectionals	1 pot/potting/potted	3
Derivationals	2 pot/potty/pottery	4

These nuclears are much less attractive to derivational suffixes than those in Section 9.3. Thus a form like °riddance (°rid $\times$ ance $\rightarrow$ °riddance) is rare. Even more rare in form (but not in fact!) is °begin. This is a one-syllable nucleus which occurs only with the homely prefix °be-, as in °become. It is itself an irregular verb like °come, or more exactly like °sing (°sing/sang/sung, °-gin/-gan/-gun). Between prefix and nucleus is a plus-junction; and between the nucleus and its only V-inflection is a change-junction:

°begin × ing → °beginning

It is the homeliness of both prefix (°belong, °beside, °behave, °between) and nucleus (vowel-ringing) which is special in °begin (beloved of beginners! see also Chapter 12). In line with what I said about the lame nucleus °-moder- at the end of the last section, the more sophisticated vocabulary of English contains many verb nuclei bonded to prefixes – like °-mit- in °admit – which do not indulge in vowel-ringing and which accept derivational suffixes more readily (such as °admit/admittance, °commit/committal – see Section 28.3).

9.5   The Y-Replacement rule

This rule can be formulated as follows (Terminal-Y being defined as a final °y following a consonant letter, or, in notation, °...Cy):

Y-Replacement affects **Terminal-Y** by replacing it with °i before V-suffixes and before C-suffixes.

It differs from the other two core rules in its *application*, as it is triggered by all suffixes. It is similar to E-Deletion, but different from Consonant-Doubling, in its *distribution*, as it operates on Terminal-Y both in nuclear and in suffixal morphemes. Column II of the matrix accordingly is occupied again.

	I Acting on nuclears	II Acting on suffixals
Inflectionals	1 try/tries/tried carry/carries/carried	3 lovely/lovelier/loveliest
Derivationals	2 try/trier/trial carry/carrier/carriage	4 lovely/loveliness

In Boxes 1 and 2, Terminal-Y appears in two nuclear morphemes: °try, a monosyllabic nucleus, and, more typically, in °carry, a two-syllable nucleus (see Section 7.3). The suffixes are inflectional in Box 1 and derivational in Box 2.

In Boxes 3 and 4, Terminal-Y appears, for simplicity, in a single morpheme, °-ly. This, despite appearances, is not the adverb suffix °-ly, which forms adverbs from adjectives (already discussed in connection with °definitely in Chapter 3 and again in Section 8.2). It is a suffix of the same shape, °-ly, which attaches to nouns and forms adjectives (°love/lovely: 'a lovely day'). It has greater potentiality than the adverb suffix: it can take the adjective inflections °-er and -est (Box 3), and it can take the derivational suffix °-ness, which is very productive in forming abstract nouns from adjectives (Box 4).

In Box 1, note the absence of °trying and °carrying and the presence of °tries and °carries. As mentioned earlier, Terminal-Y is not replaced by °i before suffixes which themselves begin with °i: in this way two adjacent °i's are avoided. Another special feature of Terminal-Y is that it triggers a change on the right of the junction: °-s becomes °-es.

In Box 2 we meet the usual selectivity of derivational suffixes: the suffix °-al attaches to °try (as it does to °deny) but not to °dry (or to °rely). The suffix °-er (not in this case the adjective inflection) is very productive in forming agent/instrument nouns from verbs: °drier as a noun can also be spelt with a plus-junction (as often on hand-dryers), but °trier ('he's a good trier') is always with a change-junction. You may feel a semantic shift between °trier and °trial. This is a common experience with derivations. The relation of °carriage to °carry is not always as transparent as that of °marriage to °marry – where we have the same change-junction:

$$°marry \times age \rightarrow °marriage$$

Suffixes with Terminal-Y can be both shorter than °-ly (we met the suffix °-y in Section 8.3), and longer (for example, °-ary, °-ory, °-ity). We have not finished with °y yet!

9.6 The coherence of the three core rules

Of course, there are exceptions. °trying is an exception to the Y-Replacement rule. But in this chapter I have concentrated on the three core change-junctions as themselves a close-knit trio of exceptions to the General Pattern.

The General Pattern is that *plus-junctions are the norm*, as I said in Section 9.2. Change-junctions, however, are so central to the spelling system that they have to be treated at length. Their presence in the system has been enough to upset many learners, who have failed to master the simplicity of, for example:

$$°love + ly \quad \rightarrow °lovely$$
$$°nice + ly \quad \rightarrow °nicely$$
$$°definite + ly \quad \rightarrow °definitely$$
$$°sincere + ly \quad \rightarrow °sincerely$$
$$°commit + ment \rightarrow °commitment$$

(The misspellings *lovly and *nicly are found very early in education; *definitly a little later; *sincerly later still; *committment persists well beyond – into Minutes and Reports.) Properly stated and properly studied the three core change-junctions need not loom so large: the backdrop is there and they must be seen against it. They have the following features in common:

- They all operate at suffix boundaries, not at prefix boundaries or nuclear/nuclear boundaries.

- They all operate before inflectional suffixes, and between them they account for all the changes that occur before inflections, as well as operating before derivational suffixes.

- They all operate on a single letter, which is the nearest letter on the left of the junction – the 'left-hand letter'.

- They all obey letter-category conditions related to the left-hand letter.

- They all three respond to the nearest letter on the right of the junction – the 'right-hand letter'. Here there is a divergence: two changes, E-Deletion and Consonant-Doubling, respond to the letter category and are triggered by vowel letters only, while Y-Replacement is triggered by all letters except °i.

- They each affect the left-hand letter in a minimal fashion. Here they diverge into separate but complementary processes, the 'minimal fashion' itself knitting the three changes together:

      E-Deletion removes a letter – subtraction of one
      Consonant-Doubling inserts a letter – addition of one
      Y-Replacement replaces a letter by another – substitution of one.

- They are mutually exclusive. Terminal-E and Terminal-Y cannot be Terminal Consonants, and vice versa; Terminal-E cannot be Terminal-Y, and vice versa.

9.7   Beyond the three core rules

After the show of rigour in the last section (9.6), we can relax. Beyond the core rules are non-core rules, exceptions, exceptions to exceptions, and a host of details. But this is not a textbook, and Chapters 10, 11 and 12, while taking us further, are designed to form a bridge to Part II: they are, in order, 'Mixed doubles' (consonants), 'Longs and shorts' (vowels), and 'About "to begin" '.

In reading them, keep in mind the fact that change-junctions are themselves the first layer of exceptions to *the General Pattern of plus-junctions*, and that we are always looking for patterns and trying to order them in importance, both as regards junctions (Part I) and as regards sounds and symbols (Part II).

10 *Mixed doubles (consonants)*

10.1 Loose talk

I once had to listen to serious people using the expression 'double letters' in connection with children tackling words beginning not with one consonant letter but with two.

I know that some children and their teachers use the expression 'double writing' for cursive handwriting – generally known as 'joined-up writing'. It's a curious use of 'double' which you won't find in standard dictionaries: it's handed on orally and it's fine in its place. But that is in discourse with children.

In research seminar discourse, 'double letters' for any pair of consonant letters at the beginning of a word is symptomatic of the unformed state of our terminology for talking about the spelling system. It, too, is a curious use of 'double', because the one kind of letter pair that you will *not* find at the beginning of a word in English is two of the same consonant letter.

The spelling systems of other languages may permit initial double consonants. Spanish allows them; and if you look in a Spanish dictionary, you will find that words beginning with double L appear as a separate 'letter' between those beginning with a single L and those beginning with M. One such word has found its way into English (°llama, the animal), as have some names from Welsh (°Lloyd in particular).

But we are not concerned now with marginal phenomena in English spelling, but with the nature of the core spelling system. If you think about it, you will see that the system permits double consonant letters in the middle of words and at the end of words, but not at the beginning. That restriction is a negative feature that most children cotton on to for themselves without instruction (like the limitation embodied in double letters itself – 'treble letters' are not permitted at all:

°full × ly → °fully

– a non-core change-junction.)

There is, however, more to double letters than meets the eye. Like twins, different pairs can have different origins. Learners may not perceive this on their own, but, prompted to look beneath the surface of the spelling, they may gain useful insight into how the spelling system works.

10.2 A bit of biology

Biologists distinguish between phenotype and genotype (for some speakers °pheno- rhymes with °beano, °geno- rhymes with °benno). 'Phenotype' refers to physical manifestation, 'genotype' to inner coding – a surface/depth contrast, if you like. The context is genetics – how plant or animal characteristics are inherited.

Take dogs, for instance. One black Labrador looks like another black Labrador, but the first is the product of two black parents and the second the product of a black and a golden. As far as colour is concerned they are phenotypically the same, both visibly black, but genotypically they are not the same – the genes they carry invisibly are different. This hidden difference will manifest itself in their descendants.

Spelling is a simpler system to explore: it needs no generations to await results, no microscopes to make the invisible visible. One pair of 'double Ns' looks like any other pair of 'double Ns' (same phenotype), but they may have different structural origins (different genotype). How many different structural origins are there for double consonants? Answer: four.

Sections 10.3 and 10.6 deal in turn with the 'double consonants' in:

Case 1	°penny	(10.3)	Doubles: In-built
Case 2	°unnatural	(10.4)	Doubles: By Abutment
Case 3	°stunning	(10.5)	Doubles: By Consonant-Doubling
Case 4	°announce	(10.6)	Doubles: By Consonant-Assimilation

Listing them like that fails to bring out the fundamental difference between in-built doubles and the other three cases. A structured classification remedies this:

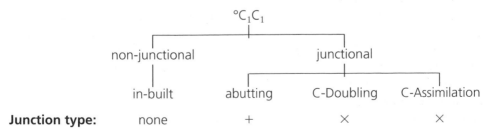

Junction type:	none	+	×	×

These four cases account for nearly all 'double consonants' – not quite all, as we saw in Section 10.1, with the marginal case of °fully (compare, and contrast, °dully).

10.3   Doubles: In-built *(Case 1)*

'Double N' in °penny is built into the spelling of the morpheme [penny], and you find it in °pennies °twopenny and °pennyfarthing. That doesn't mean to say it is completely stable (it changes in °pence) but it does mean that it isn't produced by any form of spelling junction.

°penny, with its 'double N' is a typical morpheme for inbuilt or inherent 'double consonants' (compare °banner °spinney °bonnet °dunnock). Other consonants are just as common in such two-syllable morphemes (°copper °volley °grommet °mattock), but in one-syllable morphemes the range is narrower (°boss is typical, °butt isn't).

All these morphemes are nuclear morphemes, and nuclear morphemes which can be words. In prefixes and suffixes, 'double consonants' are exceptional, but you will find 'double S' (°-less °-ness).

10.4   Doubles: By Abutment *(Case 2)*

One way of describing a plus-junction is to say that two morphemes simply abut each other. They meet end-on; no change takes place. If the left-hand letter at the junction is °n and the right-hand letter is °n, the result will be 'double N':

°un + natural → °unnatural

I am keeping 'double N' in inverted commas deliberately. The genesis of 'double N' in °unnatural is different from the genesis of 'double N' in °penny. In °penny the two °n's ('letter Ns') belong to the one morpheme; in °unnatural they belong to two different morphemes. 'Double N' may be a suitable name at the phenotypic level, but not so suitable at the genotypic level.

The plus-junction in °unnatural is between a prefix and a nuclear stem. Exactly the same result comes about between nuclear and suffix in, for example:

°keen + ness → °keenness

But check your pronunciation of this word: you will hear the two Ns (°keenness doesn't rhyme with °penis, even when the second syllable sounds

the same as that in °Guinness). You probably won't hear two Ns in °unnatural;
but how about °innate? – you may well hear them there.

We tend to avoid nuclear-to-nuclear 'double consonants': my dictionary
writes °pen name° as two words, but is happy to write °penfriend, where there
is no clash of same on same, as a single word. But the same dictionary gives
°slowworm, with a collector's piece in it – a 'double W'!

Suffixes tend to begin with vowel-letters, so the nuclear-suffix boundary is
not the best place for consonant 'doubles by abutment'. And whatever the
letter and whatever the site of the junction, we are sensitive to abutments and
are tempted to write °sub-branch, for instance, or °soul-less, with a hyphen.

10.5   Doubles: By Consonant-Doubling (*Case 3*)

There is no need for putting the word 'doubling' into sceptical quotes where
Consonant-Doubling is concerned, because doubling is precisely what
happens: the single consonant letter is doubled:

°stun × ing → °stunning

One N becomes two Ns – within the one morpheme. °stunn- is a variant form
of °stun, just as °com- is a variant form of °come, and °happi- of °happy. The
deeply ingrained printers' convention of breaking a word like °stunning at the
end of a line into 'stun-' and 'ning' has helped to obscure this. But what status
has °-ning got? Is it a variant form of the ING-inflection?

Most consonant letters (not all) undergo this doubling which occurs only at
one site, the nuclear-suffix boundary. The fact that both letters belong to one
morpheme associates this case to the first of these four, the in-built 'doubles'.
Notice, too, that the pronunciation never doubles: °stunning is pronounced
with /n/, not like °keenness with /nn/.

10.6   Doubles: By Consonant-Assimilation (*Case 4*)

With the fourth case of 'double N', exemplified by °announce, we come to a
kind of change-junction we have not so far considered at all. It is called
Consonant-Assimilation, because two consonant letters meet at the junction
and one assimilates to the other, as °d assimilates to °n in:

°ad × nounce → °announce

The nuclear morpheme here is [-nounce-], which shows up clearly in the pattern:

°announce/ annunciation
denounce/ denunciation
pronounce/pronunciation
renounce/ renunciation

The four prefixes are °ad- °de- °re- and °pro-, which are also found in the sets:

[-duce-]	[pose]
°adduce	°appose
deduce	depose
produce	propose
reduce	repose

°ad- is the base form, found before vowels (°adoption) and some consonants (before °d obviously, but also in °adhere °adjoin °administer °advantage); it assimilates before others as in °account °afflict °aggregate °alliterate °annotate °apprehend °arrogate °attenuate, and in °assimilate itself. Consonant-Assimilation accounts for both the 'double C' in °accommodation and the 'double M'.

Consonant-Assimilation complements, at prefix boundaries, the three core change-junctions, which operate at suffix boundaries. Like them, *Consonant-Assimilation affects the left-hand letter at the junction in a way which is conditioned by the right-hand letter.*

But notice that, though the result is 'double letters', the two letters belong to different morphemes. In this respect, Case 4 resembles Case 2, 'doubling by Abutment'. (See, on 'arching' symbols, Section 23.2.)

10.7   Precise talk

To call all four cases 'double letters' effaces the underlying junctional difference between °penny and °stunning on the one hand (adjacent °n's in the same morpheme), and °unnatural and °announce on the other (adjacent °n's in different morphemes); similarly, it effaces the underlying difference between °keenness (+) and °goddess (×). We should think of this when spelling out loud: how sensitive should we be to the underlying morphemes?

The loose talk I recalled in Section 10.1 was not about 'double letters' at all, but about words beginning with two assorted consonant letters. Even then, it failed to make a distinction between words like °chap and words like °clap. °ch in °chap is crucially different from °cl in °clap. This difference (traditionally the difference between a 'digraph' and a 'blend') is a matter of sound/symbol relationships, and talk about it requires a more precise shared language about sounds and symbols, of the kind I shall be using in Part II of *Insight*.

11 Longs and shorts (vowels)

11.1 Why do we learn about consonants and vowels?

Everyone learns about consonants and vowels in Primary School, and they carry this bit of knowledge-luggage with them into Secondary School, where they don't unpack it – and then they carry it with them for the rest of their lives.

Clearly there is something important about these two categories or they wouldn't have found their way into the curriculum in the first place and then maintained their place down the years and into the 1990s. So why do we learn about them? I have put this question to groups of students and got very puzzled looks in return. The only real answer I ever got (and a perfectly sensible one in the circumstances) was that we needed to know about consonants and vowels in order to decide between 'a' and 'an': 'a' before words beginning with a consonant and 'an' before words beginning with a vowel.

11.2 °a and °an

Perhaps it's a mercy that the two words °a and °an exist in English, otherwise the categories consonant and vowel might have dropped out of sight altogether. But, to digress a moment, are °a and °an two words?

There are two answers to that question, depending (as so often) on what you want to do. If you are, say, listing words of one letter and words of two letters, or listing words with the letter-profile °VC, then °an is a different word from °a. But in the *grammar* of the language, they are one and the same word – the indefinite article, to give it its traditional name. The indefinite article is a single morpheme [a], which has two spelling forms °a and °an.

To revert from grammar to spelling, what concerns me in this chapter is this: that choosing between °a and °an is a depressingly trivial reason for acquiring the concepts of 'consonant' and 'vowel', and that the concepts of 'consonant' and 'vowel' so acquired are a travesty of these two fundamental linguistic categories. I shall call this inadequate concept of the categories the 'five-vowel' or the AEIOU view of things.

The five-vowel view of things is inadequate for the following reasons:

- it fails to take account of vowel *sounds*, and therefore of the distinction between sounds and letters (Section 11.3)

- where *sounds* are concerned, the number five can be doubled to ten – and still fall far short of the total (Section 11.4)

- where *letters* are concerned, the number five must be raised to six (Section 11.5).

11.3   Vowel sounds and vowel letters

It is difficult, it is frustrating, to talk about the distinction between sounds and letters without distinct notations for the two realms – the realm of speech or auditory realm ('air') on the one hand, and the realm of writing or visual realm ('ink') on the other. That is why, in this book, I have been using a notation for sounds and other units of pronunciation signalled by slant brackets or obliques (/.../), and a notation for letters and other units of spelling signalled by the circlet (°...). Notice that the same characters (namely lower-case letters of the alphabet) are used in both notations: hence the importance of the distinctive flags, /   / and °.

Do not drop the flags! Letter °t, for example, is a different entity from sound /t/. But it is well worth noting them with the same character, when talking about our spelling system, simply because of the close association between them.

As for 'a' and 'an' – sound rules! In speech we are choosing between the two forms non-consciously all day long as we talk, using 'a' before a word beginning with a consonant *sound*, and 'an' before a word beginning with a vowel *sound*. In writing, we reflect this feature of ordinary speech, and where necessary we run counter to the five-vowel rule-of-thumb based on the letters AEIOU. Counter-instances are few in number but quite routine: for example, in 'an hour ago', the word 'hour' begins with a vowel sound but a consonant letter, whilst in 'such a one', the word 'one' begins with a vowel letter but a consonant sound.

Sounds and letters must be distinguished from each other (hence the notations), and sounds must be *talked* about as well as letters – and as easily!

11.4   Ten vowel sounds arranged in pairs

As a point of entry into the vowel sounds of English, consider the pairs of words in Table 11.1.

Table 11.1 *Derivational word-pairs 1*

°sane/sanity
°obscene/obscenity
°mime/mimic
°tone/tonic
°reduce/reduction

What we must focus on in these word-pairs are the contrasting vowel sounds. Each pair consists of a stem-word with no suffix, for example °sane, and a word derived from it by means of a derivational suffix, for example °sanity. In each case the vowel sound in the nuclear morpheme is 'long' in the stem-word and 'short' in the derived word. 'Long' and 'short' are traditional terms which will serve our purpose well enough.

In the case of these five word-pairs you will have noticed that the long values are the same as the alphabetic names of the five vowel letters, and the short values are the same as the 'phonic' names which some teachers use with beginning learners. Five different long sounds and five different short sounds makes ten different vowel sounds. That's well short of the total number of vowel sounds in English (we will operate with a list of twenty-seven of them in Part II, see Section 20.5), but *it's a good start.* You can memorise them on the basis of the five letter-names and the long/short regularity.

But what is the nature of that regularity? What links the long and the short *sounds*? The answer to that is *word-pairs like* °sane/sanity °obscene/obscenity °mime/mimic and so on, *where the two sounds are morphemically linked*, that is to say, linked by the *grammar* of the language. In Table 11.2 are some more examples of words exhibiting the same vowel pairs: the word-pairs are not all so simple in structure as those in Table 11.1, but each pair, like those, consists of words with the same nuclear morpheme.

Table 11.2 *Derivational word-pairs 2*

I	II
°nation/national	°pale/pallor
°plenary/plenitude	°deep/depth
°crisis/critical	°crime/criminal
°melodious/melodic	°compose/compositor
°student/study	°numerous/number

It is because the sounds are paired *morphemically* that the spelling system uses the same vowel letter for both sounds. This makes the spelling more stable

than the pronunciation, a characteristic of the spelling system which will
become more apparent in Part II.

In the meantime, if we want to talk about these vowel pairs, which we can
think of as core vowel sounds of English, we need a notation for them. We can
nickname the five pairs the A-pair, the E-pair, the I-pair, the O-pair and the
U-pair, and notate them as in Columns I and II in Table 11.3.

Table 11.3 *Notations for 10 core vowel sounds*

	I		II	III
	Sound notations			Pedagogical
	Short		Long	Word-pairs
A-pair	/a/		/ae/	°mat/mate
E-pair	/e/		/ee/	°pet/Pete
I-pair	/i/		/ie/	°kit/kite
O-pair	/o/		/oe/	°mop/mope
U-pair	/u/		/ue/	°cub/cube

Each vowel letter is associated with its short/long pair of sounds in exactly the
same way that °t is associated with /t/ – through sheer frequency of
correspondence in the spelling system. These correspondences are the source
of the transparent notations for the short sounds in Column I and for the long
sounds in Column II, reinforced in Column III by the kind of word-pairs used
in the Infant School classroom.

These pedagogical word-pairs in Column III differ profoundly from the
word-pairs in Tables 11.1 and 2: they are not derivational pairs. There is no
relation in grammar between the words °mat and °mate: they are just unrelated
morphemes. This doesn't render them useless: word-pairs like them are
familiar from their use in the classroom to teach the systematic series of
spelling symbols based on the letters AEIOU set out in Table 11.4.

Table 11.4

Pedagogical word-pairs	Spelling symbols	
°mat/mate	°a	°a.e
°pet/Pete	°e	°e.e
°kit/kite	°i	°i.e
°mop/mope	°o	°o.e
°cub/cube	°u	°u.e

There is a great deal to say about these spelling symbols: but it must wait until
Part II. What matters now is the inadequacy of the five-vowel view of things,
despite the appealing tidiness of Table 11.4.

11.5   Six vowel letters

Ever since Section 5.3 it has been obvious that °y is a vowel letter. If it is, then there are six vowel letters in the alphabet, not five.

I won't at this point recap the evidence about °y as a vowel from earlier chapters. It is enough to look at the additional word-pairs in Table 11.5.

Table 11.5 *Derivational word-pairs from tables 11.1 and 11.2* **plus Y-pairs**

°sane/sanity	°nation/national	°pale/pallor
°obscene/obscenity	°plenary/plenitude	°deep/depth
°mime/mimic	°crisis/critical	°vine/vineyard
°tone/tonic	°melodious/melodic	°compose/compositor
°reduce/reduction	°student/study	°numerous/number
°type/typical	**°cycle/encyclical**	**°analyse/analytic**

It is obvious that °y behaves just like °a, °e, °i, °o and °u and acts as the leading letter in vowel symbols in nuclear morphemes (°y and °y.e), and furthermore is associated with a short/long pair of vowel sounds, the same pair as °i (which leads to homophones like °rhyme and °rime, and °gym and °Jim).

In the face of all the evidence that it is a vowel letter, you may like to figure out reasons why it is customarily not recognised as one. Here are three to start you off:

- it does not have its own pair of vowel values: °i has a first claim on /i/ and /ie/.

- it's not easy to find a pedagogical (°mat/mate) pair for °y.

- in any case, as an initial letter, °y is, equally obviously, a consonant letter, as in °yak °yet °yippee °yoghurt and °yuk – and *there* is vindication of the five-vowel view: it's 'a yak', not 'an yak'!

These are reasons why °y is not *recognised* as a vowel letter. But the fact remains: it *is* a vowel letter – and the five-vowel view is doomed. It may satisfy adults; it shouldn't satisfy children who do set theory. In Part II, I shall treat °y under both categories (Section 18.6).

11.6   Five vowels/flat Earth

What we learn in Primary School about consonants and vowels is not an adequate basis for understanding the spelling system. The five-vowel view of things stifles thought and is incompatible with a curriculum which embraces scientific inquiry from Year 1.

I have not mentioned junctions in this chapter, but they have not been far away as we shall see in Chapter 12, which ends Part I of this book.

12 *About 'to begin'*

12.1 Learning from the learner

In probing a person's spelling or their conceptions about spelling, you must be prepared to be startled. You mustn't reveal your astonishment, of course: you can discover more, and thereby help more, by being unsurprisable.

I learnt this from a first-year student who wrote °begun consistently as *begune. She didn't pronounce it to rhyme with °tune, so why did she, so to speak, write it to rhyme with °tune? When I pointed the misspelling out to her, she told me she'd always spelt it that way and no-one had ever commented on it.

'But how could you possibly spell it like that? I mean, you don't pronounce it like that, do you?' I asked.

'Well,' she said, 'I just thought it was one of those funny things you get in English spelling.'

That was significant enough. I remembered a friend of mine who had spelt my surname *Montford, without a °u, on exactly the same grounds. Proper names, so important in our lives, have a lot to answer for – beginning, as I have hinted before, with °John. But this student's stumbling-block was a common verb, and I asked her innocently, with the aid of the blackboard:

'Did it never strike you as very odd to have *begin* and *began* and then to have *begune*?'

'Oh,' she said, 'I spell them with an E too.'

How could this be? She wrote neatly, she wrote quite well, but nobody, through all those years of school and sixth form, had drawn her attention to this aberration. Or perhaps someone had attended to it, but not to *her* – marked it, but not *talked* about it. You can't expect long-practised misspellings to be remedied at the stroke of a pen. It takes time and conscious effort. But the will should have been there: she was training to be a teacher.

12.2   Grammar, pronunciation, and spelling

Learners are more interesting than words, but this is a book about words –
each one a unique amalgam of grammar, pronunciation and spelling:

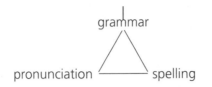

In this diagram, grammar is at the apex because grammar is the link to meaning
(and that's what words are for), pronunciation is given precedence to the left
(since speech is primary, writing secondary), and spelling is in third position
on the right (the subject of this book in proper perspective).

   I shall round off this first part of *Insight* (Part I: 'Junctions') by looking at
the spelling of one word in the light of the linguistic triangle in the diagram.
It's a word which causes difficulty to some learners, though usually junctional
difficulty (*beggining) rather than sound/symbol difficulty (*begune). It's the
word, or rather the verb, 'begin'.

   I say 'the verb "begin" ' because there's more to it than the word 'begin':
besides 'begin' itself, there's 'begins', 'beginning', 'began' and 'begun'. All
these words (or verb-forms, Section 6.2) belong to the verb 'begin'.

12.3   Spelling

I start with spelling because that is the focus of this book, and I shall first of all
recapitulate what I said about 'begin' in Section 9.4.

   We can say straightaway that the first two verb-forms are perfectly regular
(see Section 6.2):

$$°\text{begin} + \text{s} \quad \rightarrow °\text{begins} \qquad \text{Plus-junction}$$
$$°\text{begin} \times \text{ing} \rightarrow °\text{beginning} \quad \text{Consonant-Doubling}$$

The plus-junction calls for no comment. As for the Consonant-Doubling, we
note (as we did in Section 9.4) that °begin itself contains a spelling junction:

$$°\text{be} + \text{gin} \rightarrow °\text{begin}$$

°be- is a prefix; the nuclear is °-gin-, thus fulfilling both conditions mentioned
in Section 9.4, namely that as well as ending in the letter profile °...CVC, the

nuclear morpheme must be a monosyllable. Hence the doubling of °n in °beginning.

Identifying °be- as a prefix (also found in similar verbs: °become °belong °behave) accounts both for the single °g and for the double °n in the nuclear of °beginning. What is wrong with the misspelling *beggining is that it doesn't treat °be- as a prefix. Once you recognise it as a prefix, double °g becomes impossible. Morphemes in English don't begin with double consonant letters, either in-built or as the result of doubling (see Chapter 10); and there's no °beg- form of °be-, just as there is no °def- form of the prefix °de- (*deffinitely: see Chapter 3) and no °tom- form of the prefix °to (see Chapter 2: the error is just like the error in *tommorow).

Now let's go a step further in notation, using the contrast between 'outline' and 'profile' introduced in Section 7.3.

Outline	**Profile**
[— —]	[— [—]
2 morphemes	2 morphemes, nucleus no. 2
[be | gin]	[be[gin]

Remember, this tells us nothing about syllables: the morphemic outline and profile of 'tomorrow' (a three-syllable word) are exactly the same as those of 'begin' (a two-syllable word):

Outline	**Profile**
[— —]	[— [—]
2 morphemes	2 morphemes, nucleus no. 2
[to | morrow]	[to[morrow]

As explained in Chapter 4, morphemes are grammatical – units of grammar; syllables are phonological – units of pronunciation. (See Chapter 19.)

12.4   Pronunciation

More specifically, syllables are units of rhythm (Section 6.1), and in English every word, pronounced on its own, has one syllable which carries 'the stress'. This syllable, often called 'the stressed syllable', is marked in dictionaries in a variety of ways, but we can benefit from our outline-and-profile notation as it enables us to group together at a glance words which share the same configurations.

To emphasise the physical nature of rhythm, which has no analogue in the spelling system, I think it is better to use the terms 'rhythmic outline' and 'rhythmic profile' rather than 'syllable outline' and 'syllable profile'.

The rhythmic profile of 'begin' parallels the morphemic profile:

Rhythmic profile	Morphemic profile
/– ⁄/	[— [—]
2 syllables, stress on no. 2	2 morphemes, nucleus no. 2

With this 'no. 2 no. 2' pattern, let us contrast the pattern we find in the word 'begging':

Rhythmic profile	Morphemic profile
/⁄ –/	[—] —]
2 syllables, stress on no. 1	2 morphemes, nucleus no. 1

This is a 'no. 1 no. 1' pattern.

This is a more basic pattern – a one-syllable nucleus with a one-syllable inflection; that is to say, the affix follows the nucleus in °begging, whereas in °begin the affix precedes the nucleus. The grammatical inflection in °begging is perfectly regular and the spelling junction is a perfectly regular change-junction:

$$°beg \times ing \rightarrow °begging$$

The rhythm too is perfectly regular, for inflectional suffixes never affect stress. All of which makes °begging an 'easier' word than °begin.

This brings us to one of the most characteristic and complicating features of English words. Every syllable contains a vowel sound, and it is the vowel sound in a stressed syllable that gives the syllable most of its prominence. When they are stressed, vowels sound like themselves only more so; but when they are non-stressed, they may either retain their colour or, especially next to a stressed syllable, lose it and become the equivalent of a shade of grey.

This is what happens in both 'begging' and 'begin'. Their respective rhythmic profiles are:

°begging	°begin
/⁄ –/	/– ⁄/

Compare the first syllables. In 'begging' °e has its ordinary short value, /e/, as in °beg itself. In 'begin' °e does not have this value; instead it is like the first syllable of 'bikini'. (Imagine these two words written as °b'gin and °b'kini.) We need to notate the weak vowel sound in these reduced syllables, and I shall use /ı/, a form of undotted °i. The vowel correspondence in °begging, then, is °e – /e/, while in °begin it is °e – /ı/.

There's more to vowel reduction than this, as we shall see in Part II, for there is more than one shade of grey (Section 20.5). But for the present, just contrast the second syllables in our two words 'begging' /ˊ –/ and 'begin' /– ˊ/. It's more a question of rhythm than of actual sound quality, and this reduced status is very common in prefixes and suffixes including inflections, especially immediately before or after a stressed syllable. In 'bikini' /– ˊ –/, with stress on the middle syllable, the first and the third syllables both have this low status – though (see Section 7.3) we are used to °y, rather than °i, at the end of words, as in °itsy °bitsy °teeny °weeny!

The letter-profile of 'begin' is °CVCVC°. This snaps one-to-one on to the sound-profile, which is /CVCVC/:

°beg i n
°CVCVC°
/CVCVC/

But this apparent simplicity does not reveal the crucial fact that °be- is a prefix (grammar) and the first syllable is reduced or weakened (pronunciation).

12.5   Grammar

The last two sections have both been about the grammar of English – not about the structure of sentences (syntax) but about the structure of words (morphology: see Section 4.3). In Section 12.3 we analysed parts of the verb 'begin' in written form, and in Section 12.4 we analysed parts of it in spoken form. There is much more to say about the grammar (the morphemes) of this one word.

For instance, the prefix 'be-' is not unusual, compared to other prefixes (like 'de-', 're-'), in not being stressed, but it is unusual in never being stressed. It's unusual too in being found as a prefix both in Content Words and in Function Words (see Section 8.1):

I Content Words	II Function Words
become	because
behave	before
belong	behind
befriend	beside
behead	beyond
bestride	between

In Column I the meaning of 'be-' seems to be to make a verb, and in Column II to make a preposition or a conjunction.

As for the nuclear morpheme '-gin', this is unusual, not because it never appears on its own (it's a lame nuclear: see Section 4.5), but because it appears only in the verb 'begin'. As the nucleus of an irregular verb (see Section 6.2), it shows a familiar pattern of 'vowel-ringing':

sing	sang	sung
spin	span	spun
swim	swam	swum
begin	began	begun

What is grammar about? It is about the patterns and parallels that can be found in language, linking form to meaning.

12.6 Teaching from the teacher

This section title is a kind of pun, a sort of syntactic pun. In Section 12.1 'Learning from the learner', I was calling for the teacher to learn. In 'Teaching from the teacher' I am calling for the teacher to teach. That requires as much knowledge as the teacher can acquire about the matter to be taught, though it requires much else besides.

Knowledge of the spelling system is more than knowing how to spell (although it includes that). It reposes upon the linguistic triangle in Section 12.2:

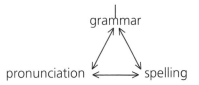

It is not just the three points that are significant: the three double-headed arrows are significant too. Part I of *Insight*, now coming to an end, has been focused on the spelling/grammar relation; Part II will be focused on the spelling/pronunciation relation. The significance of the remaining relation, the grammar/pronunciation relation, can be gauged from Section 12.4. I draw upon that side as needed, but it lies outside the scope of this book.

Conceptions about language will always underlie language teaching – and advancing learners' literacy is part of language teaching. So I will end this chapter with a little reflection about the student who started it off. Remember – as I said at the end of Chapter 1 – we use the spelling system in reading just as much as we do in writing. You are using it now.

12.7 Reflection

In Section 12.1 above I spoke of *begune (not to mention *begine and
*begane) as an aberration. From the standpoint of the standard spelling system,
it *is* an aberration (there are plenty more serious aberrations in life!) and one
that, as I indicated, should have been picked up and put right long before the
girl reached college. But teachers – people, that is – were not her only resource.
All through school and sixth form she had been *reading* – and she will never
have met *begune in print. She will only have seen °begun.

The same applies to the student in Chapter 1, with whom we began – she
will only have seen °coming.

PART

Symbols

CHAPTERS

What is a symbol?

13.1 Introduction

This chapter ('What is a symbol?') and the two that follow ('What is a sound?' and 'What is a correspondence?') are designed to put some precision into the expression 'sound/symbol correspondence'. All three terms will figure in all three chapters, but each chapter will have one of the three as its main focus. This chapter is focused on 'symbol' – the unit which gives Part II its title.

13.2 Symbols consist of letters

There are other expressions which are used for this aspect (the Part II aspect) of the spelling system, ranging from the teacher's 'phonics' to the researcher's 'grapheme-phoneme relationships'. Somewhere in between these two comes 'letter-to-sound matching', and that gives me my starting-point for 'symbol' in the expression 'sound/symbol correspondence'. *Symbols consist of letters*. This is no abstract sense of the word 'symbol': it is more a matter of simple arithmetic.

In the spelling system of English it isn't always single letters that correspond to sounds; sometimes it is two letters, or three, or even four. Take the four words in Table 13.1 overleaf.

Every word in English (not just /CVC/ monosyllables) can be treated in this way: the number of letters can be counted (Column II); the number of sounds counted (Columns III and IV); the letters matched to the sounds (Columns V and VI); and a 'symbol-size profile' produced (Column VII), the digits of which will add up to the number in Column II.

You can think of this treatment either as *cutting the word up* into symbols or as *grouping the letters* into symbols: it comes to the same thing – Columns V and VI are merely equivalent notations. It is called 'symbol segmentation', and you can start experimenting with it straightaway (start with easy words –

Table 13.1 *Words divided into symbols*

I	II	III	IV	V	VI	VII
	Number of	Sound	Number of	Symbols		Symbol-size
Word	letters	profile	sounds	(spaced)	(underlined)	profile
°cat	3	/CVC/	3	°c a t	°<u>c</u> <u>a</u> <u>t</u>	111
°chat	4	/CVC/	3	°ch a t	°<u>ch</u> <u>a</u> <u>t</u>	211
°catch	5	/CVC/	3	°c a tch	°<u>c</u> <u>a</u> <u>tch</u>	113
°caught	6	/CVC/	3	°c augh t	°<u>c</u> <u>augh</u> <u>t</u>	141

don't despise them!). You may need some guidance, you will certainly need plenty of practice, and you will need experience in order to overcome the snags. But if you explore, if you press on, if you *talk* with your fellow explorers, you will gain an insight into the symbols of the spelling system, into the sounds of the pronunciation system, and into the correspondences that exist between the two.

13.3   Symbols consist of 1, 2, 3 or 4 letters

There are six different symbols in the four words in Table 13.1: it's best to call them 'distinct' symbols, as in Table 13.2.

Table 13.2 *Distinct symbols in Table 13.1*

Symbol size	Symbol	No. of 'in-line' occurrences	Words
1-letter	°<u>a</u>	3	°cat chat catch
	°<u>c</u>	3	°cat catch caught
	°<u>t</u>	3	°cat chat caught
2-letter	°<u>ch</u>	1	°chat
3-letter	°<u>tch</u>	1	°catch
4-letter	°<u>augh</u>	1	°caught

Symbols consist of letters – of one, two, three or, the longest, four letters. Cutting up words into symbols ('symbol segmentation') is unproblematic for thousands of words.

The most frequent size of symbol is the shortest, 1-letter, and the least frequent is the longest, 4-letters. The four words in Table 13.1 were not chosen to illustrate frequency but it so happens that they do. Of the twelve 'in-line' symbols in the four words, nine are 1-letter symbols. That's three-quarters, and we shall see later that a ratio of 3 to 1 (three 1-letter symbols to one multi-letter symbol) is found in English sentences.

The prevalence of 1-letter symbols is fittingly illustrated by the word °unproblematic itself. The symbol segmentation of this word shows 13 1-letter symbols in a row:

Symbol segmentation	Symbol-size profile
°u n p r o b l e m a t i c	1111111111111

Words which are 'all ones' are quite common, and, as you can see, they don't have to be short words like °cat.

But 'all ones' are not a majority. A word like °unphotogenic, with its digraph °ph, is nearer to the normal ratio than °unproblematic, while each of the words °photo °gateau and °brought actually embodies the ratio:

Symbol segmentation	Symbol-size profile
°u n ph o t o g e n i c	°11211111111°
°ph o t o	°2111°
°g a t eau	°1113°
°b r ough t	°1141°

(Remember, the ratio is the ratio of 1-letter to multiletter symbols, counting what I have called 'in-line' symbols. In °photo there are 4 *in-line* symbols but only 3 *distinct* symbols, because °o occurs twice.) I've added a circlet at the end of the symbol-size profiles: this will signal profiles concerned with symbols (as distinct from letters) and spare us underlining within these profiles.

Counting – counting letters and counting symbols – has been the keynote of this section. The next section has a conceptual bias.

13.4 Symbols consist only of letters

Symbols consist of letters, and *only* of letters. I'm not thinking here of accents on letters or of apostrophes. I mean simply that *a symbol is a symbol and not a sound*.

°c and °h ('letter C and letter H'), taken together, do not make the sound /ch/; they make the symbol °ch ('the symbol C-H'). The symbol °ch ('C-H') enters into a number of correspondences with sounds, but it is not itself a sound. The following words all contain the symbol °ch:

°chat °chic °chloride °chord °enchant °loch °lochs
°machine °macho °mechanic °rich °riches °school °squelch

In each of these fourteen words the consonant letters °ch constitute a symbol corresponding to a consonant sound: the symbol is one and the same, °ch. Later, in Chapters 21 and 23 we shall see the different consonantal values it can have. You can tabulate the fourteen words now, if you like, according to the sound-value of °ch, by way of preparation. But as you do so, keep reminding yourself that you have fourteen in-line occurrences of one and the same symbol, whatever its sound-value.

Symbols are arrived at by segmentation and it will help if we take just one of the fourteen words, one which is a well-known stumbling-block (in the elementary stages, I hasten to add): the word °school. The symbol segmentation is °s ch oo l. Here is a full-blown analysis of the word, as in Table 13.1:

I	II	III	IV	V	VI	VII
	Number of	Sound	Number of	Symbols		Symbol-size
Word	letters	profile	sounds	(spaced)	(underlined)	profile
°school	6	/CCVC/	4	°s ch oo l	°s ch oo l	1221

What you must note is that all this display still does not give a specific sound-value for °ch ('Symbol C-H'), only a category value: that is to say, it's a consonant symbol, not a vowel symbol. The other consonant symbols are °s ('Symbol S') and °l ('Symbol L'), and the vowel symbol is °oo (Symbol OO, to be read as 'Symbol O-O', unless you prefer 'Symbol Double-O').

Symbols are easy to name, because they can be named unambiguously by the letters that constitute them: Symbol S, Symbol CH, Symbol OO, Symbol L. These names are important, for symbols consist only of letters, not of sounds.

13.5 Every letter belongs to a symbol

The secret of symbol segmentation is that *every letter belongs to a symbol*. I will illustrate this from two words in Table 13.1. Take °chat and °catch. In pronunciation they have a consonant sound in common, which we can notate /ch/. The symbol for this sound in °chat is °ch, giving the segmentation:

°ch a t

with all four letters accounted for. The correspondence involved is the familiar one:

°ch – /ch/   ('CH with the value /ch/')

If we were then to use this symbol in the analysis of °catch we would leave °t unaccounted for in the middle: °c a t ch. But if we think of pairs of words like °rich/witch or °such/hutch, it is obvious that °ch and °tch are symbols for the same sound, /ch/. So the symbol segmentation of °catch is

°c a tch

with all five letters accounted for. The correspondence involved is

°tch – /ch/   ('TCH with the value /ch/')

You are probably already familiar with this as a symbol and with the different distributions of °ch and °tch: typically °ch is morpheme-initial and °tch is morpheme-final, as in °chat and °catch.

The example of °catch illustrates the principle that every letter in a word belongs to a symbol (in this case, two 1-letter symbols and one 3-letter symbol). It is this principle which gives segmentation its thrust: with a 'spare' letter like °t in °catch, we are forced to decide which way to assign it, to the left or to the right. (You may like to explore the consequences of assigning it to the left and setting up a vowel symbol °at in °catch; and then choose between the two analyses.)

At the same time, these two symbols serve to demonstrate how important it is to name symbols by their correct names. Neither of these symbols is called /ch/: one is called 'C-H' and the other is called 'T-C-H'. Symbols are not sounds; they are units in the spelling system which correspond to sounds – that is, to units in the pronunciation system.

We now turn to sounds.

14 *What is a sound?*

14.1 Consonants and vowels

Here is Table 13.1 from the last chapter, shorn of Columns VI and VII, which we do not need. We do not really need Column V, but some readers may find it helpful to have it here (remember, those are *symbols*, not *sounds*: they only *correspond* to sounds).

Table 14.1 *Words divided into sounds*

I Word	II Number of letters	III Sound profile	IV Number of sounds	V Symbols spaced
°cat	3	/CVC/	3	°c a t
°chat	4	/CVC/	3	°ch a t
°catch	5	/CVC/	3	°c a tch
°caught	6	/CVC/	3	°c augh t

This chapter is about Columns III and IV – about the sounds in words. As you already know, each of the four words is made up of a succession of three sounds: the first a consonant sound, the second a vowel sound and the third a consonant sound. All this is compactly indicated in Column III by C for consonant and V for vowel within the slanting brackets used for 'phonemic notation': /CVC/.

'Phoneme' is the more technical term I could use instead of 'sound'. It's the term used by linguists when they analyse the sound system of a language and list its consonants (sounds, not letters) and its vowels (sounds, not letters). 'Phoneme' is simply the general name for the consonants and vowels in the sound system of a language. This is the meaning of 'sound' in the expression 'sound/symbol correspondence' and I shall stick to the term 'sound' as the focus for this chapter.

'Sound', then, is the superordinate term:

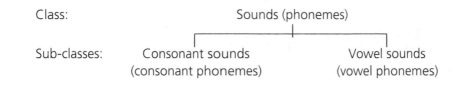

Class:		Sounds (phonemes)	
Sub-classes:	Consonant sounds (consonant phonemes)		Vowel sounds (vowel phonemes)

'Consonant' and 'vowel' are two contrasting categories which apply alike

1   to sounds (where the two categories originate)

2   to symbols

3   to correspondences

4   to letters (where we all meet the words 'consonant' and 'vowel' for the first time)

and I shall refer to them as 'categories' – the two fundamental categories common to the pronunciation system and the spelling system.

14.2   Sound profiles

Every word has a sound profile, like the sound profiles in Column III of Table 14.1. I ought to call these, more precisely, 'sound-category profiles' since they consist only of Cs and Vs, but 'sound profile' will do, as long as we understand it to refer to categories and not to specific sounds like /kat/.

You can do a lot with sound profiles. When two of you, in talking about spelling, agree on a sound profile for a word, you are agreeing on the succession of C-sounds and V-sounds that make up the word. And that is a big step forward. It is halfway to identifying the individual sounds. The essential activity here (as I keep saying) is *talk*.

The succession of C-sounds and V-sounds in English words has an interesting characteristic. /C/ and /V/ alternate, but not on equal terms: there are more /C/s than /V/s, so that successive /C/s are common, while successive /V/s are rare. For the rest of this section, I shall illustrate this from words of one syllable.

A syllable must contain a V-sound as its nucleus; that V-sound may have one or more C-sounds before it, or after it, or both. Two or more C-sounds before or after the vowel nucleus are called a consonant cluster. To over-simplify usefully: C-sounds cluster, V-sounds don't.

You can build up the possible sound profiles for words of one syllable by modelling with Cs and Vs, but, as these are *sound profiles*, remember to enclose each one in obliques (slant brackets). Here, in Table 14.2, is one systematic arrangement of possible profiles.

Table 14.2 *Sound profiles for English monosyllables*

1-Place	2-Place	3-Place	4-Place	5-Place	6-Place	7-Place
/V/	/CV/ /VC/	/CCV/ /CVC/ /VCC/	/CCCV/ /CCVC/ /CVCC/ /VCCC/	/CCCVC/ /CCVCC/ /CVCCC/	/CCCVCC/ /CCVCCC/ /CVCCCC/	/CCCVCCC/ /CCVCCCC/

These 18 profiles cover everything from 'a' to 'glimpsed'!

You can now experiment with these profiles in two ways: either select a profile as a template and find words to fit it; or think of words and assign them to their profiles. Either way, you will be isolating sounds and categorising them – and, as I suggested above, this is halfway to identifying them.

You will have to make certain decisions as you go along. Take, for instance, that unusual word I have just mentioned – °glimpsed (unusual only because words ending in /...CCCC/ *are* unusual). It highlights two problem areas which call for discussion and agreement.

In the first place, °glimpse, the base form, raises no problems: it is (recalling Section 4.3) monomorphemic – a single morpheme, °glimpse. But is the inflected form, °glimpsed, acceptable? It is a monosyllable all right, but it contains two morphemes (bimorphemic):

°glimpse × ed → °glimpsed

Are you going to distinguish between monomorphemic and bimorphemic words? Is it only inflected forms which create this problem? Or are there some derivational forms amongst the 'monosyllables' (Chapter 8) of English? Explore! Most words will be unproblematic.

In the second place, you may all agree on the pronunciation of °glimpse, as /CCVCCC/ ending in /...mps/; but are you all agreed on your pronunciation of °glimpsed? Is it:

1 /CCVCCCC/

or **2** /CCVCCC/

Does it end in **1** /...mpst/ or in **2** /...mst/? Does it matter?

You must explore. The domain of pronunciation is a huge one, and I can only touch on it, as I have said before (Section 12.2). Many words will be unproblematic, but many will need discussion – even monosyllabic ones.

Here, in Table 14.3, are 100 monomorphemic monosyllables for you to practise on. All that is needed for each word is a sound profile, one from Table 14.2. Don't skip the easy ones: get used to writing the obliques *every time*.

Table 14.3 *Monosyllables for sound profiles practice*

°a	dawn	gin	lamp	prowl
act	desk	glade	lapse	quack
aid	die	glance	loin	quilt
an	drought	gnat	mall	reel
and	dumb	go	mink	right
ape	dunce	ground	minx	row
awe	edge	guilt	mix	sauce
back	eight	gym	mount	scent
bang	elm	hatch	my	school
beast	eye	have	myth	squat
black	faint	his	nest	stray
broad	faith	hunch	nil	stretch
cake	field	if	notch	talk
chick	fight	ice	oath	text
cinch	flash	ink	of	thaw
class	flaunt	jam	oust	tray
could	free	joule	phrase	urn
count	freeze	kilt	plump	vague
crust	from	know	prompt	yield

Discuss any controversial items, and number your alternative solutions (it makes them easier to talk about).

14.3 Profiles and outlines

I said just now that when two of you agree on a sound profile for a word, you are agreeing on the succession of C-sounds and V-sounds that make up the word. You are also agreeing on something even more basic – the *number* of sounds in the word. That is the first thing to check if you are in disagreement about a profile: have you got the same number of sounds? Have you got the same sound outline?

A *sound outline* is simply a notation which shows the number of sounds without showing the categories. Here are the sound outlines for a selection of words from Table 14.3.

Don't be surprised if you find it easier to work from the profile to the more abstract outline. That's perfectly normal. What is important to grasp is the difference between the two, between profiles and outlines, since this has general application. *Outlines* are quantitative: the outlines in Table 14.4 give only the number of sounds. *Profiles* are qualitative: the profiles in Table 14.4 give the nature (as well as the number) of the sounds – that is to say, their C/V categories.

Table 14.4 *Sound outlines and sound profiles*

I Word	II Sound outline	III Sound profile
°an	/- -/	/VC/
°eight	/- -/	/VC/
°my	/- -/	/CV/
°thaw	/- -/	/CV/
°oust	/- - -/	/VCC/
°talk	/- - -/	/CVC/
°tray	/- - -/	/CCV/
°mount	/- - - -/	/CVCC/
°freeze	/- - - -/	/CCVC/
°stray	/- - - -/	/CCCV/
°minx	/- - - - -/	/CVCCC/
°stretch	/- - - - -/	/CCCVC/

14.4 Rhythmic profiles

We turn now to another aspect of English pronunciation, already introduced in Part I (Sections 7.3, 12.4), which will help us to move on from monosyllables. It's another application of the outline/profile distinction and concerns another aspect of speech – its rhythm.

The unit of rhythm in speech is the *syllable*. Each word in English has a particular rhythm – a rhythmic pattern which it shares with other words. It has a particular number of syllables and one of these is stressed: one syllable carries a stronger stress than any other syllable in the word. (Notice that 'stress' is a much more precise word than 'emphasis'.) Every word, pronounced in isolation, carries 'primary stress' on one of its syllables.

If the word is a monosyllable, there is only one syllable that can carry primary stress, but for two-syllable words there are two possible patterns, for three-syllable words there are three, and so on. This can be compactly stated in notation, as in Table 14.5.

Syllables are units in the sound-structure (or phonology) of the language, so we use oblique brackets, as for sounds. But whereas sounds were notated in Table 14.4 by hyphens, which are short, syllables are notated by dashes, which are long.

Table 14.5 *Rhythmic outlines and profiles (up to 4 syllables)*

Rhythmic outline	Possible rhythmic profiles	Specimen words
/–/ /– –/	/⸍/ /⸍ –/ /– ⸍/	°cat chat catch caught a my with °kitten chitchat catcher purple camel begging comet London °begin connect canal possess again balloon commit refer champagne
/– – –/	/⸍ – –/ /– ⸍ –/ /– – ⸍/	°educate polyglot Paddington Canada Birmingham biblical granary restlessness subaltern suddenly °banana committee possession akimbo seductive °interfere referee cockatoo disappear
/– – – –/	/⸍ – – –/ /– ⸍ – –/ /– – ⸍ –/ /– – – ⸍/	°cumulative tributary covetousness °comparative geology periphery °hypodermic reverential impetigo distribution °hullabaloo

At the very least this should reinforce the distinction, much neglected, between hyphens and dashes in standard punctuation. But its purpose here, of course, is quite different: it is to give some initial grasp of the complexity of English pronunciation, a topic to be pursued in the next chapter.

15 *What is a correspondence?*

15.1 Symbols and sounds

The French have a word for it: *les données* – the 'givens' of a situation, of a problem. The givens for us now are the spelling of a word and its pronunciation. Each is represented by a sequence of units: the letters of the spelling and the sounds of the pronunciation. But, of course, the letters do not match to the sounds until they are organised into symbols.

The spelling is certainly 'given' – highly standardised, accessibly codified, with minimal variation in the system.

Pronunciation, by contrast, feels like a complex of givens, which include variations between groups, large and small, of English speakers (British/American, English/Scottish, Liverpool/West Country, Indian/West Indian), variations between individuals in the groups, and variation within each individual, for example according to how fast they're talking, and who to, and according to where a word comes/what its neighbours are.

But this is a lopsided view, which looks at variation at the expense of conservation – that is, what is conserved through all the variations. Variations of a word are variations of that word precisely because something essential about it stays recognisably the same. Part of that something is its meaning and its grammar, but those two are married to its essential make-up of sounds. That make-up must be different from the 'make-ups' – the specific sound profiles – of the other words in the language, words made up differently *from the same set of sounds.*

Despite all the variation due to accent, tempo, occasion and context, one word differs from another through its selection of, and maintenance of, a particular sequence of specific /C/s and /V/s. Those are the 'sounds of its pronunciation' with which we have to deal.

Nor is it only the spellings which are 'standardised and codified'; meanings, grammar and pronunciations are too. Our ordinary dictionaries codify precisely those words, tens of thousands of them, which have over the centuries become standardised by usage – in their meanings, their grammar, their spelling and their pronunciation. And for the purpose of exploring symbol-to-sound correspondences in our spelling system, it is the pronunciation given in British English dictionaries that I shall use.

Real-life pronunciation is not standardised, as we all know, and never has been. What the dictionaries give is a *reference pronunciation*, in Britain a British one, in the USA an American one. Since this is a British book, its reference pronunciation (its 'RefP') is the one generally found in British dictionaries.

While British dictionaries tend to give the same reference pronunciation, they do so in a whole variety of sound notations, usually, though not always, intended to be easy for readers to understand. I shall take my pick among these, bearing in mind the very particular intention of this book, namely to offer insight into the spelling system. I have used some notations for sounds already, nearly always for individual sounds (rather than whole words), and I would urge readers not to be frightened by sound notations. Adapt mine, if you feel the need, or invent your own; arrive at them by discussion and agreement. But never omit the slanting brackets: they are the positive signal of *sounds*.

The equally positive signal of *symbols*, on the other hand, is the combination of the circlet and underlining which I used in Chapter 13. Never omit these either. The circlet indicates focus on spelling and signals letters; *underlining* of the letters signals symbols.

A correspondence consists of a symbol and a sound.

15.2   Matching in-line symbols and sounds

Do you remember the word °unproblematic in Chapter 13? Its symbol-size profile was 'all ones': °1111111111111° (Section 13.3). That means that each letter in this 13-letter word was acting as a symbol. We can categorise those symbols into consonant and vowel symbols: the symbol-category profile is °VCCCVCCVCVCVC°. Written like that, in a sentence in a paragraph, it's difficult to check. The secret is to use vertical matching:

1   °unproblematic
      | | | | | | | | | | | | |
2   °VCCCVCCVCVCVC°

The symbol-category profile in turn matches to the sound-category profile one-to-one:

```
1   °unproblematic
    | | | | | | | | | | | | | |
2   °VCCCVCCVCVCVC°
    | | | | | | | | | | | | | |
3   /VCCCVCCVCVCVC/
```

and that in turn to the specific sounds, as shown in Table 15.1:

Table 15.1 *Vertical matching – fully displayed*

1 °unproblematic | | | | | | | | | | | | | |	Spelling (letter specification)
2 °VCCCVCCVCVCVC° | | | | | | | | | | | | | |	Symbol-category profile
3 /VCCCVCCVCVCVC/ | | | | | | | | | | | | | |	Sound-category profile
4 /unproblematik/	Pronunciation (sound specification)

(You can have too much even of a good thing like vertical matching! Incidentally, /e/ and /i/ are used loosely in line 4.) The key line in this is line no. 2. If all words were like °unproblematic, if all letters matched one-to-one to sounds, there would be no need for line no. 2, no need for symbols; that layer of organisation just wouldn't exist.

But it is one of the givens of our spelling system that in-line letters *don't* match to in-line sounds in this simple way. For every word like °unproblematic there's another, probably two others, in which there are more letters than sounds. Here in Table 15.2 are the words from Chapter 13, this time vertically displayed.

Table 15.2 *Vertical matching – reduced display*

```
1 °c a t    3    °cha t   4    °c atch   5    ° caugh t   6    ° schoo l    6
2  | | |           \/ | |        | |\_/        |\_/ |           |\/\/ |
3 /CVC/ 3         /CVC/ 3       /CV C/ 3      /C V C/ 3       /CC V C/ 4


1 °pho t o   5    °g a teau  6    °b rough t   7    °unpho tog e n i c    12
2  \/ | | |          | | |\/        | |\_/ |          | | \/ | | | | | | | |
3 /C VCV/ 4        /CVC V / 4      /CC V C/ 4       /VC C VCVCVCVC/ 11
```

°cat is like °unproblematic: its symbols appear as a little row of vertical bars (3 letters, 3 sounds). But the other words have wedges as well as bars (more letters than sounds). Line 2, the 'matching' line, organises the letters – *all* the letters – of line 1 into symbols, and points each in-line symbol to an in-line sound.

In short, every in-line letter belongs to a symbol (see Section 13.5), and every symbol corresponds to an in-line sound.

15.3 Listing distinct correspondences

Table 15.2 is very compact and gives only the sound categories, not the specific sounds. As I said in Section 14.2, deciding on the category profile (the succession of Cs and Vs) is half the battle. You can attack that categorisation from both sides, segmenting the letters of the spelling into symbols and, at the same time, segmenting (learning to segment) the sounds of your pronunciation. For any word, the symbol-category profile (between circlets – see Section 13.3) and the sound-category profile (between slants) should show the same succession of Cs and Vs. Exceptions are largely confined to °x.

Now for the specific sounds. Here in Table 15.3 are the correspondences that occur in the words in Table 15.2.

Table 15.3 *Distinct correspondences from Table 15.2*
Note Read the correspondences like the following example:

°c – /k/ 'Symbol C with the value /k/'

If you want to avoid pronouncing the isolated sound /k/, you can say 'Symbol C with the value of Letter C in "cat" '. For sound notations, see Tables 20.4 and 20.8.

Consonant correspondences

°c – /k/	°cat catch caught unphotogenic
°t – /t/	°cat chat caught photo gateau brought unphotogenic
°ch – /ch/	°chat
°tch – /ch/	°catch
°s – /s/	°school
°ch – /k/	°school
°l – /l/	°school
°ph – /f/	°photo unphotogenic
°g – /g/	°gateau
°b – /b/	°brought
°r – /r/	°brought
°n – /n/	°unphotogenic (twice)
°g – /j/	°unphotogenic

Vowel correspondences

°a – /a/	°cat chat catch gateau
°augh – /aw/	°caught
°oo – /oo/	°school
°o – /oe/	°photo (twice) unphotogenic (twice)
°eau – /oe/	°gateau
°ough – /aw/	°brought
°u – /u/	°unphotogenic
°e – /e/	°unphotogenic
°i – /i/	°unphotogenic

Table 15.3 is a list of distinct correspondences. After the division by category (C and V), they are listed in order of their first appearance in Table 15.2. Categorising them into C-symbols and V-symbols is a first act of control: C-symbols and their correspondences are simpler than V-symbols and their correspondences in several ways.

The order of appearance, however, is basically random. We can gain greater control by two kinds of sorting: we can sort the symbols by alphabetical order and by size. Both of these are intrinsic to the symbol itself, which is made up of one, two, three, or four letters of the alphabet.

Table 15.4 *Correspondences from Table 15.3, listed alphabetically*

Consonant correspondences

°b – /b/	°brought
°c – /k/	°cat catch caught unphotogenic
°ch – /ch/	°chat
°ch – /k/	°school
°g – /g/	°gateau
°g – /j/	°unphotogenic
°l – /l/	°school
°n – /n/	°unphotogenic (twice)
°ph – /f/	°photo unphotogenic
°r – /r/	°brought
°s – /s/	°school
°t – /t/	°cat chat caught photo gateau brought unphotogenic
°tch – /ch/	°catch

Vowel correspondences

°a – /a/	°cat chat catch gateau
°augh – /aw/	°caught
°e – /e/	°unphotogenic
°eau – /oe/	°gateau
°i – /i/	°unphotogenic
°o – /oe/	°photo (twice) unphotogenic (twice)
°oo – /oo/	°school
°ough – /aw/	°brought
°u – /u/	°unphotogenic

As you can see, alphabetical ordering takes care automatically of symbol-size. Everyone (who knows their alphabet) can arrive reliably at the same order for the symbols.

But these are correspondences: we are not just ordering symbols. To repeat: *A correspondence consists of a symbol and a sound.* So in Table 15.4 you find, for instance, these two correspondences next to each other:

°g – /g/ ('Symbol G with the value /g/')
°g – /j/ ('Symbol G with the value /j/')

The words in which they occurred were °gateau and °unphotogenic respectively; they will be known to some of you as 'hard G' (as in °gun) and 'soft G' (as in °gem). 'Hard G' takes precedence: I shall explain why in Section 28.5.

More to the point now is the question: what *are* 'hard G' and 'soft G'? Answer: they are the *names of correspondences*:

Correspondence	Name of correspondence
°g – /g/	Hard G
°g – /j/	Soft G

Likewise the more familiar pair, 'hard C' and 'soft C', are the names of correspondences:

Correspondence	Name of correspondence	
°c – /k/	Hard C	(as in °cat)
°c – /s/	Soft C	(as in °cell)

As we come to the end of these three chapters ('What is a symbol?', 'What is a sound?', 'What is a correspondence?'), it is important to note, first of all, that 'hard C', 'hard G' and 'soft C', 'soft G' are not the names of symbols, nor the names of sounds, but the names of correspondences.

They are not the names of letters either; but we should note, secondly, that letters do have names, and this makes them easy to refer to and talk about. Symbols, sounds and correspondences need names too, if we are to refer to them, *talk* about them, and get to know them as individuals.

15.4 How many correspondences are there?

Getting to know the correspondences individually will seem pretty daunting when I tell you there are just over 400 of them: their multiplicity is one of the 'givens' of English spelling. However, we shall approach them, in the chapters that follow, by way of the symbols: these are fewer in number and much more manageable.

15.5   Coda: °John/Johnny

The name °John is pronounced /jon/. It contains 'one of those funny things you get in English spelling', as the student put it in Section 12.1. Is the funny thing just the °h? No. With symbols, sounds, and correspondences in place, we can be more precise.

There are four letters in the spelling of °John to be matched to the three sounds /CVC/ in the pronunciation. This gives us the three symbols: °j oh n – one symbol per sound. Of the consonant symbols, °j has its primary value /j/; °n has its primary value /n/. Ordinary symbols, ordinary sounds, ordinary correspondences:

$$°j \ – /j/$$
$$°n – /n/$$

But where the vowel symbol is concerned, only the sound is ordinary: /o/ (Short O) as in °on. The symbol °oh is a rare one, and the correspondence even rarer. The more expected correspondence, with the value /oe/ (Long O), is encountered often enough in the exclamation °Oh!, but otherwise is found in °ohm and °kohl, which are not exactly everyday words:

$$°oh – /oe/$$

If that correspondence is rare, the correspondence in °John is even rarer:

$$°oh – /o/$$

It's unique to °John.

Symbol, sound and correspondence can reveal the unfamiliar in the familiar. But their chief function is to make the familiar more precise: the two straight consonant correspondences just mentioned, °j – /j/ and °n – /n/, are much more important than a freak vowel correspondence.

Before leaving °John, let us look at °Johnny and link these three chapters (13–15) back to Part I. In °Johnny we have the suffix °-y, used as a diminutive ending, as in °Bill/Billy. Its pronunciation is the unstressed sound /ı/ (see Section 12.4), giving the correspondence

$$°y – /ı/$$

But there has been a change in the symbol for /n/: we now have the correspondence

$$°nn – /n/$$

There is nothing unusual about either the symbol or the correspondence. What is unusual is the change-junction that produces the symbol:

$$°John \times y \rightarrow °Johnny$$

The two consonant-letters at the end of the nuclear °John should rule out Consonant-Doubling, but uniquely in °Johnny they don't. What we have to remember is that the hundreds of rule-governed Consonant-Doublings (°sun/sunny, for instance, and its exact parallel °fun/funny) are far more important than this freak counter-example.

In Part III you will find that the vowel correspondence in °friend is almost as freakish as the one in °John; and at the same time (Section 29.2) I shall show that, in such cases, we really mean morphemes, not words – linking back again to Part I.

Symbols, sounds, correspondences, morphemes, junctions – all are required in order to construct a precise general framework against which freaks, exceptions, counter-examples and counter-patterns can be systematically seen. °John/Johnny is a one-off case. I am ignoring some larger counter-patterns in pursuit of the most general patterns.

Symbols in text

16.1 The importance of text

Symbols (Chapter 13), sounds (Chapter 14), correspondences (Chapter 15) – of these three entities, only symbols are on the page. They are in front of you now as you read. Our writing system doesn't demarcate them for us in the way in which it demarcates words and, in print, letters. But they are there and we can get used to seeing them.

Here is a passage of text from Darwin's autobiography; the scene is the mountains of North Wales, the date is the 1830s.

> On this tour I had a striking instance how easy it is to overlook phenomena, however conspicuous, before they have been observed by anyone. We spent many hours in Cwm Idwal, examining all the rocks with extreme care, as Sedgwick was anxious to find fossils in them; but neither of us saw a trace of the wonderful glacial phenomena all around us; we did not notice the plainly scored rocks, the perched boulders, the lateral and terminal moraines. Yet these phenomena are so conspicuous, that . . . a house burnt down by fire did not tell its story more plainly than did this valley.

The important thing for us is that this is *text* (see Section 8.1). It is language in use, language in sentences; and though the passage is only 100 words long, there's a great deal we can learn from it about words in text and about spelling-symbols in text.

16.2 The frequency of Function Words in text

Because we are looking at text rather than at single words, we can take a much more grammatical view of things. Words can be divided into two basic categories: Content Words (CW) and Function Words (FW). What I said about them in Section 8.1 can be represented by a structured classification: 10 word-classes – 4 CW, 6 FW:

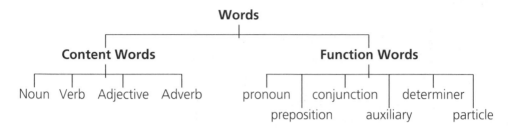

Function Words are typically short and high-frequency – a few of them very high frequency indeed ('VHF'). Twelve of them are said to account for one quarter of the words in ordinary texts (one quarter of the in-line words). These twelve 'VHF' words are: °a °and °he °I °in °is °it °of °that °the °to °was.

Here is the text again, with all its Function Words underlined.

On this tour I had a striking instance how easy it is to overlook phenomena, however conspicuous, before they have been observed by anyone. We spent many hours in Cwm Idwal, examining all the rocks with extreme care, as Sedgwick was anxious to find fossils in them; but neither of us saw a trace of the wonderful glacial phenomena all around us; we did not notice the plainly scored rocks, the perched boulders, the lateral and terminal moraines. Yet these phenomena are so conspicuous, that . . . a house burnt down by fire did not tell its story more plainly than did this valley.

Eleven of the twelve VHF words are there and they account for 20 of the in-line words, or 20% of the text – not a quarter but quite close (the missing one is °he). The total of Function Words can be quickly counted: it is 59 in-line words out of 100. Less quickly, by doing a tally, we can count the number of distinct Function Words: there are 37, or half of the total of 73 distinct words overall.

Some symbols, then, will be high in frequency because they appear in high-frequency Function Words, especially as they appear in Content Words too.

16.3 The inflection of Content Words in text

Because we are looking at words in text and not at words in a list, as in a dictionary, we find not only Function Words at work but also Content Words at work. In sentences Function Words get used over and over again; Content

Words get inflected. Grammatical aspects of a Content Word in a sentence are signalled by the absence or the presence of an inflection (see Sections 6.2–3). It is the inflected forms that concern us now.

Here is the text with the Function Words removed and inflected forms of the Content Words underlined.

> tour <u>striking</u> instance easy overlook <u>phenomena</u> conspicuous, <u>observed</u> spent <u>hours</u> <u>examining</u> <u>rocks</u> extreme care, Sedgwick anxious find <u>fossils</u> saw trace wonderful glacial <u>phenomena</u> notice plainly <u>scored</u> <u>rocks</u>, <u>perched</u> <u>boulders</u>, lateral terminal <u>moraines</u>. <u>phenomena</u> conspicuous, house <u>burnt</u> fire tell story plainly valley.

(Again, a reminder from Section 4.4, that °rock and °rocks are distinct words. It is not true to say, for instance, that °ck 'only occurs at the end of words', since the word °rocks ends with the plural morpheme °-s (and °rocked ends with °-ed, and °rocking with °-ing). It is nearer the truth to say that °ck only occurs at the end of morphemes. See °friends, Section 29.2.)

I will take the classes of Content Words from the above in turn.

Nouns   The noun plural shows up well. We find the S-inflection in °hours °rocks(2) °fossils °boulders °moraines; °phenomena(2) is a minor (not irregular) pattern of plural inflection. Only a handful of nouns have irregular plural forms in English (for example °men °women °children – and °feet, Section 4.4) and none occur in this passage.

Verbs   The ING-form and the ED-form of verbs both occur more than once: °striking °examining; °observed °scored °perched. The S-inflection, marking the present tense (third person singular), doesn't occur at all in this first-person past-tense narrative.

Since most of the passage is in the past tense, we might expect more ED-forms. Why aren't they there? For two reasons: the number of irregular verbs in English is much larger than the number of irregular nouns. Of the 200 or so such verbs, many of them very common verbs, some belong to the pattern shown by °spent (from 'spend') and some are highly irregular like °saw (from 'see'). Four other past tenses are expressed in °had °was and °did(2).

The ED-forms we have got are all used with passive meaning: 'phenomena [which have not been] observed by anyone' 'boulders [which have been] perched' 'rocks [which have been] scored'. But any extended past tense narrative – historical, fictional, or reports of various kinds – will yield past tenses in °-ed in abundance.

Adjectives and Adverbs   There are nine Content adjectives but no ER-forms or EST-forms. In fact the only comparative expression is the adverbial one 'more plainly'.

Adverbial °-ly is an interesting suffix. As explained in Section 8.2, it is not an inflectional suffix, since it changes the word-class or 'part of speech', changing adjectives into adverbs; on the other hand it is like the inflections in being universal – it attaches (in principle) to all adjectives. Derivational suffixes, as you can see from °-al °-ful °-ous in this passage, are very selective (there are no English words *conspicual* *laterous* or *anxiful*; see Section 9.3).

16.4 Text frequency versus list frequency

A common word is a word that is used a lot: it occurs frequently in text – that is, in language in use, language in sentences, typically, for us at the moment, continuous prose, since we are concerned with the spelling system. In the same way, common morphemes are ones that are used a lot: we are not usually aware of them in the way we are aware of words, but we can become aware of them. And the same applies to symbols: common symbols are ones that are used a lot, and we can become aware of these too. At the other end of the scale there are rare words, rare morphemes and rare symbols: that is to say, words, morphemes and symbols which occur *in*frequently in text.

The frequency of a morpheme will depend upon the frequency of the words in which it appears, and the frequency of a symbol will, in turn, depend upon the frequency of the morphemes in which it appears – *in* text. Let me illustrate this with the symbol °th. If you were to go through 'all the words in the dictionary', by which I mean the head-words, the symbol °th would not be a particularly common symbol. It's not uncommon, like °rh, but it's not as common as °sh or °ch. That is true of °th in words *in a list*. But do a tally of the symbols in words *in a text*, and °th scores higher, due to its occurrence in Function Words. In the 'Cwm Idwal' text it occurs 14 times – far more frequently than any other 2-letter symbol (the runner-up is °er, which occurs 8 times). In fact all the symbols which occur more frequently than °th are 1-letter symbols (see Section 13.3), namely the consonant symbols °n °s and °t, and the vowel symbols °a °e °i and °o.

16.5 A symbol is a symbol is a symbol

I will use °n to demonstrate once again the crucial difference between symbol and letter.

If you count the letters in the text of 'Cwm Idwal' – the in-line letters – you will find there are 456. If you do a tally, you will find that the number of distinct letters is 23 (the missing letters are °j, °q and °z). °n occurs 37 times.

In Chapter 17 I shall segment the text of 'Cwm Idwal' into symbols, count the in-line symbols, and do a tally to find the distinct symbols. We shall find there are 369 in-line symbols and 57 distinct symbols. °n ('symbol N') occurs 35 times. It is in fact the most-occurring symbol in the text – close on 10% of the total. But that doesn't account for all the occurrences of °n ('letter N'), only for 35 out of the 37. The other two occurrences of °n are in the symbol °ng, in °striking and °examining.

   Symbols are the units which correspond to sounds. Where °n on its own corresponds to a sound, as it does most of the time, it constitutes a symbol, a 1-letter symbol. Otherwise it can only be part of a larger symbol – in this case the 2-letter symbol °ng. *Letters are the constituents of symbols* – of 1-letter, 2-letter, 3-letter and 4-letter symbols.

17 Segmenting text into symbols

17.1 'Cwm Idwal': Segmented into symbols

The secret of symbol segmentation, as I said in Section 13.5, is that *every letter is assigned to a symbol*. The practical value of this will soon become apparent; the theoretical value of it will be explained in Part III (Chapter 25). Here follows a 'symbol-segmented' presentation of 'Cwm Idwal'. (Taking the Welsh place-name out of the text makes the number of words exactly one hundred. 'Cwm', incidentally, is 'combe' in English, meaning a valley.)

'Cwm Idwal', symbol-segmented (normal text in Section 16.1)

```
      on this tour i had a striking
      instance how easy it is to
      overlook phenomena, however
 4    conspicuous, before they have
      been observed by anyone. we
      spent many hours in [Cwm Idwal]
      examining all the rocks with
 8    extreme care, as sedgwick was
      anxious to find fossils in them;
      but neither of us saw a trace
      of the wonderful glacial
12    phenomena all around us; we did
      not notice the plainly scored
      rocks, the perched boulders, the
      lateral and terminal moraines.
16    yet these phenomena are so
      conspicuous, that ... a house burnt
      down by fire did not tell its
      story more plainly than did this
20    valley.
```

You can see at a glance the *high proportion of 1-letter symbols*, and also how 2-letter symbols are a routine feature, three or four to a line. 3-letter symbols are thin on the ground, and there is just one 4-letter symbol. 'Statistics', for this infinitesimal fragment of English will come in Section 17.2.

You can also see at a glance, because of the 'swags' (‿) underneath them, the presence of *discontinuous symbols*, about one every two lines. These all link Terminal-E to preceding vowel letters. Terminal-E is a prominent feature of the English spelling system, discussed in Part I of this book in connection with junctions. In Table 11.4 I used notations like °a.e and °e.e because, in respect of sound-value, Terminal-E is systematically associated with the preceding vowel letter as in derivational pairs like °sane/sanity – a fact which is also recognised in pedagogical pairs such as °mat/mate.

In symbol segmentation these notations become discontinuous symbols – °a.e °e.e and so on, with the names 'A dot E', 'E dot E' and so on. Apart from their discontinuity, these symbols are just like other multiletter symbols: they consist of letters – a minimum of two – and they can have more than one value. For example, the symbol °a.e has, in three different occurrences in the text, three different values – in °trace °have and °instance. These values are related to each other in the grammar: to °sane/sanity, add °instance/instant/instantiate. But the point to grasp now is that °a.e *is one and the same symbol in all three words* °trace °have °instance.

Discontinuity is confined to Terminal-E, and Terminal-E is always discontinuous: it is always the last letter of a vowel symbol. The symbol itself may be longer than two letters, as in °house, and more than one consonant letter may intervene, as in °instance, but the typical discontinuous symbol is a 2-letter symbol split by a single consonant letter, as in °trace °extreme and °notice.

It is no accident that in this section I have had to highlight a class of vowel symbols. Vowel symbols are more complex than consonant symbols, as the rest of this chapter will make clear.

17.2 'Cwm Idwal': the management of symbols

There are 369 in-line symbols in 'Cwm Idwal'. These break down by size as follows:

1-letter	293	(79.4%)
2 letter	67	(18.1%)
3-letter	8	(2.2%)
4-letter	1	(0.3%)
Total	369	(100.0%)

In round figures, ordinary texts show the following percentages for the four different sizes of symbol: 75% 1-letter, 20% 2-letter, 4% 3-letter, 1% 4-letter. This amounts to an unmistakable majority of 1-letter symbols in text, mingled with a substantial minority of longer symbols mostly of two letters. As for in-line letters, there are 456 of them in 'Cwm Idwal', giving an average of $1\frac{1}{4}$ letters per symbol.

The 369 in-line symbols reduce to 56 distinct symbols, which break down by size as follows:

1-letter	23	(41.0%)
2 letter	26	(46.5%)
3-letter	6	(10.7%)
4-letter	1	(1.8%)
Total	56	(100.0%)

These figures are not very significant, but they do indicate how quickly, in text, the number of distinct multiletter symbols (33) overtakes the number of distinct 1-letter symbols (23), since the latter, of course, cannot exceed 26 (the number of letters in the alphabet). 2-letter symbols are the most numerous, but it is reassuring to know that of the 676 possible combinations of two letters (26 × 26), only a limited number operate as symbols in the spelling system.

The symbols found by segmentation need to be arranged and classified. The first step in this management of the symbols is to cut them by category into C-symbols and V-symbols, as follows:

	I In-line	II Distinct
C-symbols	218 (59%)	28
V-symbols	151 (41%)	29

As explained in Section 14.2, C-sounds cluster routinely, V-sounds don't; a word like °spent has the sound profile /CCVCC/, and even a word like °had, with no actual cluster, has the sound profile /CVC/, with two Cs to one V. In-line C-symbols, then, are bound to outnumber V-symbols, as in Column I. But in Column II we find that within a markedly smaller total, the variety of V-symbols is as great, even slightly greater – a tendency which would be more manifest in a longer text.

To display the variety of symbols in an easily manageable way, and to compare the limited variety found in C-symbols with the greater variety found in V-symbols, we take advantage of the fact that symbols consist of letters – of one, two, three or four letters. We simply arrange them, as we did in Table

15.4, alphabetically and by size (number of letters). In the next two sections this is done for the symbols in 'Cwm Idwal'. Consonant symbols come first in Section 17.3, as they are simpler and make up more of the data; vowel symbols follow in Section 17.4.

17.3   'Cwm Idwal': Consonant symbols

In Tables 17.1 (C-symbols) and 17.2 (V-symbols) the figure beside each symbol gives the number of occurrences of that symbol in the 'Cwm Idwal' text; these add up to the in-line totals at the bottom, where the number of distinct symbols is given in parentheses. (# indicates a 'cross-category' symbol in each table.)

Of the 28 distinct C-symbols, the four highest scorers (°n 32, °s 31, °t 21 and °th 14) account for more than half of the in-line C-symbols (101 out of 185). The high frequencies of these symbols are related to their occurrence in

Table 17.1 *'Cwm Idwal': Consonant symbols, with number of occurrences*

	1-letter		2-letter	
B	°b	8		
C	°c	10	°ch	1
			°ck	3
D	°d	13	°dg	1
#E			°ed	3
F	°f	7		
G	°g	1		
H	°h	5		
K	°k	2		
L	°l	13	°ll	4
M	°m	10		
N	°n	35	°ng	2
P	°p	6	°ph	3
R	°r	9		
S	°s	31	°ss	1
T	°t	21	°th	14
V	°v	5		
W	°w	6		
X	°x	2	°xi	1
Y	°y	1		
Totals		185(18)		33(10)

In aggregate: 218 in-line (28 distinct).

Function Words and in affixes (°th occurs only in Function Words in this text – see Section 16.4). 1-letter symbols amount to 85% of the in-line C-symbols; the other 15% in this text are all 2-letter symbols.

I shall survey C-symbols in general in Chapter 21. Here I will only draw attention to four symbols in Table 17.1, three of which are snags whichever way they are approached. But you must not let the problematical overshadow the unproblematical: symbol segmentation is mostly trouble-free when you get into it.

°x: °x as a symbol on its own is peculiar in its correspondences, as its commonest value is a sequence of two sounds /CC/: /ks/ in °extreme (line 8), /gz/ in °examining (line 7). But this is not a problem in symbol segmentation: like the letters on either side of it in these two words, °x is just a 1-letter symbol.

°dg: This 2-letter symbol may look less familiar than the others in the column, but it presents no problem of segmentation – compare °Sedgwick with °judgment.

°ed: The -ED inflection (like the S-inflection) creates unavoidable, but not insoluble, difficulties. At this point I will just give guidance. The word °perched forces you to segment °p er ch ed: you should segment in the same way wherever °-ed has its *consonantal* pronunciation (/t/ in °perched, /d/ in °observed and °scored; see Section 6.2), *regardless of whether there's a plus-junction or a change-junction*:

$$°perch + ed \rightarrow °perched \qquad\qquad °p\ er\ ch\ ed$$
$$°observe \times ed \rightarrow °observed \qquad\qquad °o\ b\ s\ er\ v\ ed$$
$$°score \times ed \rightarrow °scored \qquad\qquad °s\ c\ or\ ed$$

If °-ed has its *syllabic* pronunciation, as in °waisted or °wasted, there is no segmentation problem, since there are two 1-letter symbols, °e and °d.

°xi: This symbol is one solution to the problems which arise in the word °anxious (line 9). This is a real problem of segmentation: °i in °anxious has no sound-value of its own (contrast °anxiety) and we have to choose between assigning °i to the left, making a consonant symbol °xi, and assigning °i to the right, making a vowel symbol °iou. And then add to that some peculiarities of correspondence . . .

Of 218 in-line C-symbols, only one (°xi) presents a real problem of segmentation. Of 33 distinct C-symbols, two (°xi and °ed) present structural peculiarities.

17.4 'Cwm Idwal': Vowel symbols

The six vowel letters (AEIOUY – see Chapter 11) of the English spelling system provide the control column on the left of Table 17.3. Even in a text of 100 words, some of the six serve as leading letters to quite large families of symbols: 6 A-symbols, 7 E-symbols, 3 I-symbols, 9 O-symbols, 2 U-symbols and 1 Y-symbol – 28 distinct symbols. The intrusion of H, making 29 distinct symbols in all, is like the intrusion of E in the consonant control column in Table 17.2: 'cross-category' symbols work both ways.

Table 17.2 *Cwm Idwal: Vowel symbols, with number of occurrences*

	1-letter		2-letter		3-letter		4-letter	
A	°a̱	25	°a̱.e	3				
			°a̱i	2	°a̱i.e	1		
					°a̱re	2		
			°a̱w	1				
E	°e̱	23	°e̱.e	2				
			°e̱a	1				
			°e̱e	1				
			°e̱i	1				
			°e̱r	8				
			°e̱y	2				
#H							°hour	1
I	°i̱	24	°i̱.e	1				
					°i̱re	1		
O	°o̱	22	°o̱.e	1				
			°o̱o	1				
			°o̱r	1	°o̱re	2		
			°o̱u	5	°o̱u.e	1		
					°o̱ur	1		
			°o̱w	3				
U	°u̱	6	°u̱r	1				
Y	°y̱	8						
Totals		108(6)		34(16)		8(6)		1(1)

In aggregate: 151 in-line (29 distinct).

Compared to the consonant symbols in the 'Cwm Idwal' text, there are two obvious structural extensions: *'long symbols'* of three or four letters, and *discontinuous symbols*. A less visible, but pervasive, structural feature is the presence of consonant letters in the trailing letters of 11 of the 29 vowel symbols, especially °r (in 8 of the 11): as the 'Cwm Idwal' text suggests, *mixed symbols* such as these are much more characteristic of vowel symbols than of consonant symbols.

17.5 Symbols have structure

What we learn from Tables 17.2 and 17.3 is that *spelling symbols have structure*. They have structure in terms of:

- the number of constituent letters
- the order of those letters within the symbol
- the C/V categories of those letters.

Making use of the fundamental categories, C and V, we can now generalise as follows: The structure of a symbol is related, in a very obvious way, to sound-value: symbols with consonant values begin with a consonant letter and consist of consonant letters; symbols with vowel values begin with a vowel letter and consist of vowel letters.

This is the most general statement we can make. It captures a huge amount of the data. But it is the statement of a norm, not of a law. It is like the claim in Part I (Section 9.2) that plus-junctions are the norm: it provides a general positive background against which we can chart the counter-patterns. The main counter-pattern is found in *mixed symbols*, multiletter symbols in which the trailing letters include a letter or letters of the opposite category. A more extreme counter-pattern is found in *cross-category symbols*, a subset of mixed symbols in which the leading letter itself, but not the trailing letters, is a letter of the opposite category to that of the sound-value.

In the chapters which follow, I shall show that such counter-patterns cannot be avoided, any more than change-junctions can be avoided. But they are counter-patterns. Of the 369 in-line symbols in 'Cwm Idwal', 352 belong to the general pattern, leaving less than 5% counter.

The structures of symbols are forced on us by the principle of exhaustive segmentation – that every letter belongs to a symbol (Section 13.5). This principle is an important one and I shall take it further in Part III (Chapter 25). Here, to end with, is one application of it which you may or may not have noticed in the 'Cwm Idwal' text.

°o.e looks innocent enough in Table 17.2 in company with °a.e °e.e and °i.e; and the symbol structure of °one (occurring as a morpheme in the word °anyone, line 5) is the same as that of °ape °eve °ice or °ode. The anomaly of °one lies in the correspondence °o.e – /wu/; normality returns with °n – /n/. What we have done is to pinpoint the anomaly, instead of regarding °one as an unanalysable freak. Freak it certainly is – its letter profile is °VCV, while its sound profile is /CVC/ – but it is not unanalysable.

The words °anyone and °anxiety both contain the kind of snags I gave warning of in Section 13.2. But they are only two words out of a hundred.

18 An overview of symbols

18.1 How many symbols are there?

I shall work with a combined set of some 235 consonant and vowel symbols. There's nothing definitive about this number. If you rank the symbols in order of importance, then somewhere in the 100s you are into a long tail of low-scorers, and by 200 you are into marginal symbols. These are symbols which only appear in marginal words. Let me give an extreme example – a symbol and a word so marginal that I have happily discarded them.

I did not set up a class of 6-letter symbols, partly because it would have had only one member (and that's a consideration in itself), and partly because of the word in which this monster symbol uniquely appears:

°<u>schsch</u> – /sh/   as in °eschscholtzia

There's no doubt that this is a symbol: /sh/ is a single segment of sound, and that sequence of six letters corresponds to that sound in that word. But the word is marginal – not part of the mainstream vocabulary, which is large enough on its own to keep us fully occupied. Do not, however, dismiss the word as 'unimportant'. One man's marginal word is another man's daily bread: words, especially nouns (and you will have guessed, if you're meeting it for the first time, that 'eschscholtzia' is a noun) – words exist because of their functional importance to some group, large or small, of people, in the vast variety of human activities, and their existence should lead us on, not put us off.

Nevertheless, for the simple purposes of this book, °eschscholtzia is out, while °poppy (eschscholtzia is the Californian poppy) is in.

Of the 235 symbols, 87 are consonant symbols and the rest, 148, are vowel symbols (that's 37%, or three-eighths, are C-symbols, while 63%, or five-eighths, are V-symbols). The size breakdown is given in Table 18.1.

Table 18.1 *Symbols by category and size (percentages in parentheses)*

	1-letter	2-letter	3-letter	4-letter	Total
C-symbols	22 (9.4)	56 (23.8)	9 (3.8)	–	87 (37.0)
V-symbols	6 (2.5)	55 (23.4)	69 (29.4)	18 (7.7)	148 (63.0)
Total	28 (11.9)	111 (47.2)	78 (33.2)	18 (7.7)	235 (100%)

All percentages are percentages of 235. The curiosity of 28 1-letter symbols when there are only 26 letters in the alphabet arises from two letters having dual category. One of these is °y – a thread running through Part I; the other is °u, as will be explained later in this chapter (Section 18.6).

What Table 18.1 does is to show that the greater variety of V-symbols over C-symbols (148 distinct symbols as against 87) is centred in the 'long' symbols (symbols of 3 or 4 letters). The percentage of long C-symbols is negligible, 3.8% (9 symbols out of 87), while the percentage of long V-symbols is nearly ten times as high, 37% (87 symbols out of 148). It is worth reminding oneself sharply that these are list proportions; in real-life text (see Chapter 16), long symbols of both categories amount to only 5% of in-line symbols.

In any case, until we know the numbers of C-*sounds* and V-*sounds*, we cannot judge the nature of the excess of V-symbols over C-symbols: the symbol ratio might merely reflect the sound ratio. It doesn't.

18.2   How many sounds?

I shall begin with a set of 24 consonant sounds. I would like to partner that with a set of 24 vowel sounds, because the balance would be so easily memorable. But languages are untidy things, not given to symmetry, and alongside my set of 24 consonant sounds, I shall adopt a set of 27 vowel sounds. (One might make the two sets equal by, say, beefing up the consonants with /wh/ in °whale and maybe /hj/ in °huge, and dropping /oir/ in °coir from the vowels, but ... Well, for a start, /wh/ isn't in the RefP, not regularly.) 'Round about 25' for both categories is an easily memorable indicator of magnitudes, especially for the vowel sounds, about which there are widespread misconceptions. People need to know that, in the sound system of English, there's neither an infinite number of vowel sounds nor a little clutch of five.

The 24 C-sounds can be notated with 18 consonant letters from the alphabet, each with its expected value, plus four familiar digraphs and two unfamiliar ones. These last two are: /zh/ for the consonant sound in the middle of °vision, and /dh/ for the consonant sound in the middle of °bother –

contrast /th/ in °both. Segmenting word pronunciations into sounds needs practice and some guidance, but the notation for consonant sounds need not be a discouragement. If consonants next to each other ('clusters', including what are traditionally known as 'blends') – give trouble, exploit the spelling: °chain and °train may sound very alike, especially in children's mouths, but we are focusing on the spelling system not on the physical facts of pronunciation. (The notation for the consonant sounds will be found set out in Table 20.3.)

Turning to the 27 vowel sounds, we can almost manage with the five traditional vowel letters, plus °w and °r. These seven letters, in combinations of twos or threes, can cope easily with all 20 long vowel sounds, for example:

/oe/ in °hope and °soap
/oo/ in °hoop and °soup
/ow/ in °down and °out
/oer/ in °ore and °oar.

For the remaining seven vowel sounds (all short, or more precisely six short and one minimal) we want single-letter notations, of which five are ready to hand in the alphabet (see Section 11.4 on short/long vowel pairs). The sixth short vowel sound is the fully-coloured sound in °push °pull °could °would, and it is best to borrow a foreign letter for this: ø. As for the minimal vowel – it does not have the same status as The Six, as it never occurs in stressed syllables. In its most typical form it is the colourless, or 'grey', vowel sound, heard for instance in the first and last syllables of °aroma. As notation for it, I shall be unconventional and use the 'at' character which is already on the keyboard: /@/. My main purpose is the statement of correspondences, and for this we do not need to distinguish between 'shades of grey' (Sections 12.4 and 20.6). (The notation for the vowel sounds will be found set out in Table 20.8.)

The short/long distinction in the vowel sounds, then, is reflected systematically in their notations, just as it is reflected, though less systematically, in their spelling symbols. How 'long' the long vowel sounds are doesn't really matter, nor how 'pure'. English is well-known for its diphthongs – long vowel sounds which change in quality over their length. But, as I say, our concern is not with the physical facts of pronunciation, but first and foremost with the contrast between consonant sounds and vowel sounds reflected in the spelling system.

That is not to say that the physical facts – the physiology and the physics – of human speech are a matter of indifference: far from it. But we are segmenting pronunciation *to gain insight into a spelling system*, not into sounds and their production.

The long vowel sounds, then, all receive a two-character or three-character notation, for example /ee/ for the vowel sound in °fee, and /eer/ for the vowel sound in /fear/. Daunting complications flow from variations in pronunciation and from the effects of rhythm, both of which are concentrated in the vowels, as opposed to the consonants. The effects of rhythm are felt strongly within the RefP, which tends to minimise vowel sounds more than other accents do. (See Sections 12.4 and 19.8.) But with 27 vowel sounds, together with 24 consonant sounds, we need not be daunted.

18.3   How many correspondences?

The answer I gave to this question in Section 15.4 was 'just over 400'. I shall leave it at that. It gives the right order of magnitude, and any precise number is the product of the symbols you segment, the pronunciations you recognise, and the sounds you segment them into – and the words you admit. These are all variable, and even spelling can be: the two spellings °eschscholtzia and °eschscholzia in the dictionary yield the correspondences °z̲ – /s/ and °z̲ – /ts/ respectively. I shall ignore spelling variation, because in the great mainstream corpus of English words it's of marginal importance. So, too, is the exact number of correspondences.

Of greater interest is the way in which 400-odd correspondences are distributed among roughly half that number of symbols. At this point it is appropriate to give the distribution data for the symbols as well, so that it can be compared with that of the correspondences. In these tables symbols are simply counted in groups according to their leading letter and also categorised C or V by their leading letter (°y counting as a vowel letter). This could be refined, but refinement would not affect what the rank-ordering is telling us.

In Table 18.2 the five traditional vowels take the first five places: symbols beginning with these letters account for 59% of all symbols, and symbols beginning with the 'big three' account for 45% of all symbols. In Table 18.3 we see the same story, but pitched up a bit: the same five account for 69% of all correspondences, and the 'big three' account for 55% of all correspondences.

We are dealing here solely with numbers, not with individual symbols or with the correspondences that go with them. As a conclusion to this bout of numbers, Table 18.4 shows some averages contrasting the two categories. These averages give no hint of the uneven distributions revealed in Tables 18.2 and 18.3, highlighted there by the 'big three' vowels. The fertility of the six vowel letters is proclaimed in line 2 of Table 18.4.

Table 18.2 *Numbers of symbols per leading letter, rank-ordered*

	°C	°V	
A		38	the
O		37	big
E		33	three
I		19	
U		14	
C	10		
S	10		
G	7		
P	7		
T	7		
D	6		
Y		6	
H	5		
R	5		
B	4		
K	4		
M	4		
N	4		
F	3		
L	3		
W	3		
Q	2		
V	2		
X	2		
Z	2		
J	1		
	91	147	=238
	(38%)	(62%)	

Table 18.3 *Numbers of correspondences per symbol group as in Table 18.2, rank-ordered*

	°C	°V	
O		78	the
A		73	big
E		71	three
I		30	
U		28	
S	16		
C	14		
G	13		
T	11		
Y		9	
P	7		
D	6		
H	5		
N	5		
R	5		
X	5		
B	4		
F	4		
K	4		
M	4		
W	4		
L	3		
J	2		
Q	2		
V	2		
Z	2		
	118	289	=407
	(29%)	(71%)	

Table 18.4 *Symbols per leading letter and correspondences per symbol*

		Leading letters	Symbols	
1	C:	20	91	average of 4.6 symbols per leading letter
2	V:	6	147	average of 24.5 symbols per leading letter
		26	238	

		Symbols	Correspondences	
3	C:	91	118	average of 1.3 correspondences per symbol
4	V:	147	289	average of 2.0 correspondences per symbol
		238	407	

18.4   'Eschscholtzia' problems

I have already explained in Section 18.1 that there is nothing definitive about my list of symbols; it's a comprehensive list, but not exhaustive. There are three kinds of problem which beset anyone constructing such a list: 'eschscholtzia' problems (this Section), segmentation problems (Section 18.5), and categorisation problems (Section 18.6).

Eschscholtzia problems. Marginal words, marginal morphemes, marginal symbols, marginal correspondences. What does one do, for instance, with °rendezvous? It's not a marginal word like °eschscholtzia, and it doesn't contain a marginal monster symbol (see Section 18.1). Is it one morpheme, two or three? If the C-symbols are straightforward (°r °n °d °v), what about the three vowel symbols °e °ez and °ous? The correspondences of the last two are clear – for one pronunciation of the word, at least:

°ez – /ae/

°ous – /oo/

but are they worth including in a non-exhaustive list? As for °e, do we plump for the correspondence °e – /o/, °rend- rhyming with °pond, or do we try to accommodate, with a symbol °en, the in-between sound (nasalised) which you sometimes also hear in the first syllable of °envelope?

There are many of these marginal decisions to make, because that is the nature of language and of our experience of it. That is the insight to be gained at this point. Whether a word is regarded as marginal or not depends on the community concerned and on the activity engaged in. The margins of our individual vocabularies expand from infancy onwards. Education is the chief, but not the only, engine of that expansion.

18.5   Segmentation problems

There is one area in particular, of segmentation, where I have let uncertainty persist. It is seen at its simplest in connection with °t in °action. Two segmentations are possible:

1	°a c t io n	°t – /sh/	°io – /ə/
2	°a c ti o n	°ti – /sh/	°o – /ə/

Number 1 respects the morpheme boundary between °act and °-ion (and the symbol °io is needed anyway in °fashion, with the same minimal vowel value);

number 2 has a certain appeal. The decision has to be made in the light of similar boundaries: in °passion °fusion °coercion °fluxion °cautious °gracious °herbaceous °anxious (see Section 17.3), °partial °special °religion/religious °righteous and others. Clearly there is an interdependency between °t and the two 'soft' vowels °e and °i (hence the appeal of number 2); but, while interdependencies can cross morpheme boundaries, as in °critical/criticise (Section 28.5), symbols shouldn't (but they sometimes do – Section 23.2). (I have not included all the possible symbols arising from this uncertainty in the lists which appear in the following chapters.)

18.6   Categorisation problems

We happily think of consonant symbols as symbols with consonant values, and vowel symbols as symbols with vowel values, and this is fine 95% of the time. Mixed symbols, as such (for instance °gu in °guide or °igh in °sigh) are no problem, since the 'mix' is confined to the trailing letters. Where problems do arise, however, is firstly with cross-category symbols, where leading letter and value are in conflict (namely °ho °hour °heir °le °re and, in the opposite direction, °ed; see Section 17.5) and, secondly, with the dual categorisation of °y.

Cross-category symbols I shall treat separately from the rest and I shall give precedence to their sound-value by calling the three H-symbols and °le and °re 'vowel symbols', and °ed a 'consonant symbol', emphasising their anomalous nature.

Y-symbols I shall treat in both lists, since °y has dual categorisation (in °yearly, the °y at the beginning, coming before a vowel symbol, is acting as a consonant symbol, while the °y at the end, following a consonant symbol, is acting as a vowel symbol; see Section 11.5). This would be well displayed by the following alphabet array:

$$°V$$
$$a$$
$$e$$
$$i$$
$$o$$
$$u$$

°C: b c d f g h j k l m n p q r s t v w x y z

This shows °y at the intersection of the two letter-classes. I like this display as it drives home strongly the unique nature of this much misunderstood letter (see Sections 7.3 and 8.3). But though it tells the truth, it doesn't tell the whole truth – which is that °y is not, in fact, unique in having dual categorisation. Here is another array which allows for *two* letters in the intersecting set:

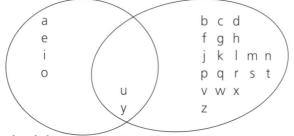

Note that both letters are primarily vowel letters.

°u is very restricted in its role as a consonant letter, so much so that this aspect of °u is often overlooked altogether. Nevertheless that is its role in words like °language, °linguistic, °anguish. Its value in these cases is /w/. There is nothing far-fetched about this correspondence: we all encountered it early in literacy in words like °quick (see Keith's story in Section 19.3). It is the traditional doctrine about 'Q and U going together' that blinds us – or shuts our ears – to this simple fact: °qu . . . in °quick is not a symbol; it is a sequence of two 1-letter symbols.

°y is also restricted as a consonant letter. In this capacity it is typically the first letter of a word immediately followed by a vowel letter (but never by °y!) – or more accurately, the first letter of a morpheme, as in °yon/yonder/be-yond. The important difference between these two dual-category letters is that there is no other consonant letter with primary value /y/ – hence the traditional ranking of °y as a consonant letter; whereas there is a consonant letter with primary value /w/, namely °w.

I shall treat °u, like °y, under both categories, but in both cases the bigger entry will be under vowels.

18.7   Coda: How to spell °consonant

The two categories consonant and vowel are so woven into the fabric of language that the next chapter (Chapter 19) will be a further probe into their ubiquitous role in the structure of English – in grammar with the morpheme, in pronunciation with the syllable, in spelling with the symbol (see Section 12.2).

But let me end the present chapter on a particular rather than on a general note. (This section is a rather long coda to an already long chapter, and some readers may prefer to go straight to Chapter 19.) It is interesting how some students in teacher training – students who have passed through our school system – in writing about vowels and consonants use the misspelling *constonant. It appears to be a mis-linking to °constant, when the link should really be to °sonic or other related forms. The nuclear morpheme [son-] is seen in:

°sonic

sonorous

resonate

resonant

consonant

(not to mention links to 'son et lumière', 'sonata', and to 'SOuNd itself').

The structure is [Prefix[Nuclear]Suffix] and the junctions are plus-junctions:

$$°con + son + ant \rightarrow °consonant$$

The prefix °con- commutes, as it often does, with °dis-, in °dissonant, reminding us that °consonant is also an adjective, as in committee parlance 'consonant with our avowed goals' or whatever.

But both as noun and adjective, °consonant is stressed on the first syllable. Here is its rhythmic profile (see Section 7.3):

/´ – –/ ('three syllables, stress on the first')

Syllable number 1 is stressed, and its vowel sound (/o/ as in °cot) is fully coloured, as it must be in a stressed syllable. Syllables number 2 and 3 have no stress at all; they are weak syllables and their vowel sounds have no colour – in Section 12.4 I called them 'grey'. They both have the same shade of grey.

The underlying colour in the nuclear morpheme can be recovered by reference to °sonic – to a related form in which the syllable is stressed and the vowel sound is exhibited, so to speak, in full colour (/o/ as in °cot, again). The underlying colour in the suffix morpheme can also be recovered, in the adjectival form °consonantal, another exhibitory related form (or 'ERF' for short). Here is its rhythmic profile:

/– – ´ –/ ('four syllables, stress on the third')

The vowel sound is /a/, as in °cat.

The spelling system keeps the shape of the morphemes constant, and this yields the correspondences:

°a̱ – /a/	°o̱ – /o/	full-colour vowel sounds ('maximal' in Chapter 20)
°a̱ – /ə/	°o̱ – /ə/	neutral/grey vowel sound ('minimal' in Chapter 20)

Syllables next to primary-stress syllables tend to be weakest, and their vowel sounds the most minimised, as in °hist'ry, °p'liceman, °sep'rate (the ERF for °hist'ry is °historical; °sep'rate has no ERF; as for the morpheme [police], BBC news-readers never indulge in the one-syllable pronunciation that the rest of us use, but is there an ERF?).

Notice that in °consonantal, syllable number 1 retains colour; its vowel sound is still /o/; it has secondary stress. We can notate the whole rhythmic profile more delicately to show these details, if we wish:

Rhythmic profile	More delicate rhythmic profile
/– – ∠ –/	/⌐ ⌣ ∠ ⌣/

with /⌐/ indicating secondary stress, and /⌣/ indicating weak syllable with minimised vowel sound.

The word °consonantal, of course, can serve as an ERF for those spellers who write *consonent. I don't think I have yet met *constonent, but there's no reason at all why the two errors shouldn't co-occur!

Morphemes versus syllables

19.1   Consonants and vowels again

Before I go on to treat consonant symbols and vowel symbols separately, it is time to say something more about the fundamental categories, consonant and vowel, and the units to which they belong.

We saw in Section 14.1 that the two categories, C and V, apply alike

1   to sounds (or phonemes; this is where C and V originate),

2   to symbols

3   to correspondences

4   to letters (where we all meet the terms 'consonant' and 'vowel' for the first time).

I'm now going to suggest, at the risk of a huge over-simplification, that in speech, C and V units constitute *syllables*, and in writing C and V units constitute *morphemes*.

I've put syllables first, at this point, because speech comes before writing (in more senses than one) and the two categories started life as two classes of *sounds* which structure the *syllable* which is a unit of *speech*. In English (as explained in Section 14.2), a syllable must contain a vowel sound and may also contain one or more consonant sounds before and/or after the vowel sound; by contrast, many of the world's languages have only very simple syllables, all

/CV/. C and V sounds, then, are the *direct constituents of syllables*. A syllable consists of (is constituted by) one or more sounds (phonemes), of which one, and only one, is a vowel sound.

In writing, however, in the spelling system of English, the direct constituents of morphemes are C and V symbols, not C and V letters. Letters are only indirect constituents of morphemes via the symbols. That is to say: symbols are the direct constituents of morphemes, and letters are the direct constituents of symbols, as in Figure 19.1 (see also Chapter 25).

Speech	Writing	
syllable	morpheme	
sounds	symbols	← *level of correspondences*
	letters	

Figure 19.1   *Low-level units in speech and writing*

At this point I might sum up the whole of Part II of *Insight* as follows. In English, the lowest-level unit in speech is the sound and the lowest-level unit in writing is the letter, but that does not make the letter the unit of correspondence to sounds; letters are the constituents of symbols, and the *symbol* (consisting of one, two, three or four letters) is the unit of correspondence to sounds.

But while Figure 19.1 gives a good insight into sounds, symbols and letters, and the relations between them, it may be suggesting quite the wrong idea about syllables and morphemes.

19.2   Bringing the morpheme on-stage

My statement just now that 'in speech, C and V units constitute *syllables*, and in writing C and V units constitute *morphemes*' is meant as a corrective (an exaggerated corrective) to a longstanding tradition that the only unit intermediate between the word and the letter is the syllable. Both units, the syllable and the morpheme, are intermediate, in speech and in writing respectively, between the word and its smallest constituents, but they must not be confused with each other. Still less must the familiar one, the syllable, be allowed to drive off-stage the less familiar one, the morpheme.

Let me illustrate the difference between the two units by means of a very short example, °squirting (Section 19.3), and a longer example of the same phenomenon, °refrigerator (Section 19.5).

19.3 °squirting

Keith asked me 'How do you spell "squirt"?' I said 'How do you start it?'

Keith: SQ.
Me: Well then, what's your next letter?
Keith: *(Hesitantly)* E?
Me, looking at what he'd written and pointing to °quick: No.
Which letter always follows Q?
Keith: Oh – U!
Me: Yes, SQU – that gives you /skw/ in 'squirt', just as QU gives you /kw/ in 'quick'. The next sound is the tricky one – /ur/. I'll give it you: it's written IR. *(Keith writes.)* Can you give me another word with IR in it, sounding /ur/?
Keith: *(Puzzled)* D'you, d'you mean here, in what I've written?
Me: No. *(Looking out of the window)* What about the things that you see flying about, in the sky?
Keith: Aeroplanes?
Me: No! Small. Much smaller. *(Inspired)* With feathers.
Keith: Birds!
Me: Yes. Birds. Birds. How do you spell 'bird'?
Keith: BIRD.
Me: That's right. There's your IR, same as in 'squirt'. *(Looking at his script I see that, in adding °ir to his °squ, Keith added on °t at the same time.)* Good! That's how you spell 'squirt'. Now, what is it you're saying here? Let's see.

Together we read what he'd just been writing: 'The firemen were quick to come. They were squirt . . .'. 'Ah!' I said. 'What do you need to write next?'
Keith said /ting/, but he wrote °ing.

19.4 Syllabic division and morphemic division

We have here two conflicting divisions of the word:

1 **Syllabic division**	2 **Morphemic division**
squir-ting	squirt-ing

Number 1 reflects how we break words up into separate syllables when we feel the need to; it doesn't reflect our normal pronunciation. Number 2 reflects the grammatical structure of the word which is also reflected in the spelling system:

$$°squirt + ing \rightarrow °squirting$$

They're not really in conflict with each other; they're just doing different things. But the difference between the two needs to be clearly grasped. A longer word will help.

19.5   °refrigerator

Barnaby was asked to spell 'refrigerator'. Enthusiastically, he did, grouping the letters as follows:

RE FRI DGE RA TOR

This was a good spelling – not a correct spelling, but a good one. Asked how many syllables there were, Barnaby counted five, in accordance with his letter grouping. He also ventured the view that a weaker speller might end with TER instead of TOR, misled (the weaker speller) by his own pronunciation.

Barnaby has grouped the letters by syllables.

19.6   Morphemic versus syllabic grouping of letters

Syllables are, of course, units of speech, and Barnaby's syllables all fall into the structural pattern /C(C)V/ (they are all /CV/ except the second, which is /CCV/).

How about morphemes? How congruent are Barnaby's syllable groupings with the groupings we would make (in spelling analysis) at the level of the morpheme? One morphemic analysis (of the standard spelling) is:

[re[friger]at]or]

To compare the two groupings we can display them like this:

	S:	1	2	3	4	5
Syllable groupings:		RE	FRIGE		RA	TOR
Morpheme groupings:		RE	FRIGER		AT	OR
	M:	1	2		3	4

Things are fine to begin with: S1 and M1 are congruent with each other, and therefore the start of S2 and the start of M2 are congruent. After that, it is not the discrepancy in the counts that concerns us (5 syllables but 4 morphemes – M2 is a bisyllabic morpheme); it is the displacement of the numbering. The units aren't in line vertically: the start of M3 is later than that of the syllable above it; the start of M4 likewise.

(Just in case the discrepancy in the counts is muddling, let us remove it. Another, more delicate, analysis will give us five morphemes, with 'frig-', as in 'frigid', identified as the nuclear morpheme:

	S:	1	2	3	4	5
Syllable groupings:		RE	FRI	GE	RA	TOR
Morpheme groupings:		RE	FRIG	ER	AT	OR
	M:	1	2	3	4	5

Though the numbers are now matched, this is no improvement in terms of congruency: the displacement now begins earlier, since the G is part of the nuclear morpheme number 2, and Barnaby's G (or DG) belongs to syllable number 3.)

Returning to the first display (it's simpler if we do), here is the junction analysis, which helps in identifying the morphemes:

$$°re + friger + ate \times or \rightarrow °refrigerator$$

The word belongs to a derivation set which is repeated over and over again in English:

> °refrigerate
> refrigeration
> refrigerator

Take almost any verb formed with the verb-suffix °-ate, such as °refrigerate, and you will be able to form an abstract noun with the suffix °-ion and an agent noun with the suffix °-or. For example:

°dictate	°indicate	°prevaricate	°speculate
dictation	indication	prevarication	speculation
dictator	indicator	prevaricator	speculator

°demonstrate/demonstration/demonstrator, and so on. (Use an ordinary forward dictionary, or, much better, use *Walker's* reverse dictionary – see Chapters 3–4.)

19.7   Initial consonantising of syllables

What Barnaby is doing with °refrigeration is what Keith did with °squirting: he is starting syllables (units of pronunciation, remember) with a consonant sound wherever he can. This is what we like to do in English: this is why we talk about the syllable '-tion', pronounced /shun/, instead of the morpheme [-ion] which is not so convenient to pronounce in isolation. It is natural for us to do this with syllables. But we mustn't mistake the syllables for morphemes.

The word-ending '-tion' is the most glaring example of how syllables have overshadowed morphemes. Whatever the symbol analysis should be of words like °action, the junction analysis is beyond dispute:

$$°act + ion → °action$$

Compare: $$°act + ive → °active$$

This doesn't mean to say the syllable division is wrong; as I said above, it's just doing a different job. It is as natural for us to divide, for instance, the word 'action' between the two consonant sounds /k/ and /sh/ as it was for Keith to divide 'squirting' between the vowel sound /ur/ and the consonant sound /t/. But in both cases the nuclear morpheme loses a consonant and the suffix morpheme gains one:

1 **Syllabic division**	2 **Morphemic division**
squir-ting	squirt-ing
ac-tion	act-ion

I shall call this natural tendency of ours 'initial consonantising'. It's not harmful in itself.

19.8   Syllable distortion

What is harmful is the distortion of pronunciation which usually accompanies deliberate syllable division in speech. The rhythmic profile (see Section 14.4) of 'squirting' and 'action' is the same – two syllables, stress on the first:

°squirting   /⌣ –/
°action   /⌣ –/

When people pronounce the syllables separately, they stress each syllable in turn, altering the rhythm of the word. In altering the rhythm you can alter the consonant profile of the word: if you say 'getting' slowly as 'get-ting', the effect can be to double the /t/ sound (in pursuit of initial consonantising). But much more seriously, and much more commonly, you alter the vowel quality.

This is best seen in 'refrigerator'. If it is divided as Barnaby divided it and pronounced as a sequence of five stressed syllables (if it is 'stretched'), each syllable is given a full vowel sound and the five vowel sounds come out as in line 2:

		re	fri	ge	ra	tor
1	Syllable groupings					
2	Vowel sounds under stress:	/e/	/i/	/ur/	/ae/	/oer/

But the rhythmic profile of 'refrigerator' is not (and cannot be)

	/ᴗ ᴗ ᴗ ᴗ ᴗ/	(=a distorted profile)
It is	/– ᴗ – – –/	(=the normal profile)

One syllable, and only one syllable, must bear primary stress, and in 'refrigerator' it is syllable number 2, with full vowel /i/ as in 'fridge'. The only other full vowel sound is in syllable number 4: /ae/ as in 'rate'; this syllable may bear secondary stress. The remaining three syllables contain 'minimised' vowels; they bear no stress at all, but merely fill in the rhythm.

Deliberate syllable division nearly always involves syllable distortion: stress on each syllable overrides the normal rhythmic profile, and vowels which are normally minimised are instead, and quite artificially, maximised. This is what has happened in line 2 above. Other distortions can be inflicted on words in the name of pedagogic distinctness, but vowel maximisation is the chief one. It's done from the best of motives – to help learners cope with the spelling.

19.9   Keeping the morpheme on-stage

Syllable distortion is doubly harmful. It distorts the sound-structure of words so that it gives no insight into pronunciation. At the same time, it distorts the morpheme structure of words, effectively driving the morpheme out of sight; in this way it gives no insight into spelling.

Both Keith and Barnaby were ten years old, or thereabouts. Barnaby was much more advanced in spelling. Yet we find Keith non-consciously operating with the morpheme [-ing] – he didn't write °-ting, you see, though he said it – and we find Barnaby not operating consciously with morphemes at all. When he said that other children might end °refrigerator with TER not TOR he was spelling a syllable, not the agent morpheme [-or] which commutes with [-ion] as in °actor/action (°refrigerator/refrigeration).

Learning about morphemes (not necessarily under that name) can begin as

soon as the spelling system makes words not only visible but segmentable –
°cats and °coming and °crocodiles. Words in their spoken form are
segmentable, of course, but they are not visible and they are not neatly sliced
into discrete minimal units. And they are not stationary; audio-recording can
reproduce the pronunciation of a word and repeat it and repeat it, but it cannot
make it stand still like the written word. It's no accident that the word
'grammar' comes from the Greek word meaning 'write' (our morphemes
[graph] and [gram-]).

I am not happy, as I said in Chapter 18, that human speech, its physiology
(so accessible – we carry it around with us, a personal laboratory of cause and
effect) and its other facets are not part of the school curriculum. But I would
argue that the spelling system can provide the starting-point of such study, just
as it can provide the starting-point of the study of grammar.

The morpheme is as much a unit in the grammar of spoken language as it is a
unit in the grammar of written language. It is not, however, a unit in the
structure of speech in the way that it is a unit in the structure of the spelling
system. Morphemes in speech undergo much more variation than they do in
writing: they are not only fugitive, they fluctuate.

Conversely, the syllable is present in the spelling of English, but not as a
unit of physical rhythm – there is nothing analogous to that on the page – nor
as an indispensable unit in the spelling system. 'Syllabification' has sometimes
figured in the school curriculum (especially across the Atlantic), largely as an
arid preoccupation with word-breaking based on printers' rules. In the
teaching of literacy, the syllable has a profoundly important role – that is, the
real syllable, the unit of rhythm, which, when we use it in the rhythmic
profiles of words, is intermediate between word and sound.

I therefore stand by my huge overstatement in Sections 1 and 2 that in
speech C and V units constitute *syllables*, and in writing C and V units
constitute *morphemes*. In the next chapter (Chapter 20), we must look more
closely at pronunciation, since in Chapters 21–24 I shall be presenting the C
and V symbols together with their sound values and giving examples of their
correspondences in morphemes.

20 *Symbols and their sound-values*

20.1 Look and talk

Written text is abundantly available and highly accessible in our immediate world. If we want to look at English spelling and *talk* about it, we can. There is nothing to stop us being observant about the spelling system and, with suitable terminology and notation, exploring it in discussion. At the same time, we can be observant about pronunciation and explore that too.

In this chapter, I am preparing the way for the four final chapters of Part II, which display consonant symbols and vowel symbols (Chapters 21, 22) and consonant correspondences and vowel correspondences (Chapter 23, 24). The choice of direction, from symbols to sounds (and not the reverse, from sounds to symbols) is deliberate and is another way of summing up the whole of Part II. In the spelling system there are symbols, but no sounds. There are no sounds in text on the page. Deaf people who have never heard the sounds can read; the rest of us bring the sounds to the text. Indeed this choice of direction can be said to sum up Parts I and II together, since the junction phenomena described in Part I were phenomena on the page, not in the ear.

In these five chapters (20–24), to the end of Part II, you will be faced with more and more tables and less and less prose text; in fact, the four final ones are really lists posing as chapters. There is no way round this: Part II has been about 'symbols' in the simple non-abstract sense explained in Chapter 13 – 'symbol' as a unit in the spelling system. There are over two hundred such symbols, and these tables and lists identify them individually, classifying them by category and by structure. They also relate the symbols to sounds with the aid of a *sound-notation based on the spelling system* – a convergent rather than a divergent notation. But while the tables and lists, and the 'matrices' in Chapters 21 and 22, may make it possible to see both the wood and the trees, they fall far short of mapping the wood and charting the paths and intersections within it.

There is nothing definitive about the tables or the lists. The process by which they were produced – symbol segmentation – is far more important than the tables and lists themselves. And more important still are the words and morphemes realised in text by the sequences of symbols. You don't get the meaning if you don't get the morpheme!

In this chapter, I list the consonant symbols (Section 20.2) and sounds (20.3), followed by the vowel symbols (20.4) and sounds (20.5–7).

20.2   Consonant symbols

Here is an overview of the consonant symbols.

Table 20.1 *Consonant symbols (80) in alphabetical order. Underlining omitted*

B	°b		°gi		°pn	T	°t
	bb		gn		pp		tch
	bu		gu		pph		th
C	c	H	h		ps		ts
	cc	J	j		pt		tt
	cch	K	k	Q	q		tw
	ch		kh		qu	V	v
	ci		kk	R	r		vv
	ck		kn		rh	W	w
	cq	L	l		rr		wh
	cqu		ll		rrh		wr
D	d	M	m	S	s	X	x
	dd		mb		sc		xh
	dg		mm		sch		xi
	dj		mn		sci	Y	y
F	f	N	n		sh	Z	z
	ff		ng		sp		zz
	ft		ngu		ss		
G	g		nn		st		
	gg	P	p		sth		
	gh		ph		sw		

Much could be said about the structure of these 80 symbols – how many of each size, how many 'mixed', how many 'double' and so on; but much more important by way of preparation for the next chapter is a similar overview of the consonant *sounds* and their notation.

Just before moving on to the sounds, however, it is worth pausing to note that there are 21 single-letter consonant symbols. That means that each of the consonant letters acts as a symbol on its own. That may seem so obvious as not to be worth stating. But bear in mind that it could be different. Think how the role of °h as a trailing letter, in °ch °sh °th and others, is far greater that its role as a 1-letter symbol. And think how °q has traditionally not been taught as a 1-letter symbol (see Section 18.6).

20.3   Consonant sounds

The consonant symbols of Table 20.1 are listed again in Table 20.2, but this time each symbol is accompanied by the sounds to which it can correspond. This is, then, a bird's-eye view of all the consonant correspondences, without sample words or morphemes – you'll find those in Chapter 23, complete with systematic names for the correspondences.

Table 20.2 *Consonant symbols with sound-values. Underlining omitted*

°b	/b/	°gg	/g/	°pn	/n/	°sw	/s/		
°bb	/b/		/j/	°pp	/p/	°t	/t/		
°bu	/b/	°gh	/g/	°pph	/f/		/ch/		
°c	/k/		/f/	°ps	/s/	°tch	/ch/		
	/s/	°gi	/j/	°pt	/t/	°th	/th/		
	/ch/	°gn	/n/	°q	/k/		/dh/		
°cc	/k/		/n-y/	°qu	/k/	°ts	/z/		
°cch	/k/	°gu	/g/	°r	/r/	°tt	/t/		
°ch	/ch/	°h	/h/	°rh	/r/	°tw	/t/		
	/k/	°j	/j/	°rr	/r/	°v	/v/		
	/sh/	°k	/k/	°rrh	/r/	°vv	/v/		
°ci	/sh/	°kh	/k/	°s	/s/	°w	/w/		
°ck	/k/	°kk	/k/		/z/	°wh	/w/		
°cq	/k/	°kn	/n/		/sh/		/h/		
°cqu	/k/	°l	/l/		/zh/	°wr	/r/		
°d	/d/	°ll	/l/	°sc	/s/	°x	/k-s/		
°dd	/d/	°m	/m/	°sch	/s/		/g-z/		
°dg	/j/	°mb	/m/		/sh/		/z/		
°dj	/j/	°mm	/m/	°sci	/sh/		/k/		
°f	/f/	°mn	/m/	°sh	/sh/		/k-sh/		
	/v/	°n	/n/	°sp	/z/	°xh	/g-z/		
°ff	/f/	°ng	/ng/	°ss	/s/	°xi	/k-sh/		
°ft	/f/	°ngu	/ng/		/z/	°y	/y/		
°g	/g/	°nn	/n/		/sh/	°z	/z/		
	/j/	°p	/p/	°st	/s/		/s/		
	/zh/	°ph	/f/	°sth	/s/	°zz	/z/		

If you make a tally of the sound notations in Table 20.2, you will find there are 24 of them. In Table 20.3, I have arranged the 24 notations in alphabetical order and added sample words or morphemes.

Table 20.3 *Consonant-sound notations (24) arranged alphabetically, with sample morphemes (mostly Function Words)*

/b/	°but	/ng/	°-ing
/ch/	such much	/p/	upon pre-
/d/	do	/r/	re-
/dh/	the	/s/	such so
/f/	for	/sh/	shall
/g/	go	/t/	to
/h/	have has	/th/	through
/j/	just	/v/	over of very
/k/	can	/w/	will why
/l/	let	/y/	yet
/m/	my	/z/	as has was
/n/	not	/zh/	rouge

Alphabetical order, being familiar, makes the 24 notations easier to master, but it throws no light on the sounds themselves. In Chapter 11 we established a bridgehead among the vowel sounds of English by grouping ten of them into five short/long pairs (11.4). We can establish a larger bridgehead among the consonant sounds by grouping into pairs no fewer than 16 of them (that's two-thirds of the 24). The members of each pair are physically related to each other as sounds – they are, to use the phoneticians' terms, voiceless/voiced pairs. They are also related to each other in the grammar: note, for example, /t/ and /d/ for the morpheme °-ed in °hissed and °buzzed, /s/ and /z/ in the plurals °griefs and °thieves, /f/ and /v/ in °thief (noun) and °thieve (verb).

The eight pairs of consonant sounds are shown in Table 20.4 (opposite), in Columns I and II. To experience the physical affinity and difference involved, experiment with the voiceless sound /s/ in °hiss and its twin, the voiced sound /z/ in °buzz. You can turn the resonance ('voicing' in the larynx) on, to change °hiss to °his, and off, to change °buzz to °bus.

Table 20.4 *Consonant sounds arranged with voiceless/voiced pairs as the core (Note:* −......+ *indicates voiceless/voiced pair)*

Plosives		Continuants		
I **Stops** −......+	**II** **Fricatives** −......+	**Nasals**	**Liquids**	**Onsets** **only**
/p/.../b/	/f/.../v/ /th/.../dh/	/m/		/w-/
/t/.../d/ /ch/.../j/	/s/.../z/ /sh/.../-zh/	/n/	/l/ /r/	/y-/
/k/.../g/		/-ng/		/h-/
Sample words				
°pin bin	°fat vat thin that	°map		°wail
tin din chin jut	sip zip ship rouge	nap	°lap rap	yale
kin gut		pang		hail

Note: Two of the sounds have a hyphen on the left to indicate that they do not start words in English: /ng/ is a very common sound in the RefP, typically morpheme-final as (twice) in °singing; /zh/ is a rare sound, commonest in mid-word position, as in °television and °pleasure, in both of which it's morpheme-final, as it is in °rouge, a rather fading word. (If °vat strikes you as fading – though it's not, in fact – think of VAT.) I must leave the phonetic headings to speak for themselves.

20.4   Vowel symbols

Here is an overview, in alphabetical order, of the vowel symbols I shall use in the matrices in Chapter 22 and in the correspondences listed in Chapter 24. Again, there is nothing definitive about this list, but it is pretty comprehensive. It shows graphically the high proportion of symbols which have °a °e or °o as leading letter – the 'big three' of Tables 18.2 and 18.3.

There are 140 symbols in Table 20.5, and in such numbers they are rather daunting, much more daunting than the consonant symbols. That should not stop you having fun contextualising ones which catch your eye – that is to say, finding words (or morphemes) in which they appear.

Much more important, though, is to realise how rare in text most of them

Table 20.5 *Vowel symbols (140) in alphabetical order. Underlining omitted*

A	E	I	O	U	Y
°a	°e	°i	°o	°u	°y
aa	e.e	i.e	o.e	u.e	y.e
aar	ea	ia.e	oa	ub	ye
ach	ea.e	ic	oar	uch	yr
ae	ear	ie	oar.e	ue	yre
a.e	ear.e	ie.e	oe	ui	yrrh
ah	eau	ier	oeu	ui.e	
ai	eb	ier.e	og	ur	
ai.e	ed	ieu	oh	ur.e	
aigh	ee	iew	oi	ure	
air	ee.e	igh	oi.e	urr	
ais.e	eer	io	oir	ueue	
al	eg	ir	ois	ueur	
al.e	ei	ir.e	ol		
ao	ei.e	ire	oo		
ar	eigh	irr	oo.e		
are	eir	is	oor		
ar.e	eo	is.e	or		
arr	er		ore		
arre	er.e		orps		
arrh	ere		orr		
au	err		os		
au.e	et		ot		
augh	eu		ou		
aul	eu.e		ou.e		
aur	eur		oub		
aw	ew		ough		
awe	ewe		oul		
aw.e	ewer		oup		
awer	ey		our		
ay	eye		our.e		
aye	ez		ous		
ayer			ow		
ayor			ow.e		
			owe		
			oy		
			oy.e		

are (on 'text' see Section 16.1), and how frequent in text a few of them are (see Section 16.2). Important, too, to distinguish between *frequency in text* and *incidence in list* (see Section 16.4). For example, the symbol °oul will only appear in three words in the dictionary (that is, it has very low incidence), but those three words are Function Words (see Section 16.2); they are the common verb-auxiliaries °could °would °should, so the frequency of the symbol °oul is going to be higher than its incidence might suggest.

However, I am going to leave such quantitative aspects to the reader's observation, judgment and experience, being more concerned with the *conceptual framework* and the means for *talking* about vowel symbols, vowel sounds, and the correspondences between them. Talking about the vowel phenomena is a more demanding task than talking about the consonant phenomena, but the same conceptual framework will see us through.

In each of the six columns in Table 20.5 you can see symbols of different structures. Classifying the symbols by those structures imposes a greater degree of order than alphabetical listing on its own. At the same time, in Table 20.6, I can enter against each symbol the number of different correspondences it enters into.

Table 20.6 *Vowel symbols classified by structure with number of correspondences for each symbol (Note: l. = letter; disc. = discontinuous). Underlining omitted*

1l.	2l. disc.	2 solid	3l. disc.	3 solid	4l. disc.	4 solid
°a 7	°a.e 5	°aa 1	°ai.e 1	°aar 1	°ais.e 1	°aigh 1
		ae 3	al.e 1	ach 1		arre 1
		ah 3	ar.e 2	air 1		arrh 1
		ai 4	au.e 3	are 2		augh 1
		al 3	aw.e 1	arr 1		awer 1
		ao 1		aul 1		ayer 1
		ar 3		aur 1		ayor 1
		au 5		awe 1		
		aw 1		aye 1		
		ay 4				
°e 6	°e.e 2	°ee 4	°ee.e 1	°ear 4	°ear.e 1	°eigh 2
		ea 3	ea.e 1	eau 3		ewer 1
		eb 1	ei.e 1	eer 1		
		ed 2	er.e 1	eir 2		
		eg 1	eu.e 1	ere 3		
		ei 4		err 1		
		eo 4		eur 2		
		er 3		ewe 1		
		et 1		eye 1		
		eu 2				
		ew 3				
		ey 4				
		ez 1				

Table 20.6 continued →

Table 20.6 *continued*

1l.	2l. disc.	2 solid	3l. disc.	3 solid	4l. disc.	4 solid
°i 4	°i.e 5	°ic 1	°ia.e 1	°ier 1	°ier.e 1	
		ie 4	ie.e 1	ieu 2		
		io 1	ir.e 1	iew 1		
		ir 2	is.e 1	igh 1		
		is 1		ire 1		
				irr 1		
°o 7	°o.e 5	°oa 2	°oi.e 2	°oar 1	°oar.e 1	°orps 1
		oe 4	oo.e 2	oeu 1	our.e 2	ough 5
		og 1	ou.e 1	oir 3		
		oh 1	ow.e 1	ois 1		
		oi 2	oy.e 1	oor 2		
		ol 1		ore 1		
		oo 4		orr 1		
		or 3		oub 1		
		os 1		oul 1		
		ot 1		oup 1		
		ou 6		our 5		
		ow 3		ous 1		
		oy 1		owe 1		
°u 7	°u.e 3	°ub 1	°ui.e 1	°uch 1	– – – –	°ueue 1
		ue 2	ur.e 1	ure 3		ueur 1
		ui 2		urr 1		
		up 1				
		ur 2				
°y 3	°y.e 1	°ye 1	– – –	°yre 1	– – – –	°yrrh 1
		yr 2				

If you tot up the number of correspondences, they come to 281, twice the number of symbols – an average therefore of two correspondences per symbol, but unevenly distributed. On the page opposite, for comparison, is the equivalent table for the consonant symbols, wrenched for this purpose from its rightful place in Section 20.2.

Here we have 104 correspondences to 80 symbols, an average of 1.25 per symbol. Note in both tables the high proportion of symbols with only one value.

Returning to the vowel symbols, I ought at this point to list them all with their sound-values (to parallel the consonant list in Table 20.2 above): but en masse they are too overwhelming – too many for a bird's-eye view. Such a list occupies the whole of Chapter 24, in the form of a long alphabetical list of vowel correspondences, complete with sample words or morphemes. Before

Table 20.7 *Consonant symbols in alphabetical order with number of correspondences for each symbol (derived from Table 20.2). Underlining omitted*

B	°b	1		°gh	2	P	°p	1		°st	1
	bb	1		gi	1		ph	1		sth	1
	bu	1		gn	2		pn	1		sw	1
C	c	3		gu	1		pp	1	T	t	2
	cc	1	H	h	1		pph	1		tch	1
	cch	1	J	j	1		ps	1		th	2
	ch	3	K	k	1		pt	1		ts	1
	ci	1		kh	1	Q	q	1		tt	1
	ck	1		kk	1		qu	1		tw	1
	cq	1		kn	1	R	r	1	V	v	1
	cqu	1	L	l	1		rh	1		vv	1
D	d	1		ll	1		rr	1	W	w	1
	dd	1	M	m	1		rrh	1		wh	2
	dg	1		mb	1	S	s	4		wr	1
	dj	1		mm	1		sc	1	X	x	5
F	f	2		mn	1		sch	2		xh	1
	ff	1	N	n	1		sci	1		xi	1
	ft	1		ng	1		sh	1	Y	y	1
G	g	3		ngu	1		sp	1	Z	z	2
	gg	2		nn	1		ss	3		zz	1

that, in Chapter 22, the vowel symbols are divided into six groups by leading letter (as in Table 20.6 above) and by another structural feature, namely the presence or absence of °r as a trailing letter. This makes it possible to display each symbol's set of sound-values within a manageable matrix of symbols (on the vertical axis) and sounds (on the horizontal axis).

But even before tackling the vowel matrices, some of which are quite large, you can acclimatise yourself to this way of presenting symbols and their sound-values with the help of the consonant matrices in Chapter 21, backed up by the alphabetical list of consonant correspondences in Chapter 23. The consonant matrices are much smaller, much simpler, and they give good practice in reading a convergent notation for the sounds. With a convergent notation, the symbols of the spelling system can become stepping-stones to a memorisation and mastery of the sounds.

20.5 Vowel sounds: Overall

Anyone who just compared the two last tables – Table 20.6 (vowels) and Table 20.7 (consonants) – could be forgiven for thinking that there must be many more vowel sounds than consonant sounds. If 80 consonant symbols, by way of 104 correspondences, relate to 24 consonant sounds, then 140 vowel symbols, by way of 281 correspondences, must relate to perhaps 40 or 50 vowel sounds.

Of course, this is not so, as I made clear in Section 18.2. There I suggested that we could almost get by with a balancing set of 24 vowel sounds – especially if we ignored the pervasive minimal vowel, which is what much of the syllable distortion, mentioned in Section 19.8, attempts to do. However, 24 vowel sounds are not quite enough for the RefP (reference pronunciation), and I shall use, as I said, a set of 27 vowel sounds – 26 'maximal vowel sounds' and one consolidated 'minimal vowel sound'.

Table 20.8 presents the whole set of 27 vowel sounds in an arrangement based on the bridgehead of short/long pairs established in Chapter 11 (see Table 11.3). Those short/long pairs are expanded now to triplets, making 15; one more short vowel and ten more long vowels are added to the maximals, making 26; and all 26 maximals, the vowel sounds which can carry stress, are contrasted with a single minimal, which can't.

Table 20.8 *Display of all 27 vowel sounds (For sample words, see Table 20.9)*

Maximal vowel sounds (1.Short 2.Long 3.R-coloured)					Minimal
Core short/long pairs and triplets	6th triplet	Paired longs		Single longs	
1. /a/ /e/ /i/ /o/ /u/	/ø/				/ə/
2. /ae/ /ee/ /ie/ /oe/ /ue/	/oo/	/aa/ /oi/ /ow/		/aw/	
3. /aer/ /eer/ /ier/ /oer/ /uer/	/oor/	/aar/ /oir/ /owr/		/ur/	

These 27 sound notations will suffice for all the 281 vowel correspondences that will be listed. This is a very important consideration: it suggests that getting to know the vowel sounds both collectively and individually may not be a much heavier task than getting to know the consonant sounds. And once again there is a convergent notation to help (it is in regard to the vowel sounds that notations designed to give phonetic information are most at odds with the spelling system – most divergent – though using many of the same familiar letters).

As with the morphemes in Part I, so with the sounds: move from the known gradually into the unknown, and don't be afraid to explore – or you will be unable to encourage other learners to explore. Above all, *talk* about your discoveries and your difficulties. Your knowledge of sound/symbol relations must never stand still, any more than your knowledge of words and word structures.

Lastly, remember that *you use this system of vowel sounds*, or a system very like it, when you talk, both in speaking and listening. If you don't know the system of vowel sounds that you operate as a speaker of English, now is your chance to discover this part of yourself. But cut your teeth, as it were, with the consonant sounds – and use all the help the spelling system can give.

Table 20.9, which follows, is a companion list to Table 20.3 (consonant-sound notations). The 27 vowel sound notations are given in near-alphabetical order together with sample words or morphemes – Function Words where possible.

Table 20.9 *Vowel-sound notations arranged alphabetically, with sample morphemes (mostly Function Words)*

/a/	°and °that		/o/	°not
/ae/	°may °they		/oe/	°no °go °though
/aer/	°dare °there		/oer/	°or °for °nor
/aa/	°can't		/ø/	°would °good
/aar/	°aren't °are		/oo/	°do °through
			/oor/	°poor
/aw/	°taught °ought			
			/ow/	°how
/e/	°get °any °said		/owr/	°our
/ee/	°me			
/eer/	°here		/oi/	°noise
			/oir/	°coir
/i/	°it °with			
/ie/	°I °my °might		/u/	°us °but
/ier/	°wire °lyre		/ue/	°used
			/uer/	°pure
			/ur/	°her °fir °fur °word
/ə/	(only in unstressed syllables)			
	°about °away °-al °-ion °-en °-er °-or °con-		(shwa)	
	°enough °beyond °-ing °-ed °-est °-ly °-y °-ive °de-		(shwi)	

In the next section I give an account of two features which complicate the vowel sounds by comparison with the consonant sounds, namely the R-coloured vowels in the bottom row of Table 20.8 and the minimal vowel at the bottom of Table 20.9 (and in the rightmost column of Table 20.8).

20.6   Vowel sounds: R-coloured and minimal

R-coloured vowels and Trailing-R symbols

In principle, all the sounds in Table 20.8 are distinct from each other, but in fact, in the RefP, /aa/ in °father sounds the same as /aar/ in °farther, and /aw/ in °caught sounds the same as /oer/ in °court. In these chapters we are getting at sound notations by way of the spelling symbols in order to gain insight into the spelling system, and my list of 27 sound notations is a compromise. The two sounds /aar/ and /oer/ belong to a set of 10 sounds, the 'R-coloured vowel sounds', which correspond to a large, structurally distinct group of symbols, namely symbols which contain °r in their trailing letters and which we can call 'Trailing-R symbols'.

These symbols can be picked out from Table 20.5. Essentially they are mixed symbols, with a vowel-letter as leading letter and the consonant-letter °r as trailing letter, for example °<u>ar</u> in °jar. Such a °r is certainly still a consonant letter (and not halfway to being a vowel letter like °w in °jaw), since it obeys the Consonant-Doubling rule (Chapter 9):

$$°jar \times ing \rightarrow jarring$$

In the 3-letter symbols also, the junction rules are obeyed:

$$°peer + ing \rightarrow °peering \quad \text{(Plus-junction)}$$
$$°purr + ing \rightarrow °purring \quad \text{(Plus-junction)}$$
$$°pore \times ing \rightarrow °poring \quad \text{(E-Deletion)}$$

What is more, in speech, the consonant sound /r/ reappears in the pronunciation of these four inflected forms, indicating that it is latent in the pronunciation of the vowel sounds in the base forms:

°jar	/aar/
°peer	/eer/
°purr	/ur/
°pore	/oer/

In short, the spelling system maintains the presence of the letter °r in such morphemes; the pronunciation, by contrast, varies between absence of the sound /r/ in the base form and its presence in the inflected form.

In the absence of consonantal /r/ in the base forms, these words have the sound profile /CV/. That is what forces us to recognise °<u>ar</u> °<u>eer</u> °<u>urr</u> °<u>ore</u> as symbols. °fear, for instance, has the same sound profile as °fee, /CV/, not as

°feel, /CVC/. At the same time °fear does not rhyme with °fee; the two V-sounds are different. What makes /eer/ in °fear different from /ee/ in °fee is the effect of the latent /r/: that is why it, and the nine other vowel sounds in the bottom row of Table 20.8, are called 'R-coloured'.

Here are the ten sounds in words all with the same syllabic sound frame (just about! – you may be able to find a better frame):

Table 20.10 *R-coloured vowel sounds (10)*

/aer/	°m<u>are</u>	/aar/	°m<u>ar</u>
/eer/	°m<u>ere</u>	/oor/	°m<u>oor</u>
/ier/	°m<u>ire</u>	/oir/	°M<u>oir</u>
/oer/	°m<u>ore</u>	/owr/	°M<u>auer</u>/°<u>our</u>
/uer/	°M<u>uir</u>	/ur/	°m<u>yrrh</u>/°<u>err</u>

The R-coloured sounds commute with each other in this frame in step with Trailing-R symbols. The latent /r/ is revealed in the vowel sound and in its reappearance as a consonant sound when a vowel sound follows, as in 'hare and hounds' 'fear and trembling' and so on – a phenomenon known as 'linking R'. Even where the vowel sound is unrevealing, as it can be in /aar/ and /oer/, consonantal /r/ is recovered as linking R, as in 'far away' and 'core an apple'. The same sounds and symbols also commute in step in syllables where the vowel sound is closed in by a following consonant sound, as in °farther and °court. Accordingly, in support of /aar/ in °farther we can cite /ur/ in °further, and in support of /oer/ in °court we can cite /ur/ in °curt – the latent /r/ in such words having no chance to reveal itself before a following vowel sound.

Dictionaries differ in how they deal with the problem of 'post-vocalic R' (as it is called – meaning '/r/ following a vowel sound'). It is a problem for the RefP in British dictionaries, less of a problem for accents of English which 'sound their Rs' – meaning their post-vocalic Rs. For the RefP it presents a certain limited problem in symbol segmentation, which can be summed up by saying that, in the RefP, °fearing doesn't rhyme with °key-ring. But this is a problem for sound/symbol matching, not a problem for the spelling system. Trailing-R symbols simply maintain distinctive morpheme shapes, both where morpheme pronunciation is constant in the RefP (°fear/feared/fearful) and where it is not (°fear/fearing). They have another, wider role in relation to the variety of accents of English both in Britain and around the world, but that lies beyond the scope of this book.

The minimal vowel and vowel symbols

Pronunciation as a whole lies beyond the scope of this book, and the abnormal length of this chapter hints at how big a topic it is. My aim in treating it is to

explain certain features in the notation I have adopted, in the next four
chapters, for the sound-values of symbols. Like the R-coloured vowels, the
minimal vowel is a characteristic of the RefP which requires special attention.

Minimal vowels crop up the moment one leaves the safety of monosyllables
(see Section 7.4). Take the following three words from the 'Cwm Idwal'
passage (Chapter 16):

	Rhythmic outline	Rhythmic profile	
°striking	/– –/	/⊿ –/	'2 syllables, stress on no. 1'
instance	/– –/	/⊿ –/	'2 syllables, stress on no. 1'
terminal	/– – –/	/⊿ – –/	'3 syllables, stress on no. 1'

The rhythmic outline (Chapter 6) gives the number of syllables; the rhythmic
profile (Sections 7.3 and 14.4) classifies the syllables into stressed and non-
stressed.

Now, in these three words all the non-stressed syllables are weak syllables,
like the first syllable of °begin and °bikini discussed in Section 12.4, or the
second syllable of °begging, also discussed there. We can indicate weak
syllables in notation by a refinement to the rhythmic profile:

	Rhythmic outline	Rhythmic profile	More delicate rhythmic profile
°striking	/– –/	/⊿ –/	/⊿ ˘/
instance	/– –/	/⊿ –/	/⊿ ˘/
terminal	/– – –/	/⊿ – –/	/⊿ ˘ ˘/

This is a positive notation for weak syllables. After you have learnt to
recognise the stressed syllable (the one syllable in each word which carries
greater stress than any other syllable), you need to learn to recognise the
weak syllables – so important are they as a characteristic of English word-
rhythm.

Stressed syllables only have maximal, weak syllables only have minimal
vowel sounds. Here are all the vowel sounds in the three words (one per
syllable, as always):

	Rhythmic profile 2	Vowel sounds
°striking	/⊿ ˘/	/ie/ /ɪ/
instance	/⊿ ˘/	/i/ /ə/
terminal	/⊿ ˘ ˘/	/ur/ /ɪ/ /ə/

What are /ɪ/ ('shwi') and /ə/ ('shwa')? They are the 'two shades of grey' (Section 18.2) of the minimal vowel, and they can both be replaced in these words by the undifferentiated notation /ə/:

	Rhythmic profile 2	Vowel sounds
°striking	/⸍ ⸌/	/ie/ /ə/
instance	/⸍ ⸌/	/i/ /ə/
terminal	/⸍ ⸌ ⸌/	/ur/ /ə/ /ə/

Very often it doesn't matter which quality of minimal vowel you use in a weak syllable: basically it's a rhythm-filler, as I suggested in Section 19.8, keeping consonants apart and counting (± consonants) as a syllable. This is the case with the middle syllable of °terminal: you may find it difficult to decide what your pronunciation is – whether you use shwi or shwa in that syllable. (You will think that you use shwi because of °i in the spelling.) The point is that *it doesn't matter*. And when it doesn't matter, the notation /ə/ will do.

   Traditionally the minimal vowel has been identified with the 'neutral vowel sound' and given its own notation /ə/, known as shwa. You will find this in some dictionaries. The same dictionaries often do not recognise shwi, and they give it the same notation as they give to the full vowel /i/. But rhythmically the two sounds, shwa and shwi, have the same low status, restricted to weak syllables – typically immediately before and immediately after a stressed syllable and typically in suffixes and prefixes.

   In fact, shwi is as ubiquitous as shwa, though there is a lot of variation from person to person and from accent to accent. If we list all the Content Words (of more than one syllable) from 'Cwm Idwal', as in Table 20.11 overleaf, we find them evenly balanced – as it happens, there are 15 of each.

   In discussing pronunciations, make sure you agree on the number of syllables (Column I): °glacial can be two syllables, with /ae/ in the first; the middle syllable of °lateral is easily elided (omitted) as in °hist'ry (Section 18.7). Make sure, too, you agree where the primary stress falls (Column II): in 3-syllable words like °wonderful and °overlook, where there is another maximal vowel one syllable away from the primary stress, it's easy, in starting out, to put a secondary stress on it, and then mistake it for the primary stress; in both words, grammar is an important guide (look at all the words with °over- as a prefix in the dictionary, and at all the words with °-ful as a suffix in the reverse dictionary (Section 4.1), for their stress-patterns or rhythmic profiles). Thirdly, note any differences about whether a syllable is weak or not (Column III): some speakers will use a maximal vowel in the first syllable of °conspicuous /kon-/, and °observed /ob-/, or of °extreme /eks-/, and °examining /eks-/ or /egz-/, or in the first syllable of °moraines /o/, because of its unfamiliarity.

Table 20.11 *The minimal vowel in Content Words from 'Cwm Idwal'*

	I Rhythmic outline	II Rhythmic profile	III Rhythmic profile 2	IV Vowel sounds			
2-syllable							
striking	/– –/	/́– –/	/́– ̀–/	/ie/	/ɪ/		
instance	/– –/	/́– –/	/́– ̀–/	/i/	/ə/		
easy	/– –/	/́– –/	/́– ̀–/	/ee/	/ɪ/		
Sedgwick	/– –/	/́– –/	/́– ̀–/	/e/	/ɪ/		
anxious	/– –/	/́– –/	/́– ̀–/	/a/	/ə/		
fossils	/– –/	/́– –/	/́– ̀–/	/o/	/ə/		
notice	/– –/	/́– –/	/́– ̀–/	/oe/	/ɪ/		
plainly	/– –/	/́– –/	/́– ̀–/	/ae/	/ɪ/		
boulders	/– –/	/́– –/	/́– ̀–/	/oe/	/ə/		
story	/– –/	/́– –/	/́– ̀–/	/oer/	/ɪ/		
valley	/– –/	/́– –/	/́– ̀–/	/a/	/ɪ/		
observed	/– –/	/– ́–/	/̀– ́–/	/ə/	/ur/		
extreme	/– –/	/– ́–/	/̀– ́–/	/ɪ/	/ee/		
moraines	/– –/	/– ́–/	/̀– ́–/	/ə/	/ae/		
3-syllable							
wonderful	/– – –/	/́– – –/	/́– ̀– –/	/u/	/ə/	/ø/	
glacial	/– – –/	/́– – –/	/́– ̀– ̀–/	/a/	/ɪ/	/ə/	
lateral	/– – –/	/́– – –/	/́– ̀– ̀–/	/a/	/ə/	/ə/	
terminal	/– – –/	/́– – –/	/́– ̀– ̀–/	/ur/	/ɪ/	/ə/	
overlook	/– – –/	/– – ́–/	/́– ̀– ́–/	/oe/	/ə/	/ø/	
4-syllable							
phenomena	/– – – –/	/– ́– – –/	/̀– ́– ̀– ̀–/	/ɪ/	/o/	/ɪ/	/ə/
conspicuous	/– – – –/	/– ́– – –/	/̀– ́– – ̀–/	/ə/	/i/	/ue/	/ə/
examining	/– – – –/	/– ́– – –/	/̀– ́– ̀– ̀–/	/ɪ/	/a/	/ɪ/	/ɪ/

As to shwa and shwi (Column IV), there isn't much room for variation in this list. All but one of the inflections with °e have shwi in the RefP, as does the inflection °-ing in the list; the exception is °-er, which is always shwa, as in °boulders (where °...er is not, of course, an inflection but is built-in to the nuclear morpheme). The suffixes °-ance °-al °-a and °-ous in the list are always shwa; the suffixes °-y and °-ly, also in the list, are always shwi. The physical quality of both sounds varies considerably, especially of word-final shwi, which for some speakers it is close to /ee/.

In morpheme-final position the choice between shwa and shwi can be critical (as in °copper/copy °coppers/copies), and occasionally elsewhere.

Much more could be said, but the essential point is to recognise that weak syllables are ever-present in the rhythm of English and the minimal vowel is a central feature of that rhythm, not a marginal feature.

I call it the minimal vowel, embracing shwa and shwi, because what the two sounds have in common in rhythmic status is much more important than their difference in quality, which very often doesn't matter at all. Using the unitary notation /ə/ can be a handy and quite legitimate device in analysing word-pronunciations. But more importantly, in the chapters which follow, the distinction between shwa and shwi can be a positive hindrance in stating the sound-values of vowel symbols. What needs to be stated is that a symbol can have minimal value in addition to whatever maximal values it has, and this can be done by a single correspondence to /ə/. This saves a very large number of correspondences, as well as saving a column in most of the sound/symbol matrices. The reason is that most vowel symbols have dual value as between maximal and minimal value, and, as in the case of the Trailing-R symbols, this dual value is functional at certain places in the spelling system in maintaining the shape of morphemes.

In Section 18.7 I used the example of °consonant/consonantal to illustrate this last point. Going back to Chapters 3 and 4, we might remember °define/definite/definitive/definition.

20.7   Vowel sounds: Bit by bit

This section goes back to Table 20.8 as a whole and builds it up gradually. Readers who are exhausted by the length of this chapter should skip it and, if they have the strength, go straight to Chapter 21.

In Section 11.4 I presented, as a point of entry into the vowel sounds of English, ten vowel sounds arranged in five short/long pairs:

Table 20.12   *Core pairs of vowel sounds*

Core short/long pairs				
Short /a/ /e/ /i/ /o/ /u/				
Long /ae/ /ee/ /ie/ /oe/ /ue/				
°mat met nit not nut				
°mate meet mite moat mute				

To these we can now add five of the R-coloured vowels, making 15 sounds, and taking us over halfway to our total:

Table 20.13 *Core pairs of vowel sounds with associated R-coloured vowel sounds*

	A	E	I	O	U
Short	/a/	/e/	/i/	/o/	/u/
Long	/ae/	/ee/	/ie/	/oe/	/ue/
R-coloured	/aer/	/eer/	/ier/	/oer/	/uer/
	A	E	I	O	U
Sample	°air	°ear	°ire	°ore	°Ure
words for	°mare	°mere	°mire	°more	°cure
symbols	°pair	°peer	°pyre	°pore	°pure
of R-	°fair	°weir			°Muir
coloured		°deer		°door	
vowels				°four	
				°for	

The rationale for the notation of the short/long pairs was established in Chapter 11: each pair consists of two morphemically related sounds, their relationship signalled by the spelling system. For example, the spelling of °grain and °granary associates both of the vowel sounds in the nuclear morpheme [grain/gran-] with °a, which is the leading letter in the two symbols °<u>ai</u> and °<u>a</u>. Hence the two sound notations, /ae/ and /a/.

The vowel sound in °air is also associated with A-symbols (symbols with °a as leading letter), as indicated in the words in the A-column in Table 20.9 – hence the notation /aer/ for the R-coloured vowel, making a series /a/ /ae/ /aer/. Similar steps lead to similar notations in the E I O and U columns (no separate column for Y, since the sounds are the same as those in the I column – hence the example °pyre).

With these fifteen sounds and their notations in place, we can add a sixth triplet of short, long and R-coloured vowel sounds. The short vowel sound is the sound in °put (rhyming with °foot) and in °push and °pull, and its notation is /ø/ (see Section 18.2). With this sound in place, the short vowel sounds of the RefP are complete. There are only six of them:

/a/	/e/	/i/	/o/	/u/	/ø/
°pat	°pet	°pit	°pot	°putt	°put

(°putt, as in golf).

This last short vowel sound has much lower incidence than the main five; in some accents of English it's more restricted than in others, and in some accents the three sounds /u/ /ø/ and /oo/ of the RefP (°buck °book and °boot) are merged in various ways into two sounds. The junior grade of /ø/ can be felt in its having no letter of its own like the other five – which is why I have gone abroad for the sound notation.

The long sound of this sixth triplet is /oo/ as in °moo, and the R-coloured sound is /oor/ as in °moor. /ø/ and /oo/ don't alternate in morphemes like the other short/long pairs, but they are associated with each other as sounds, while /oor/ has the same relationship to /oo/ as /uer/ in °cure has to /ue/ in °cue.

So the first eighteen vowel sounds can be set out as in Table 20.14:

Table 20.14 *Pattern of 18 vowel sounds*

	Core pairs, and triplets					6th triplet	
Short	/a/	/e/	/i/	/o/	/u/	/ø/	(in °bull)
Long	/ae/	/ee/	/ie/	/oe/	/ue/	/oo/	(in °boot)
R-coloured	/aer/	/eer/	/ier/	/oer/	/uer/	/oor/	(in °boor)
	Sample words for symbols of R-coloured vowels				°Ure °cure °pure °Muir	°sure °tour °poor °moor	

These eighteen sounds in Table 20.14 are all (as I called them earlier) 'maximal' vowel sounds. Maximal vowel sounds can serve as vowel sounds in stressed monosyllables. In such words the short vowel sounds always need, in English, a consonant to 'close' the syllable. The longer ones (long and R-coloured – the R-coloured vowel sounds are the longest) can serve in 'open' syllables, that is without a final consonant sound. There are eight more maximal sounds to come – four long ones and four R-coloured ones. Six of these can take their places as pairs:

Table 20.15 *Display of 24 vowel sounds*

	Core pairs, and triplets					6th triplet	Paired longs		
Short	/a/	/e/	/i/	/o/	/u/	/ø/			
Long	/ae/	/ee/	/ie/	/oe/	/ue/	/oo/	/aa/	/oi/	/ow/
R-coloured	/aer/	/eer/	/ier/	/oer/	/uer/	/oor/	/aar/	/oir/	/owr/
					Sample words		°br a °b ar	°c oy °c oir	°s ow °s our

Finally, two long but unpaired sounds, one of each kind:

Table 20.16 *Display of 26 vowel sounds*

| Maximal vowel sounds (short, long, and R-coloured) | | | | | | | | | |
Core short/long pairs, and triplets					6th triplet	Paired longs			Single longs
/a/ /e/	/i/	/o/	/u/		/ø/				
/ae/ /ee/	/ie/	/oe/	/ie/		/oo/	/aa/ /oi/	/ow/	/aw/	
/aer/ /eer/	/ier/	/oer/	/uer/		/oor/	/aar/ /oir/	/owr/		/ur/
						Sample words	°paw °purr		

The picture is not complete without the minimal vowel, so this must now be added in a separate compartment on the right-hand side of the table, contrasting with all the maximal vowel sounds. It is entered (using character ⓐ) on the same line as the short vowels, since minimal vowels are always short – indeed they are often shorter than short, and sometimes minimised to nothing (as in °hist'ry °p'liceman °sep'rate – Sections 18.7 and 20.6). Table 20.17 below goes a small step further than the full display of 27 vowel sounds in Table 20.8 in that it has a modification to the notation in the bottom line; but this refinement is not needed in the chapters which follow.

Table 20.17 *Display of all 27 vowel sounds (with ʳ)*

| | Maximal vowel sounds (1.Short 2.Long 3.R-coloured) | | | | | | | | | Minimal |
	Core short/long pairs and triplets					6th triplet	Paired longs		Single longs	
1.	/a/ /e/ /i/	/o/	/u/			/ø/				/ⓐ/
2.	/ae/ /ee/ /ie/	/oe/	/ue/			/oo/	/aa/ /oi/ /ow/		/aw/	
3.	/aeʳ/ /eeʳ/ /ieʳ/	/oeʳ/	/ueʳ/			/ooʳ/	/aaʳ/ /oiʳ/ /owʳ/		/uʳ/	

21 *Consonant symbols*

21.1 Introduction to Chapters 21–24

Preview

Every letter belongs to a symbol and every symbol corresponds to a sound.

We now have both the symbols and their notation in place, and the sounds and their notation in place too. The consonant symbols have been listed in Tables 20.1 and 20.2, and the consonant sounds in Tables 20.3 and 20.4; the vowel symbols have been listed in Tables 20.5 and 20.6, and the vowel sounds in Tables 20.8 and 20.9.

These last four chapters of Part II are:

21 Consonant symbols

22 Vowel symbols

23 Consonant correspondences

24 Vowel correspondences

Chapters 21 and 22 survey, family by family, all the symbols and their values; and Chapters 23 and 24 list, in alphabetical order, all the correspondences together with their names and sample words or morphemes.

Names

It is as important for the correspondences to have names as it is for the symbols and the letters and the sounds. In this book, letters have their familiar names, and symbols are named from the letters they contain. The names I shall suggest for the correspondences vary; strictly speaking, none of them involves 'naming the sound'. This is deliberate. Giving or naming the sounds in speech is a matter of agreement between the speakers. But it is important to be able to name them, in whatever way suits the talk-situation, when referring to them on their own or when reading out the correspondences themselves. For example:

°<u>b</u> – /b/   'Symbol B with the value /b/'

Letters, symbols, sounds and correspondences are different entities, with names (and notations) that are often similar. When necessary – and it's very often advisable – *give the entity-name first*. You will find this habit helpful in reading sentences containing notation:

read	°t	as 'the letter T'
read	°<u>t</u>	as 'the symbol T'
read	/t/	as 'the sound T'
read	°the	as 'the word "the" '
read	[-ing]	as the 'morpheme "ing" '

I give a short example of this 'entity-distinguishing discourse' in the next section.

21.2   Recapitulation

Making a clear distinction between sounds and symbols has been the key task of Part II of *Insight* – between sounds in the pronunciation of words and symbols in the spelling of words. As a necessary step towards that goal, I made the preliminary distinction between letters and symbols as follows.

In matching the spelling of a word to its pronunciation we have to segment the spelling into as many letter-groups as there are sounds. The resulting groups may contain up to four letters but most commonly contain only one. Calling these groups 'symbols' gives a precise (and down-to-earth) meaning to the term 'symbol', which is needed in talking about symbol/sound relationships in English spelling. A symbol is one letter, two letters, three letters or four letters which correspond to a sound.

The following table, taken from Chapter 13, gives examples of words segmented into symbols:

Table 21.1 *(=Table 13.1) Words divided into symbols*

I Word	II Number of letters	III Sound profile	IV Number of sounds	V Symbols (spaced)	VI (underlined)	VII Symbol-size profile
°cat	3	/CVC/	3	°c a t	°c̲a̲t̲	111
°chat	4	/CVC/	3	°ch a t	°c̲h̲ a t̲	211
°catch	5	/CVC/	3	°c a tch	°c̲ a t̲c̲h̲	113
°caught	6	/CVC/	3	°c augh t	°c̲ a̲u̲g̲h̲ t̲	141

The notation must distinguish symbols from sounds, as it does in the correspondence cited in Section 21.1: °b̲ – /b/. It must also distinguish symbols from letters. For example:

> In °by ('the word "by" ') we have °b ('letter B') acting as a 1-letter symbol, °b̲ ('symbol B').
> In °buy ('the word "buy" ') we have °b ('letter B') as one letter of the 2-letter symbol °b̲u̲ ('symbol BU').
> In °lamb ('the word "lamb" ') we have °b ('letter B') as one letter of the 2-letter symbol °m̲b̲ ('symbol MB').

Of course, this looks, and is, absurdly cumbersome, precisely because the economy of the notations in writing is being sacrificed in order to set out their spoken realisations! It's really much shorter:

> In °by we have °b acting as a 1-letter symbol, °b̲.
> In °buy we have °b as one letter of the 2-letter symbol °b̲u̲.
> In °lamb we have °b as one letter of the 2-letter symbol °m̲b̲.

Once the entities are distinguished, the real discussion can begin on just why °buy is segmented this way. The next section (21.3) will throw some light on this.

21.3 Families of symbols

Symbols can be classified and arranged in all sorts of ways. I shall set aside both internal characteristics of structure (length and composition) and external characteristics of sound value or of text-frequency, list-incidence, distribution in vocabulary, position in morpheme, or junctional site – all of which are worthy of attention. Instead, after dividing the symbols into their consonant and vowel categories, I shall present them in 'families' in two alphabetical lists, consonant symbols in the next section (21.4) and vowel symbols in Chapter 22.

A 'family' of symbols, for this purpose, is simply a group of symbols which start with the same letter: so we have the B-family followed by the C-family, and so on. This highlights the importance of the 'leading letter'. The leading letter is the first letter in the symbol, the left-most letter if there is more than one – it's purely positional. Any letters to the right are 'trailing letters'.

Thus, in the symbol °bu in °buy, °u is a trailing letter in a B-symbol, leaving °y as the leading letter (and solo letter) of a Y-symbol. We could segment °buy differently, but would a U-symbol, °uy, provide any insight?

Each family has a matrix to itself. The symbols on the left-hand side of each matrix provide a control column, and against each symbol, in columns to the right, are entered the sound-values which that symbol may have (equivalent to the correspondences it enters into, but not set out in the form of individual correspondences).

The sound-values are set out across the top of the matrix – for each family of symbols, just those sounds which are required. The sound most closely associated with the leading letter appears first, so that the top left-hand corner is the heart of each matrix. The other sound-values head the columns to the right in a generally diminishing order of association. So, for any symbol, you can look along the row and read off its range of sound-values. I've re-ordered the rows so that all symbols which have the primary sound-value of the leading letter appear before those that don't. The patterns that result can be readily seen, and convey the chief message of this chapter: that symbol families have family values.

21.4   Consonant symbol families: 22 matrices

Note 1: The three numbers in parentheses at the head of each matrix indicate, in order, the number of symbols (down the left-hand column), the number of sounds (across the top), and the number of correspondences (=the number of entries in the matrix).

Note 2: The words/morphemes on the right illustrate the sound-values given in notation in each top line (for example /b/ in °but, /k/ in °can). I have used Function Words where possible. Many more sample words/morphemes will be found in Chapter 23.

Table 21.2 *Matrices of consonant symbols, arranged in 'leading letter' families (alphabetically), with sound-values*

Symbol	Sound-values					Sounds exemplified
B (3) (1) (3)						
	/b/					°<u>but</u>
°<u>b</u>	/b/					
°<u>bb</u>	/b/					
°<u>bu</u>	/b/					
C (10) (4) (15)						
	/k/	/s/	/ch/	/sh/		°<u>c</u>an °<u>s</u>o °mu<u>ch</u> °<u>sh</u>all
°<u>c</u>	/k/	/s/	/ch/	/sh/		
°<u>ch</u>	/k/		/ch/	/sh/		
°<u>cc</u>	/k/					
°<u>cch</u>	/k/					
°<u>ck</u>	/k/					
°<u>cq</u>	/k/					
°<u>cqu</u>	/k/					
°<u>cu</u>	/k/					
°<u>ce</u>				/sh/		
°<u>ci</u>				/sh/		
D (2) (1) (2)						
	/d/					°<u>do</u>
°<u>d</u>	/d/					
°<u>dd</u>	/d/					
#E – for °<u>ed</u> see Cross-category symbols in Section 21.5.						
F (3) (2) (4)						
	/f/	/v/				°<u>f</u>or °<u>v</u>ery
°<u>f</u>	/f/	/v/				
°<u>ff</u>	/f/					
°<u>ft</u>	/f/					
G (7) (5) (12)						
	/g/	/j/	/zh/	/f/	/n/	°<u>g</u>o °<u>j</u>ust °rou<u>g</u>e °<u>f</u>or °<u>n</u>ot
°<u>g</u>	/g/	/j/	/zh/			
°<u>gg</u>	/g/	/j/				
°<u>gh</u>	/g/			/f/		
°<u>gu</u>	/g/					
°<u>ge</u>		/j/	/zh/			
°<u>gi</u>		/j/				
°<u>gn</u>					/n/	

Table 21.2 *continued*

Symbol	Sound-values	Sounds exemplified
H (1) (1) (1)		
	/h/	°has
°h̲	/h/	
	(for °h̲o °h̲eir °h̲our see Cross-category symbols in Section 21.5)	
J (1) (1) (1)		
	/j/	°just
°j̲	/j/	
K (4) (2) (4)		
	/k/ /n/	°can °not
°k̲	/k/	
°k̲k̲	/k/	
°k̲h̲	/k/	
°k̲n̲	/n/	
L (2) (1) (2)		
	/l/	°let
°l̲	/l/	
°l̲l̲	/l/	
	(for °l̲e see Cross-category symbols in Section 21.5)	
M (4) (2) (5)		
	/m/ /n/	°my °not
°m̲	/m/	
°m̲m̲	/m/	
°m̲b̲	/m/	
°m̲n̲	/m/ /n/	
N (4) (2) (5)		
	/n/ /ng/	°not °-ing
°n̲	/n/ /ng/	
°n̲n̲	/n/	
°n̲g̲	/ng/	
°n̲g̲u̲	/ng/	
P (7) (5) (7)		
	/p/ /f/ /n/ /s/ /t/	°per- °for °not °so °to
°p̲	/p/	*continued …*

Table 21.2 *continued*

Symbol	Sound-values					Sounds exemplified
continued . . .						
°pp	/p/					
°ph		/f/				
°pph		/f/				
°pn			/n/			
°ps				/s/		
°pt					/t/	
Q (2) (1) (2)						
	/k/					°can
°q	/k/					
°qu	/k/					
R (4) (1) (4)						
	/r/					°re-
°r	/r/					
°rr	/r/					
°rh	/r/					
°rrh	/r/					
						(for °re see Cross-category symbols in Section 21.5)
S (9) (4) (15)						
	/s/	/z/	/sh/	/zh/		°so °as °shall °rouge
°s	/s/	/z/	/sh/	/zh/		
°ss	/s/	/z/	/sh/			
°sc	/s/					
°st	/s/					
°sth	/s/					
°sw	/s/					
°sch	/s/		/sh/			
°sci			/sh/			
°sh			/sh/			
T (7) (5) (10)						
	/t/	/ch/	/th/	/dh/	/sh/	°to °much °through °the °shall
°t	/t/	/ch/				
°tt	/t/					
°th	/t/		/th/	/dh/		
°tw	/t/					
°tch		/ch/				
°te		/ch/				
°ti					/sh/	

Table 21.2 *continued*

Symbol	Sound-values					Sounds exemplified
U (1) (1) (1)						
	/w/					°will
°u	/w/					
V (2) (1) (2)						
	/v/					°very
°v	/v/					
°vv	/v/					
W (2) (2) (3)						
	/w/	/h/				°will °has
°w	/w/					
°wh	/w/	/h/				
X (2) (5) (6)						
	/k-s/	/g-z/	/z/	/k/	/k-sh/	°can °so °go °as °shall
°x	/k-s/	/g-z/	/z/	/k/	/k-sh/	
°xh		/g-z/				
Y (1) (1) (1)						
	/y/					°yet
°y	/y/					
Z (2) (2) (3)						
	/z/	/s/				°as °so
°z	/z/	/s/				
°zz	/z/					

In Chapter 23 you will find sample words for all the correspondences indicated in the matrices. Each matrix calls for more or less extensive comment which in the present context we have to forgo. The emphasis here must be on the concepts of *symbol* and *correspondence* and on the use of a *convergent notation* (see Section 20.1) for gaining insight into the spelling system.

Some comments follow in the next section but only on a tiny minority of counter-pattern symbols, namely the cross-category symbols.

21.5   Cross-category symbols

A cross-category symbol has a leading letter of the opposite category to its sound-value. The small number of such symbols in Table 21.3 emphasises the importance of the fundamental categories, C and V, in matching spelling to pronunciation. Reading the table may be made easier by reading the comments which follow it.

Table 21.3 *Cross-category phenomena*

Consonant leading letter	Vowel value		
°heir	/aer/		in °heir
°ho	/o/		in °honest °honour
°hour	/our/		in °hour
°le	/ə-l/		in °little °able
°re	/ə/		in °centre °meagre
Vowel leading letter	**Consonant value**		
°ed	/d/	/t/	in °rubbed °chopped
°o.e	/w-u/		in °one °once
°oir	/w-ier/	/w-aar/	in °choir °reservoir
°ois		/w-aa/	in °bourgeois

°ho is forced on us as a symbol which has a C-letter as leading letter but V-value. It is peculiar to the morpheme [hon-], the nuclear of a derivation set which includes °honest °honour °honestly °dishonour and several other words.

°ed is the converse of °ho, being a symbol which has a V-letter as leading letter but C-value. It is like °ho in being peculiar to one morpheme – in this case a high-frequency morpheme in the grammatical core of English, namely the verb inflection -ED. When this inflection has its syllabic pronunciation, as in °hunted and °hounded, °sited and °sided, there is nothing anomalous about the symbols which constitute it: they are the vowel symbol °e and the consonant symbol °d. But when the pronunciation is non-syllabic (see Section 6.1), then the letters °ed are best regarded as a 2-letter symbol, °ed, with value either /t/ or /d/. And this holds good in all junctional circumstances:

Plus-junctions:	°hissed °buzzed °lumped °numbed
	°scoffed °scorned °scooped °skewered
Change-junctions:	
E-Deletion:	°hoped °hosed °scored °secured
Consonant-Doubling:	°hopped °robbed °stunned °starred
Y-Replacement:	°tried °carried °satisfied °salaried

This analysis is not forced on us in the way °ho is, but its recognition greatly facilitates symbol segmentation in texts (see Section 17.3; a similar argument can be made for a symbol °<u>es</u> in respect of the S-inflection). °<u>ed</u> is by far the most important of these nine anomalous symbols because its function is to constitute an inflectional morpheme.

°<u>le</u>: Second in importance comes °<u>le</u>, a morpheme-final symbol (like °<u>re</u>), but one which can also constitute a morpheme on its own, as it clearly does, for instance, in °hand/handle °start/startle °spit/spittle (a derivational, not an inflectional morpheme). The real anomaly in °<u>le</u> is that its letter profile is °CV and its sound-value is the reverse, /VC/, reflected in the counter-pattern Consonant-Doubling in °spittle. (Its pronunciation is often described as 'syllabic /l/', on a par with syllabic /n/ in the usual pronunciation of 'button' and syllabic /m/ in 'rhythm': in all such cases, if the minimal vowel /ə/ is present in the syllable it will always have shwa quality /ə/, not shwi /ɪ/.)

°<u>re</u> never constitutes a morpheme but is always a morpheme-final symbol as in °centre °fibre; it has the same value as °<u>er</u> in the American spellings °center °fiber, but offers a routine Terminal-E for deletion in words like °central and °fibrous, where American spelling requires deletion of an internal °e.

°<u>heir</u> and °<u>hour</u> are unique symbols constituting free morphemes which are stable in derivations such as °heirloom °hourly; [heir] in °inherit undergoes deletion of trailing °i (see Section 29.4), while [hour] in °horology undergoes deletion of trailing °u (compare °glamour/glamorous).

°<u>o.e</u> has been remarked on already (Section 17.5). There is nothing unusual about its correspondences in other morphemes (in °bone, for instance), but in the free morpheme °one, and its derivative °once, its value is anomalous in two ways: it is a sequence of two sounds /w-u/ and the first of these is consonantal. In the derivative °only, both anomalies disappear.

°<u>oir</u> and °<u>ois</u>: the anomalous /w/ in the value of °<u>o.e</u> just mentioned is paralleled by /w/ associated with leading °o in these two symbols. Note that °<u>oir</u> in the free morpheme °choir undergoes deletion of °i in the derivative °choral (Section 29.4). With °reservoir and °bourgeois we are up against the problems of marginal symbols and marginal correspondences typified by °rendezvous (Section 18.4).

I called this section 'Cross-category symbols'. Strictly speaking, no symbol as such can be 'cross-category' (a symbol is a symbol is a symbol – Section 16.5), which is why Table 21.3 is headed 'Cross-category phenomena': the phenomena are correspondences. But throughout these chapters we are approaching these phenomena via the symbols of the spelling system, not via the sounds of the pronunciation system.

22 *Vowel symbols*

22.1 Vowel symbol families

The first three sections of Chapter 21 formed an introduction to 'families of symbols' and to matrices of symbols and their sound-values, and Section 21.4 introduced such matrices in the relatively simple circumstances of the consonant symbols. Membership of a symbol family is determined by the leading letter of each symbol. Consonant symbols begin with a consonant letter, vowel symbols begin with a vowel letter; the half-dozen exceptions to this regularity were treated as 'cross-category' symbols in Section 21.5. The six vowel letters are A E I O U Y (see Section 11.5).

The vowel symbols are more numerous than the consonant symbols, and, with only six leading letters, the families are bound to be large – as we know from Chapter 20, where the vowel symbols are set out according to their structure (Table 20.6). The structures of vowel symbols are more complicated than those of the consonant symbols, as they can be longer (up to four letters, as opposed to three) and they can be discontinuous – the 'dotted' symbols involving Terminal-E, like °a.e in °gate. These two features make for more and longer symbols but they do not complicate sound/symbol relationships. Two other features, however, do complicate these relationships.

The first is the minimal vowel (see Section 20.6, especially Table 20.11: °striking °instance °observed °extreme). This is not a feature of the spelling system but of the pronunciation system. The spelling system is not affected by it; it operates without it, which is the significant thing. When we relate symbols to sounds, then we have to recognise the complexity of the pronunciation system, and we have to provide, against a large proportion of the vowel symbols, a minimal value. This first complicating feature therefore is accommodated in the main table of matrices, Table 22.1.

The second feature is also a feature of the pronunciation system and of the RefP in particular – the R-coloured vowels (see Section 20.6: °mare °mere °mire and so on). But this feature is paralleled by the Trailing-R symbols in the spelling system: a structural feature of these symbols, namely the presence of °r as a trailing letter, corresponds to the R-colouring of the sounds. Trailing-R symbols correspond only to R-coloured vowels, which means that the

Trailing-R symbols, having no values in common with the rest of the vowel symbols (except the minimal vowel), can be treated separately, and I have set out their matrices in Table 22.2.

The sound notation for the vowels has been given in Table 20.8.

22.2   The six families: A E I O U Y matrices

Note 1: the three numbers in parentheses at the head of each matrix indicate, in order, the number of symbols (down the left-hand column), the number of sounds (across the top), and the number of correspondences (=the number of entries in the matrix).

Note 2: Sample words/morphemes for the sound-values given in the sound-notation will be found in Chapter 24.

Table 22.1 *Matrices of vowel symbols (excluding Trailing-R symbols), arranged in 'leading letter' families, with sound values*

Symbol	Values									
A (22) (10) (50)										
	/a/	/ae/	/aa/	/aw/	/@/	/o/	/oe/	/e/	/ee/	/ie/
°<u>a</u>	/a/	/ae/	/aa/	/aw/	/@/	/o/		/e/		
°<u>a.e</u>	/a/	/ae/	/aa/		/@/			/e/		
°<u>ai</u>	/a/	/ae/			/@/			/e/		
°<u>al</u>	/a/		/aa/	/aw/						
°<u>au.e</u>		/ae/		/aw/			/oe/			
°<u>ay</u>		/ae/			/@/			/e/	/ee/	
°<u>ah</u>		/ae/	/aa/		/@/					
°<u>ai.e</u>		/ae/								
°<u>aigh</u>		/ae/								
°<u>ao</u>		/ae/								
°<u>au</u>			/aa/	/aw/	/@/	/o/	/oe/			
°<u>aa</u>			/aa/							
°<u>al.e</u>			/aa/							
°<u>aul</u>				/aw/						
°<u>augh</u>				/aw/						
°<u>aw</u>				/aw/						
°<u>aw.e</u>				/aw/						
°<u>awe</u>				/aw/						
°<u>ae</u>					/@/			/e/	/ee/	
°<u>ach</u>						/o/				
°<u>aye</u>										/ie/
°<u>ais.e</u>										/ie/

Table 22.1 *continued*

Symbol	Values

E (21) (10) (48)

	/e/	/ee/	/@/	/ae/	/ie/	/i/	/ue/	/oo/	/oe/	/o/
°e	/e/	/ee/	/@/	/ae/		/i/				/o/
°ee	/e/	/ee/	/@/	/ae/						
°ea	/e/	/ee/	/@/	/ae/						
°ei	/e/	/ee/		/ae/	/ie/					
°eo	/e/	/ee/	/@/						/oe/	
°eb	/e/									
°eg	/e/									
°ey		/ee/	/@/	/ae/	/ie/					
°e.e		/ee/		/ae/						
°ee.e		/ee/								
°ea.e		/ee/								
°ei.e		/ee/								
°et				/ae/						
°ez				/ae/						
°eigh				/ae/	/ie/					
°eye					/ie/					
°ew							/ue/	/oo/	/oe/	
°eau							/ue/		/oe/	/o/
°eu							/ue/	/oo/		
°eu.e							/ue/			
°ewe							/ue/			

(for °ed see Cross-category symbols in Section 21.5)

I (13) (7) (26)

	/i/	/ie/	/@/	/ee/	/a/	/e/	/ue/
°i	/i/	/ie/	/@/	/ee/			
°i.e	/i/	/ie/	/@/	/ee/	/a/		
°ie		/ie/	/@/	/ee/		/e/	
°is		/ie/	/@/	/ee/			
°ig		/ie/					
°is.e		/ie/					
°igh		/ie/					
°ic		/ie/					
°ie.e	/i/			/ee/			
°ia.e			/@/				
°io			/@/				
°ieu							/ue/
°iew							/ue/

Table 22.1 *continued*

O (26) (11) (57)

Symbol	/o/	/oe/	/ø/	/oo/	/ow	/oi/	/ə/	/u/	/aw/	/i/	/ee/
°o	/o/	/oe/	/ø/	/oo/			/ə/	/u/		/i/	
°o.e	/o/	/oe/		/oo/			/ə/	/u/			
°ou	/o/	/oe/		/oo/	/ow/		/ə/	/u/			
°ow	/o/	/oe/			/ow/						
°og	/o/										
°oo		/oe/	/ø/	/oo/				/u/			
°ough		/oe/		/oo/	/ow/		/ə/		/aw/		
°oe		/oe/		/oo/				/u/			/ee/
°oa		/oe/							/aw/		
°oh		/oe/									
°ol		/oe/									
°os		/oe/									
°ot		/oe/									
°owe		/oe/									
°oul			/ø/								
°oo.e			/ø/	/oo/							
°oup				/oo/							
°ous				/oo/							
°oeu				/oo/							
°ou.e					/ow/						
°ow.e					/ow/						
°oub					/ow/						
°oi						/oi/	/ə/				
°oi.e						/oi/	/ə/				
°oy						/oi/					
°oy.e						/oi/					

(for °o.e as a Cross-category symbol, and for °ois, see Section 21.5)

U (8) (7) (18)

Symbol	/u/	/ue/	/ø/	/oo/	/ə/	/e/	/i/
°u	/u/	/ue/	/ø/	/oo/	/ə/	/e/	/i/
°ub	/u/						
°u.e		/ue/		/oo/	/ə/		
°ue		/ue/		/oo/			
°ui		/ue/		/oo/			
°ui.e		/ue/					
°uch		/ue/					
°ueue		/ue/					

Table 22.1 *continued*

Symbol	Values

Y (3) (3) (5)

	/i/	/ie/	/ə/
°y	/i/	/ie/	/ə/
°y.e		/ie/	
°ye		/ie/	

Table 22.2 *Matrices of vowel symbols with trailing-R, arranged in 'leading letter' families, with sound values. (See Notes preceding Table 22.2)*

Symbol	Values

A (12) (4) (16)

	/aer/	/aar/	/oer/	/ə/
°ar.e	/aer/	/aar/		
°are	/aer/	/aar/		
°air	/aer/			
°aar		/aar/		
°arr		/aar/		
°arre		/aar/		
°arrh		/aar/		
°ayer		/aar/		
°ayor		/aar/		
°ar		/aar/	/oer/	/ə/
°aur			/oer/	
°awer			/oer/	

E (10) (6) (19)

	/eer/	/aer/	/aar/	/ur/	/uer/	/ə/
°ear	/eer/	/aer/	/aar/	/ur/		
°ere	/eer/	/aer/		/ur/		
°eir	/eer/	/aer/				
°eer	/eer/					
°er			/aar/	/ur/		/ə/
°eur				/ur/		/ə/
°er.e				/ur/		
°err				/ur/		
°ear.e				/ur/		
°ewer					/uer/	

Table 22.2 *continued*

Symbol	Values

I (6) (4) (8)

	/ier/	/eer/	/ur/	/ǝ/
°<u>ire</u>	/ier/			
°<u>ir</u>		/eer/	/ur/	/ǝ/
°<u>ier</u>		/eer/		
°<u>ier.e</u>		/eer/		
°<u>ir.e</u>			/ur/	
°<u>irr</u>			/ur/	

O (11) (6) (20)

	/oer/	/oor/	/owr/	/oir/	/ur/	/ǝ/
°<u>our</u>	/oer/	/oor/	/owr/		/ur/	/ǝ/
°<u>oor</u>	/oer/	/oor/				
°<u>or</u>	/oer/				/ur/	/ǝ/
°<u>our.e</u>	/oer/				/ur/	
°<u>or.e</u>	/oer/				/ur/	
°<u>oar</u>	/oer/					
°<u>ore</u>	/oer/					
°<u>orr</u>	/oer/					
°<u>oar.e</u>	/oer/					
°<u>orps</u>	/oer/					
°<u>oir</u>				/oir/		

(for °<u>oir</u> as a Cross-category symbol see Section 21.5)

U (5) (4) (8)

	/uer/	/ur/	/oor/	/ǝ/
°<u>ure</u>	/uer/		/oor/	/ǝ/
°<u>ueur</u>	/uer/			
°<u>ur</u>		/ur/		/ǝ/
°<u>ur.e</u>		/ur/		
°<u>urr</u>		/ur/		

Y (3) (3) (4)

	/ier/	/ur/	/ǝ/
°<u>yre</u>	/ier/		
°<u>yr</u>		/ur/	/ǝ/
°<u>yrrh</u>		/ur/	

23 Consonant correspondences

> **23.1** How to read the lists of correspondences
> **23.2** Words/morphemes as sample items
> **23.3** Alphabetical list of consonant correspondences

23.1 How to read the lists of correspondences

The list of consonant correspondences in this chapter and the list of vowel correspondences in Chapter 24 are both strictly alphabetical. You will find it best to glance at the lists now in order to follow these guidance notes.

The symbols are still in 'family groups', as in Chapters 21 and 22, by virtue of their leading letters, and the three figures in parentheses at the head of each group indicate, as before, the number of symbols, the number of sound-values and the number of correspondences, in that order. Cross-category correspondences are signalled by # on their left. Correspondences where the sound-value is a sequence of two sounds, as it normally is for °x̲, are signalled by ! on their right.

Each list consists of three columns: the left-hand column contains the correspondences, the middle column gives each correspondence a name, and the right-hand column supplies words or morphemes to exemplify the correspondence.

Correspondences

Each correspondence is set out in full notation in the left-hand column, in the following form:

Symbol	Dash	Sound-value
(letter or letters with circlet and underlined)	–	(notation between two oblique brackets: /. . ./)

For example: °b̲ – /b/ ('Symbol B with the value /b/').

Names of correspondences

It is the principle of naming correspondences, like any other entities we wish to talk about, that is important. There is nothing final about the names suggested here; better ones may be available.

One part of each name is, however, determined in advance: the correspondence name must include the symbol name, which consists of the names of the constituent letters of the symbol. Something must then be added to distinguish the name of the correspondence from that of the symbol. Where a symbol enters into only one correspondence, I have used the term 'sole' as an addition ('SOLE BB'), except where the symbol and the sound-notation are the same – fully convergent – when I have used the addition 'straight' ('STRAIGHT B'). Where a symbol enters into more than one correspondence, I have used sample words to distinguish between the correspondences ('GH in GHOST' 'GH in ROUGH'). But where correspondences are related to each other, then descriptive/contrastive terms are valuable, since they tell us something systematic about the spelling system. Examples are: HARD C, SOFT C; VOICELESS S, VOICED S; SHORT A, LONG A, MINIMAL A.

Sample words/morphemes

A really informative list of sample words/morphemes could manage to indicate not only the commonness or rarity of individual correspondences, but their commonness or rarity in different morphemic environments. The lists which follow make no such attempt, either in respect of incidence or frequency (see Section 16.4) or in respect of inter- or intra-morphemic environments. The sample items are mostly cited as words, heavily biased in favour of Function Words to reinforce the theme of Section 16.2; some items appear as prefixes or suffixes, and the latter include all the inflections.

Perhaps the most significant thing about the sample lists, however, is simply the use of the term 'morpheme' in the heading.

23.2   Words/morphemes as sample items

The importance of morphemes as simultaneously units in the grammar and units in the spelling system has been emphasised throughout this book. The morpheme, not the word, is the real locus of the symbol. So there are at least three reasons why 'morpheme' must take its place beside 'word' at the top of the column of sample items.

- To say that the correspondence °ie – /e/ is only found in the word °friend may be fine at one level of discussion, but at another level it is false and conceptually inadequate. This 'unique' correspondence is found not only in the word °friend but in the words °friends °friendly °befriend and other words formed on the nuclear morpheme [friend], many of which will be found in Section 29.2. When you see the word °friend in the list, then, think of the morpheme under the skin – [friend].

- While °friend is a free morpheme, the prefix °be- is a tied morpheme. All affixes are, in principle, tied morphemes; and so are nuclears like °-gin- in °begin – that is, nuclears which cannot stand on their own as words. (In Section 4.5, I called such nuclear morphemes 'lame' in contrast to free-standing nuclears like °friend.) Some sample words, therefore, are cited for the sake of a correspondence located in an affix: MINIMAL OU, as in °famous, for instance. Because affixes tend to be weak syllables in pronunciation, their symbol make-up and their correspondences tend to get neglected.

- Morphemes are made up of symbols, and symbols are the unit of correspondence with sounds. Generally speaking, all symbols are contained within morphemes: DOUBLE T, for instance, in °catty belongs to the morpheme [cat]. This is the general pattern, part of the four-tier framework to be put forward in Chapter 25 at the beginning of Part III. Against this background we can identify counter-instances, particularly with double consonant symbols (Chapter 10 'Mixed doubles' is relevant here). Take the adverb °educationally, analysed once before. The plus-junction before the adverb suffix produces a double consonant symbol by abutment:

°educational + ly → °educationally

The two letters °l belong to different morphemes, but there is only a single sound /l/ in the pronunciation. It is commonsense to treat them as forming a two-letter symbol. Such 'arching' symbols are in fact a familiar feature in the vocabulary. Among the 3000+ adverbs in English (see Section 3.5), there are some 500 adverbs (see Section 3.5) like °educationally – °brutally °finally °normally °usually °unproblematically and so on – and another 100 like °beautifully. Double-consonant arching symbols are also regularly produced, at prefix boundaries, by Consonant Assimilation, as in °account °accredit and (twice) in °accommodation (see Section 10.6). We can state precisely the conditions under which this counter-pattern appears; and for every two-letter symbol which crosses a morpheme boundary, there are thousands which don't. Notice, furthermore, that the problem of arching symbols lies in sound/symbol relationships, not in morpheme segmentation and junctions.

Finally, in consulting the lists, always test the correspondences and the sample items for yourself, and test them against other words and morphemes. In short, grow your own examples. *And identify morphemes wherever you can* (see Section 4.5).

23.3   Alphabetical list of consonant correspondences

Correspondence	Name of correspondence	Sample words/morphemes
B (3) (1) (3)		
°b – /b/	STRAIGHT B	°be by bad but back been best both about above below before better behind beyond nobody beneath between abduct obstruct, -able eatable, -ible edible
°bb – /b/	SOLE BB	°rabbit hobble rubbing rubbed abbreviate
°bu – /b/	SOLE BU	°build buy buoy
C (10) (4) (15)		
°c – /k/	HARD C	°can across could conduct ecosystem particle, -ic tonic
°c – /s/	SOFT C	°hence since existence acid cent
°c – /ch/	C in CELLO	°cello
°c – /sh/	C in COERCION	°coercion
°cc – /k/	SOLE CC	°accredit tobacco succumb
°cch – /k/	SOLE CCH	°saccharine
°ce – /sh/	SOLE CE	°ocean herbaceous cretaceous
°ch – /ch/	STRAIGHT CH	°each much such which
°ch – /k/	CH in CHEMIST	°school ache psychology
°ch – /sh/	CH in CHIC	°niche quiche
°ci – /sh/	SOLE CI	°social official musician spacious
°ck – /k/	SOLE CK	°back wicket panicky
°cq – /k/	SOLE CQ	°acquire acquaint acquiesce
°cqu – /k/	SOLE CQU	°lacquer
°cu – /k/	SOLE CU	°circuit biscuit

D (2) (1) (2)

| °<u>d</u> – /d/ | STRAIGHT D | °<u>d</u>o and bad did had amid dare does done down good need said could round under would beside during nobody should toward decide disprove adoption, -ed sited sided |
| °<u>dd</u> – /d/ | SOLE DD | °a<u>dd</u> ladder middle kidding addict |

#ED (1) (2) (2)

| #°<u>ed</u> – /d/ | ED in BUZZED | °-ed used /zd/, rubbed hugged aimed bowed shoved breathed followed aired |
| #°<u>ed</u> – /t/ | ED in HISSED | °-ed used /st/, itched rushed wrapped racked |

F (3) (2) (4)

°<u>f</u> – /f/	STRAIGHT F	°i<u>f</u> few for from after first front before, -ful beautiful
°<u>f</u> – /v/	F in OF	°o<u>f</u>
°<u>ff</u> – /f/	SOLE FF	°o<u>ff</u> efficient suffer, ad- affix
°<u>ft</u>	SOLE FT	°so<u>ft</u>en often

G (7) (5) (12)

°<u>g</u> – /g/	HARD G	°<u>g</u>o ago get got good going again against
°<u>g</u> – /j/	SOFT G	°<u>g</u>em gin rage raging stagy magic, -ology zoology, -age luggage
°<u>g</u> – /zh/	G in ROUGE	°beige mirage
°<u>ge</u> – /j/	GE in GEORDIE	°<u>ge</u>orgette georgic
°<u>ge</u> – /zh/	GE in BOURGEOIS	°bour<u>ge</u>ois
°<u>gg</u> – /g/	GG in EGG	°e<u>gg</u> dagger begging baggage aggression
°<u>gg</u> – /j/	GG in SUGGEST	°exa<u>gg</u>erate
°<u>gh</u> – /g/	GH in GHOST	°a<u>gh</u>ast gherkin ghetto ghoul
°<u>gh</u> – /f/	GH in ROUGH	°enou<u>gh</u> cough laugh draught
°<u>gi</u> – /j/	SOLE GI	°reli<u>gi</u>ous contagious
°<u>gn</u> – /n/	SOLE GN	°<u>gn</u>ash gnarl gnat gnaw gnome
°<u>gu</u> – /g/	SOLE GU	°<u>gu</u>ess guest guide guilt guitar

H (1) (1) (1)

°h – /h/	STRAIGHT H	°he had has her him his how have here hence behind childhood
#°heir – /aer/	SOLE HEIR	°heir
#°ho – /o/	SOLE HO	°honest honour honorary
#°hour – /owr/	SOLE HOUR	°hour

J (1) (1) (1)

°j – /j/	STRAIGHT J	°just jam jest jilt join jug reject

K (4) (2) (4)

°k – /k/	STRAIGHT K	°like kale keen kiss cook coke trek
°kh – /k/	SOLE KH	°khaki
°kk – /k/	SOLE KK	°trekking
°kn – /n/	SOLE KN	°knack knee knit knuckle unknown

L (3) (2) (3)

°l – /l/	STRAIGHT L	°let lot else last less like only plus along below least until while whole little unless although, -ly madly, -al tidal
#°le – /əl/!	SOLE LE	°able little middle gargle, -able probable, -ible possible, -le handle
°ll – /l/	SOLE LL	°all till well will shall allocate beautifully, -ally drastically

M (4) (2) (5)

°m – /m/	STRAIGHT M	°am me my him may amid from many mine more most much must same some them whom among might minus middle imperil empower, -ism racism
°mb – /m/	SOLE MB	°lamb climb thumb succumb
°mm – /m/	SOLE MM	°simmer dimmer slimmed slimming commit immediate symmetry
°mn – /m/	MN in DAMN	°condemn autumn
°mn – /n/	MN in MNEMO-	°mnemo-/mnemonic

N (4) (2) (5)

°n̲ – /n/	STRAIGHT N	°an in no on and any can nor not now one been done down even many mine near need next none only than then went when again front hence minus never round since under until behind beyond enough nobody unless against another beneath between neither nothing, -en widen, -ent violent, -ence violence, -ion action, -ness coolness, in- informal, un- unfriendly
°n̲ – /ng/	N in INK	°tank sink bunk oncology income anger finger anxious
°n̲g̲ – /ng/	STRAIGHT NG	°along among during nothing everything, -ing coming going
°ngu̲ – /ng/	SOLE NGU	°tongue harangue meringue
°n̲n̲ – /n/	SOLE NN	°cannot sonnet planner inner sunny announce connect innovate ennoble

P (7) (5) (7)

°p̲ – /p/	STRAIGHT P	°up put past plus upon except pervade prevail provide supersede
°p̲h̲ – /f/	SOLE PH	°photo nephew triumph seraph
°p̲n̲ – /n/	SOLE PN	°pneumo- pneumatic pneumonia
°p̲p̲ – /p/	SOLE PP	°upper opposite dipped apply supply
°p̲p̲h̲ – /f/	SOLE PPH	°sapphire
°p̲s̲ – /s/	SOLE PS	°psycho- psychology pseudonym psychiatry psoriasis
°p̲t̲ – /t/	SOLE PT	°ptero- pterodactyl pteridophyte ptomaine ptarmigan

Q (2) (1) (2)

°q̲ – /k/	SOLE Q	°quite quack quell quick quote loquacious colloquy inquest
°qu̲ – /k/	SOLE QU	°conquer opaque grotesque quiche

R (4) (1) (4)

°r̲ – /r/	STRAIGHT R	°from very every front round across rather through stationary lottery gallantry

#°re – /ə/	SOLE RE	°centre meagre acre
°rh – /r/	SOLE RH	°rhyme rhythm rhapsody rhododendron
°rr – /r/	SOLE RR	°currant barrel marry tomorrow barring starry occurrence, arrogant irrational correction surrogate
°rrh – /r/	SOLE RRH	°haemorrhage diarrhoea

S (9) (4) (15)

°s̲ – /s/	VOICELESS S	°so us its say yes best else last just most must past plus same said says some such this thus used first least minus since worse worst beside against submit transmit, -s cats reaps, -est nicest, -ist artist, -ous famous
°s̲ – /z/	VOICED S	°as is has his was hers ours says these those whose yours theirs because opposite, -s badges badgers, -es bosses, -ise visualise, -ism idealism
°s̲ – /sh/	S in SUGAR	°sure ensure
°s̲ – /zh/	S in PLEASURE	°measure treasure leisure vision fusion occasion
°sc̲ – /s/	SOLE SC	°scent scene science nascent adolesce obsolescent
°sch̲ – /s/	SCH in SCHISM	°schism
°sch̲ – /sh/	SCH in SCHEDULE	°schedule
°sci̲ – /sh/	SOLE SCI	°conscious conscience
°sh̲ – /sh/	STRAIGHT SH	°she shall should skittish
°ss̲ – /s/	SS in PRESS	°less across unless actress helpless, -ness kindness
°ss̲ – /z/	SS in DISSOLVE	°dessert possess scissors
°ss̲ – /sh/	SS in MISSION	°passion aggression succession percussion assure pressure
°st̲ – /s/	SOLE ST	°fasten hasten castle wrestle gristle whistle apostle hustle
°sth̲ – /s/	SOLE STH	°asthma isthmus
°sw̲ – /s/	SOLE SW	°sword answer

T (7) (5) (10)

°t – /t/	STRAIGHT T	°at it to but get got its let not out too yet best just last most must next till that went what about after against first front least might quite until worst except between towards without opposite transport definite royalty joint, -est oddest, -t burnt, -ate considerate, -ist cyclist, -ity rarity
°t – /ch/	T in NATURE	°feature
°tch – /ch/	SOLE TCH	°catch fetch itch scotch hutch butcher satchel
°te – /ch/	SOLE TE	°righteous
°th – /th/	VOICELESS TH	°both thing beneath nothing through thin thick breath ether
°th – /dh/	VOICED TH	°the than that them then they this thus with other there their these those either rather thence though neither whether without although father breathe clothe smooth
°th – /t/	TH in THYME	°Thomas Thames
°ti – /sh/	SOLE TI	°cautious flirtatious differential partial
°tt – /t/	SOLE TT	°better little butter getting fatter attract, -ette laundrette
°tw – /t/	SOLE TW	°two

U (1) (1) (1)

°u – /w/	CONSONANT U	°quite quark quest quick quality quote anguish language penguin persuade suite

V (2) (1) (2)

°v – /v/	STRAIGHT V	°even ever over very above every never, -ive active
°vv – /v/	SOLE VV	°revved revving navvy

W (2) (2) (3)

°w – /w/	STRAIGHT W	°we was want well went were will with worse worst between towards wag wit wound work

°wh – /w/	NORMAL WH	°why what when where which while nowhere whether whisper
°wh – /h/	WH in WHO	°whom whose whole

X (2) (5) (6)

°x – /k-s/!	NORMAL X	°next wax vex fix box luxury buxom onyx coax axiom vixen fixture index, ex- export exhibition
°x – /g-z/!	X in EXAM	°exist exact exert example anxiety
°x – /z/	X in XYLOPHONE	°xylum xenophobia xerox
°x – /k/	X in EXCEPT	°exceed excel
°x – /k-sh/!	X in ANXIOUS	°anxious
°xh – /g-z/!	SOLE XH	°exhibit exhaust exhort

Y (1) (1) (1)

°y – /y/	CONSONANT Y	°yes yet you your yours beyond yonder yard yellow yoyo young

Z (2) (2) (3)

°z – /z/	STRAIGHT Z	°zig-zag zest zoo fez hazard, -ize polarize
°z – /s/	Z in WALTZ	°waltz spritzer
°zz – /z/	SOLE ZZ	°buzz fizz buzzard prezzie

Warning: Too many correspondences can damage your view of the recurring patterns of the spelling system. The matrices of symbols and sounds back in Chapters 21 and 22 may well be more instructive – perhaps less entertaining – than these lists of correspondences (Chapters 23 and 24) with their sample words and morphemes. Far worse than the consonant correspondences, when it comes to concealing the wood with trees, are the vowel correspondences which follow.

24 Vowel correspondences

24.1 How to read the list

The correspondences are set out in alphabetical order in exactly the same way as the consonant correspondences in Chapter 23. Sections 1 and 2 of that chapter provide a full introduction to the lists, but the following two paragraphs are repeated from Section 23.1 for convenience.

The symbols are still in 'family groups', as in Chapters 21 and 22, by virtue of their leading letters, and the three figures in parentheses at the head of each group indicate, as before, the number of symbols, the number of sound-values and the number of correspondences, in that order. Cross-category correspondences are signalled by # on the left-hand side. Correspondences where the sound-value is a sequence of two sounds, as it normally is for °x, are signalled by ! on the right-hand side.

The list consists of three columns: the left-hand column contains the correspondences, the middle column gives each correspondence a name, and the right-hand column supplies words or morphemes to exemplify the correspondence.

24.2 Alphabetical list of vowel correspondences

Correspondence	Name of correspondence	Sample words/morphemes
A (34) (13) (66)		
°a̲ – /a/	SHORT A	°am an as at and can had has back than that bad
°a̲ – /ae/	LONG A	°a communication stated amoral
°a̲ – /aa/	A in BRA	°can't last past after shan't rather
°a̲ – /aw/	A in WATER	°all although

°a̱ – /o/	A in WANT	°was what watch quarrel squash
°a̱ – /e/	A in ANY	°many
°a̱ – /ə/	MINIMAL A	°away about above again along among across around against another canoe, -al arrival, -al normal, literary numeracy
°a̱.e – /ae/	LONG A.E ('A dot E')	°same came escapade protease, ate- legislate
°a̱.e – /a/	SHORT A.E	°have axe
°a̱.e – /aa/	A.E in VASE	°massage promenade
°a̱.e – /e/	A.E in ATE	°ate
°a̱.e – /ə/	MINIMAL A.E	°literate haulage passage
°a̱a – /aa/	SOLE DOUBLE A	°baa
°a̱ar – /aar/	SOLE AAR	°bazaar
°a̱ch – /o/	SOLE ACH	°yacht
°a̱e – /ee/	AE in ANAESTHETIST	°aesthete caesar haematoma
°a̱e – /e/	AE in HAEMORRHAGE	°haemorrhage
°a̱e – /ə/	MINIMAL AE	°archaeology gynaecology
°a̱h – /ae/	AH in DAHLIA	°dahlia
°a̱h – /aa/	AH in AH!	°ah hurrah
°a̱h – /ə/	MINIMAL AH	°rajah
°a̱i – /ae/	LONG AI	°again aid grain contain
°a̱i – /a/	SHORT AI	°plaid plait
°a̱i – /e/	AI in SAID	°said against
°a̱i – /ə/	MINIMAL AI	°bargain captain villain
°a̱i.e – /a/	SOLE AI.E	°raise praise
°a̱igh – /ae/	SOLE AIGH	°straight
°a̱ir – /aer/	SOLE AIR	°air pair stair cairn
°a̱is.e – /ie/	SOLE AIS.E	°aisle
°a̱l – /aa/	AL in PALM	°half calf calm qualm
°a̱l – /aw/	AL in TALK	°walk chalk stalk
°a̱l – /a/	AL in SALMON	°salmon
°a̱l.e – /aa/	SOLE AL.E	°halve calve
°a̱o – /ae/	SOLE AO	°gaol
°a̱r – /aar/	AR in CARD	°art park argue target guard
°a̱r – /oer/	AR in WARD	°towards warm dwarf warden
°a̱r – /ə/	MINIMAL AR	°forward standard sugar
°a̱r.e – /aer/	AR.E in SCARCE	°scarce
°a̱r.e – /aar/	AR.E in CHARGE	°starve
°a̱re – /aer/	ARE in CARE	°dare flare share square
°a̱re – /aar/	ARE in ARE	°are

°arr – /aar/	SOLE ARR	°parr barred
°arre – /aar/	SOLE ARRE	°bizarre
°arrh – /aar/	SOLE ARRH	°catarrh
°au – /aw/	AU in AUTUMN	°auction fraud haunt
°au – /aa/	AU in AUNT	°aunt laugh draught
°au – /oe/	AU in CHAUFFEUR	°chauffeur
°au – /o/	AU in SAUSAGE	°cauliflower
°au – /@/	MINIMAL AU	°restaurant
°au.e – /aw/	AU.E in SAUCE	°cause gauze
°au.e – /ae/	AU.E in GAUGE	°gauge
°au.e – /oe/	AU.E in MAUVE	°mauve
°augh – /aw/	SOLE AUGH	°caught taught daughter naughty
°aul – /aw/	SOLE AUL	°baulk caulk
°aur – /oer/	SOLE AUR	°dinosaur centaur
°aw – /aw/	SOLE AW	°dawn awkward saw law
°aw.e – /aw/	SOLE AW.E	°tawse hawse
°awe – /aw/	SOLE AWE	°awe
°awer – /oer/	SOLE AWER	°drawer
°ay – /ae/	LONG AY	°may say day away stay play
°ay – /ee/	AY in QUAY	°quay
°ay – /e/	AY in SAYS	°says
°ay – /@/	MINIMAL AY	°Sunday Monday holiday
°aye – /ie/	SOLE AYE	°aye (yes)
°ayer – /aer/	SOLE AYER	°prayer
°ayor – /aer/	SOLE AYOR	°mayor

E (31) (15) (67)

°e – /ee/	LONG E	°be he me we she even, re- reprint
°e – /e/	SHORT E	°get let yes yet best ever less next them then very well went when every never better except unless whether, ex- extricate
°e – /i/	E in PRETTY	°England
°e – /ae/	E in DEBRIS	°regime precis
°e – /o/	E in RENDEZVOUS	°envelope
°e – /@/	MINIMAL E	°below every before behind beside beyond enough except because beneath between even target emission enlarge, -es bosses, -ed hunted, -en darken, ex- expose, de- depend, re- reply

°e.e – /ee/	E.E in THEME	°these eve complete athlete
°e.e – /ae/	E.E in FETE	°fete
°ea – /ee/	EA in BEAD	°bead
°ea – /e/	EA in HEAD	°instead bread tread thread
°ea – /ae/	EA in GREATLY	°great break steak
°ea.e – /ee/	SOLE EA.E	°please ease leave increase
°ear – /eer/	EAR in FEAR	°near hear clear beard
°ear – /ur/	EAR in EARTH	°learn heard early rehearsal
°ear – /aer/	EAR in SWEAR	°bear pear tear wear
°ear – /aar/	EAR in HEART	°hearth
°ear.e – /ur/	SOLE EAR.E	°hearse rehearse
°eau – /oe/	EAU in BUREAU	°gateau plateau tableau
°eau – /o/	EAU in BUREAUCRACY	°bureaucracy
°eau – /ue/	EAU in BEAUTY	°beautiful
°eb – /e/	SOLE EB	°debt
#°ed – /d/	VOICED ED	°-ed ribbed raised rowed
#°ed – /t/	VOICELESS ED	°-ed ripped raced
°ee – /ee/	LONG DOUBLE E	°been need between see meet feet, -ee refugee
°ee – /e/	SHORT DOUBLE E	°threepence Greenwich
°ee – /ae/	DOUBLE E in NEE	°fiancee
°ee – /@/	MINIMAL DOUBLE E	°coffee toffee committee
°ee.e – /ee/	SOLE EE.E	°cheese freeze sneeze
°eer – /eer/	SOLE EER	°beer peer, -eer engineer
°eg – /e/	SOLE EG	°phlegm apophthegm
°ei – /ee/	EI in DECEIT	°conceit ceiling
°ei – /e/	EI in LEISURE	°heifer
°ei – /ae/	EI in VEIN	°veil rein reign sheikh
°ei – /ie/	EI in EITHER	°neither
°ei – /@/	MINIMAL EI	°forfeit foreign sovereign
°ei.e – /ee/	SOLE EI.E	°seize receive conceive
°eigh – /ae/	EIGH in FREIGHT	°eight weigh neighbour
°eigh – /ie/	EIGH in HEIGHT	°sleight
°eir – /eer/	EIR in WEIR	°weir weird
°eir – /aer/	EIR in THEIR	°their
°eo – /ee/	EO in PEOPLE	°people
°eo – /e/	EO in LEOPARD	°jeopardy
°eo – /oe/	EO in YEOMAN	°yeoman
°eo – /@/	MINIMAL EO	°surgeon bludgeon truncheon
°er – /ur/	ER in HERB	°her person, per- permutate
°er – /aar/	ER in CLERK	°sergeant derby

°er – /@/	MINIMAL ER	°ever over after never other under better either rather neither whether father liberty, -er faster, er- smoker, per- permissive, super- supervise
°er.e – /ur/	SOLE ER.E	°serve reverse terse
°ere – /eer/	ERE in HERE	°mere sincere severe
°ere – /aer/	ERE in THERE	°where ere ampere
°ere – /ur/	ERE in WERE	°were
°err – /ur/	SOLE ERR	°err
°et – /ae/	SOLE ET	°ballet sachet ricochet
°eu – /ue/	EU in NEUTRAL	°feud pneumatic
°eu – /oo/	EU in RHEUMATISM	°rheumy rheumatics
°eu.e – /ue/	SOLE EU.E	°deuce
°eur – /ur/	EUR in CONNOISSEUR	°entrepreneur raconteur
°eur – /@/	EUR in CHAUFFEUR	°amateur
°ew – /ue/	EW in FEW	°stew newt nephew curfew
°ew – /oo/	EW in CREW	°clew blew crew eschew
°ew – /oe/	EW in SEW	°sew
°ewe – /ue/	SOLE EWE	°ewe
°ewer – /uer/	SOLE EWER	°sewer ewer
°ey – /ee/	EY in KEY	°geyser
°ey – /ae/	EY in THEY	°obey prey whey
°ey – /ie/	EY in GEYSER	°geyser
°ey – /@/	MINIMAL EY	°money journey valley
°eye – /ie/	SOLE EYE	°eye
°ez – /ae/	SOLE EZ	°rendezvous

I (19) (10) (34)

°i – /i/	SHORT I	°if in is it did him his its this till will with until which little middle
°i – /ie/	LONG I	°I minus behind china bicycle bronchitis
°i – /ee/	I in VISA	°machinery chic mosquito
°i – /@/	MINIMAL I	°going during nothing rabbit, -ing coming, -ic atomic, -ible terrible, -ity community
°i.e – /ie/	LONG I.E	°like mine quite while beside precise infantile, -ise criticise
°i.e – /i/	SHORT I.E	°since give live
°i.e – /ee/	I.E in MACHINE	°police prestige expertise
°i.e – /a/	I.E in MERINGUE	°meringue

°i.e – /ə/	MINIMAL I.E	°office definite, -ive active
°ia.e – /ə/	SOLE IA.E	°marriage carriage
°ic – /ie/	SOLE IC	°indictment
°ie – /ie/	LONG IE	°pie tie vie
°ie – /ee/	IE in FIELD	°belief relief achieving
°ie – /e/	IE in FRIEND	°friend
°ie – /ə/	MINIMAL IE	°collie prairie calorie
°ie.e – /ee/	IE.E in PIECE	°niece believe besiege piece
°ie.e – /i/	IE.E in SIEVE	°sieve
°ier – /eer/	SOLE IER	°pier cashier bombardier
°ier.e – /eer/	SOLE IER.E	°fierce pierce
°ieu – /ue/	SOLE IEU	°lieu
°iew – /ue/	SOLE IEW	°view
°ig – /ie/	SOLE IG	°sign resign benign paradigm
°igh – /ie/	SOLE IGH	°might high thigh fright
°io – /ə/	MINIMAL IO	°fashion cushion, -ion action attention tension
°ir – /ur/	IR in BIRD	°first squirt girl shirk
°ir – /eer/	IR in SOUVENIR	°kirsch kir
°ir – /ə/	IR in TAPIR	°tapir
°ir.e – /ur/	SOLE IR.E	°dirge
°ire – /ier/	SOLE IRE	°fire admire inquire empire
°irr – /ur/	SOLE IRR	°whirr chirr
°is – /ie/	IS in ISLAND	°island
°is – /ee/	IS in PRECIS	°precis
°is – /ə/	MINIMAL IS	°chassis
°is.e – /ie/	SOLE IS.E	°isle lisle

O (38) (19) (81)

°o – /o/	SHORT O	°of on got not off from along across beyond opposite nonsense
°o – /oe/	LONG O	°go no so fro both only over going nobody open, co- cohabit
°o – /oo/	O in DO	°do to who whom two
°o – /ø/	O in WOMAN	°bosom
°o – /u/	O in TON	°among front other nothing son won
°o – /i/	O in WOMEN	°women
°o – /ə/	MINIMAL O	°nobody towards opposite reason symbol atom, -dom kingdom
°o.e – /oe/	LONG O.E	°those whole home rose, -ose verbose

°<u>o.e</u> – /o/	SHORT O.E	°gone shone
°<u>o.e</u> – /oo/	O.E in MOVE	°whose lose prove
°<u>o.e</u> – /u/	O.E in LOVE	°done none some above come
°<u>o.e</u> – /wu/!	O.E in ONCE	°one once
°<u>o.e</u> – /ə/	MINIMAL O.E	°welcome Europe, -some lonesome
°<u>oa</u> – /oe/	OA in BOAT	°oak road coal coat cocoa
°<u>oa</u> – /aw/	OA in BROAD	°broad
°<u>oar</u> – /oer/	SOLE OAR	°oar soar roar board
°<u>oar.e</u> – /oer/	SOLE OAR.E	°coarse hoarse
°<u>oe</u> – /oe/	OE in TOE	°woe foe doe aloe
°<u>oe</u> – /oo/	OE in SHOE	°shoe canoe
°<u>oe</u> – /u/	OE in DOESN'T	°does doesn't
°<u>oe</u> – /ee/	OE in AMOEBA	°foetus phoenix oesophagus
°<u>oeu</u> – /oo/	SOLE OEU	°manoeuvre
°<u>og</u> – /o/	SOLE OG	°physiognomy
°<u>oh</u> – /oe/	SOLE OH	°oh! ohm
°<u>oi</u> – /oi/	OI in JOIN	°oil boil void
°<u>oi</u> – /ə/	MINIMAL OI	°connoisseur
°<u>oi.e</u> – /oi/	OI.E in VOICE	°choice noise
°<u>oi.e</u> – /ə/	MINIMAL OI.E	°tortoise
°<u>oir</u> – /oir/	OIR in COIR	°coir
#°<u>oir</u> – /wier/!	OIR in CHOIR	°choir
#°<u>oir</u> – /waar/!	OIR in RESERVOIR	°reservoir
#°<u>ois</u> – /waa/!	SOLE OIS	°bourgeois patois chamois
°<u>ol</u> – /oe/	SOLE OL	°folk yolk
°<u>oo</u> – /oe/	DOUBLE O in BROOCH	°brooch
°<u>oo</u> – /oo/	DOUBLE O in BOOM	°too noon balloon shampoo
°<u>oo</u> – /ø/	DOUBLE O in BOOK	°good took foot brook shook
°<u>oo</u> – /u/	DOUBLE O in BLOOD	°flood
°<u>oo.e</u> – /oo/	OO.E in CHOOSE	°ooze groove noose loose
°<u>oo.e</u> – /ø/	OO.E in GOOSEBERRY	°gooseberry
°<u>oor</u> – /oer/	OOR in DOOR	°floor
°<u>oor</u> – /oor/	OOR in POOR	°moor boor
°<u>or</u> – /oer/	OR in FORM	°or for nor born scorch afford
°<u>or</u> – /ur/	OR in WORD	°worst work world attorney
°<u>or</u> – /ə/	MINIMAL OR	°mirror comfort, -or actor
°<u>ore</u> – /oer/	SOLE ORE	°more before shore commodore

°<u>or</u>.e – /oer/	OR.E in HORSE	°gorse force
°<u>or</u>.e – /ur/	OR.E in WORSE	°worse
°<u>orps</u> – /oer/	SOLE ORPS	°corps
°<u>orr</u> – /oer/	SOLE ORR	°abhorred
°<u>os</u> – /oe/	SOLE OS	°apropos
°<u>ot</u> – /oe/	SOLE OT	°depot
°<u>ou</u> – /oe/	OU in SOUL	°shoulder boulder mould
°<u>ou</u> – /oo/	OU in SOUP	°you youth wound routine
°<u>ou</u> – /ow/	OU in SOUND	°out about round without south mountain
°<u>ou</u> – /o/	OU in COUGH	°trough
°<u>ou</u> – /u/	OU in TOUCH	°enough country young southern
°<u>ou</u> – /ə/	MINIMAL OU	°-ous famous marvellous
°<u>ou</u>.e – /ow/	SOLE OU.E	°house mouse blouse carouse
°<u>oub</u> – /ow/	SOLE OUB	°doubt
°<u>ough</u> – /oe/	OUGH in THOUGH	°though dough furlough
°<u>ough</u> – /oo/	OUGH in THROUGH	°through
°<u>ough</u> – /ow/	OUGH in PLOUGH	°bough
°<u>ough</u> – /aw/	OUGH in THOUGHT	°ought bought
°<u>ough</u> – /ə/	MINIMAL OUGH	°thorough borough
°<u>oul</u> – /ø/	SOLE OUL	°could would should
°<u>oup</u> – /oo/	SOLE OUP	°coup
°<u>our</u> – /owr/	OUR in SOUR	°our ours flour devour
°<u>our</u> – /oer/	OUR in FOURPENCE	°your yours four pour court mourn
°<u>our</u> – /oor/	OUR in TOUR	°bourgeois contour
°<u>our</u> – /ur/	OUR in JOURNEY	°journal courtesy
°<u>our</u> – /ə/	MINIMAL OUR	°colour favour honour
°<u>our</u>.e – /oer/	OUR.E in SOURCE	°course
°<u>our</u>.e – /ur/	OUR.E in SCOURGE	°scourge
°<u>ous</u> – /oo/	SOLE OUS	°rendezvous
°<u>ow</u> – /oe/	OW in GLOW	°below own know show window
°<u>ow</u> – /ow/	OW in GROWL	°how now down owl allow powder
°<u>ow</u> – /o/	OW in KNOWLEDGE	°knowledge
°<u>ow</u>.e – /ow/	SOLE OW.E	°browse drowse dowse
°<u>owe</u> – /oe/	SOLE OWE	°owe
°<u>oy</u> – /oi/	SOLE OY	°boy buoy employ corduroy
°<u>oy</u>.e – /oi/	SOLE OY.E	°gargoyle

U (13) (10) (26)

°<u>u</u> – /u/	SHORT U	°up us but just much must plus such thus under until unless product, sub- subject, un- untimely
°<u>u</u> – /ue/	LONG U	°used unit cubic duty student
°<u>u</u> – /oo/	U in JUNIOR	°lunar inclusive
°<u>u</u> – /ø/	U in BULL	°full pull pudding buffet
°<u>u</u> – /e/	U in BURY	°bury
°<u>u</u> – /i/	U in BUSY	°busy
°<u>u</u> – /ə/	MINIMAL U	°minus focus forum stirrup
°<u>u.e</u> – /ue/	U.E in CUBE	°use tube acute acumen
°<u>u.e</u> – /oo/	U.E in RUDE	°June brute exclude
°<u>u.e</u> – /ə/	MINIMAL U.E	°minute /ᴗ –/, lettuce
°<u>ub</u> – /u/	SOLE UB	°subtle
°<u>uch</u> – /ue/	SOLE UCH	°fuchsia
°<u>ue</u> – /ue/	UE in PURSUE	°cue due Tuesday avenue
°<u>ue</u> – /oo/	UE in BLUE	°clue glue true
°<u>ui</u> – /ue/	UI in NUISANCE	°suit
°<u>ui</u> – /oo/	UI in FRUIT	°recruit
°<u>ui.e</u> – /oo/	SOLE UI.E	°juice cruise bruise
°<u>ur</u> – /ur/	UR in BURN	°curl lurch curtain
°<u>ur</u> – /ə/	MINIMAL UR	°sulphur surprise Saturday
°<u>ur.e</u> – /ur/	SOLE UR.E	°curse curve purse urge
°<u>ure</u> – /uer/	URE in PURE	°cure endure mature caricature
°<u>ure</u> – /oor/	URE in SURE	°sure abjure
°<u>ure</u> – /ə/	MINIMAL URE	°figure, -ure pleasure
°<u>urr</u> – /ur/	SOLE URR	°purr burr
°<u>ueue</u> – /ue/	SOLE UEUE	°queue
°<u>ueur</u> – /uer/	SOLE UEUR	°liqueur

Y (6) (5) (9)

°<u>y</u> – /i/	SHORT Y	°myth rhythm symbol, syn- synthesis
°<u>y</u> – /ie/	LONG Y	°by my why try hyphen myocardial
°<u>y</u> – /ə/	MINIMAL Y	°any many only very every nobody busy, -ly madly, -y dirty
°<u>y.e</u> – /ie/	SOLE Y.E	°scythe byte
°<u>ye</u> – /ie/	SOLE YE	°bye dye rye
°<u>yr</u> – /ur/	YR in MYRTLE	°myrtle
°<u>yr</u> – /ə/	MINIMAL YR	°martyr zephyr satyr
°<u>yre</u> – /ier/	SOLE YRE	°lyre byre
°<u>yrrh</u> – /ur/	SOLE YRRH	°myrrh

Warning: These lists need you to bring words to them – especially Content Words, which I have been very niggardly with. The data of the spelling system are abundantly available to us all. Lists like these can stimulate plenty of *talk*, both where you think they have got things right and where you think you can improve them. Talk can be about words and morphemes and where they go in the lists; *but remember*: these two lists are lists of *correspondences*, and the deeper issue is what to count, and what not to count, as a correspondence.

PART

III

SOE

CHAPTERS

25 The spelling system of SOE: A four-tiered model

25.1 Unifying Part I and Part II

'SOE' (the Standard Orthography of English) is the name I shall give, in Chapter 27, to the writing-system as a whole. This system includes

1 the spelling system

2 the punctuation system

3 other elements such as the numerals 1, 2, 3 and 27 which you have just read.

The spelling system is the principal component of SOE and has already occupied 24 chapters of this book.

Chapters 1–12 (Part I) dealt with words and their grammatical constituents, morphemes, under the title 'Junctions'. Junctions are the 'joins' between morphemes in the spelling system: the morphemes in a written word can join simply

$$°go + ing → °going \qquad a\ plus\text{-}junction$$

or not so simply

$$°come × ing → °coming \qquad a\ change\text{-}junction$$

Chapters 13–24 (=Part II) dealt with sound/symbol relationships under the title 'Symbols'. Symbols are the units in the spelling of a word which match to the sounds of its pronunciation: they may consist of one letter (°c a t), two letters (°ch a t), three letters (°c a tch) or four letters (°c augh t). Letters are the constituents of symbols in the spelling system.

There is a unifying principle uniting Parts I and II: constituency.

25.2   Constituency

Words consist of morphemes; symbols consist of letters. Every word consists of one or more morphemes; every symbol consists of one or more letters. For example:

The word 'happy'	is a 1-morpheme word	[happy]
The word 'unhappy'	is a 2-morpheme word	un[happy]
The word 'unhappiness'	is a 3-morpheme word	[un[happy]ness]
The word 'unhappinesses'	is a 4-morpheme word	[un[happy]ness]es]
The symbol °c	is a 1-letter symbol	°c a t
The symbol °ch	is a 2-letter symbol	°ch a t
The symbol °tch	is a 3-letter symbol	°c a tch
The symbol °augh	is a 4-letter symbol	°c augh t

There is an exact parallel between the word/morpheme pair of units and the symbol/letter pair of units: in both pairs, every member of the larger unit consists of one or more members of the 'smaller' unit. The key to this parallelism is 'one or more': a word can consist of a single morpheme (like 'cat'), and single-morpheme words are common; a symbol can consist of a single letter (like °c and °a and °t), and single-letter symbols are even commoner (see Section 17.2).

Such single-constituent structures are characteristic of language (think of 'monosyllables'; think of words like 'a' and 'I'; think of sentences consisting of just a main clause, or of paragraphs containing only one sentence; think of one-word answers). But a model based on size ('larger/smaller') won't accommodate single-constituent structures: the word 'cat' is not larger than the morpheme [cat]; the letter °c is not smaller than the symbol °c.

If you are thinking in terms of larger and smaller it is natural to be thinking at the same time in terms of 'whole' and 'part', since a part must be smaller than a whole and a whole must be larger than a part. But this model won't do either. The morpheme [cat] is certainly part of the word 'cats'; but it is not a part of the word 'cat', it is the whole of it. In the same way, letter °c is part of the symbol °ch, but it is the whole of symbol °c.

The structural model which accommodates this feature of language is called *the constituency model*. Morphemes are the constituents of words; letters are the constituents of symbols. Instead of 'larger' and 'smaller' we speak of 'higher' and 'lower'. The higher unit in each pair (namely words and symbols) is made up of *one or more* of the lower units in each pair (words of one or more morphemes, and symbols of one or more letters).

In the next section the constituency model will enable us to unify Part I and Part II still further.

25.3   Four tiers of units

So far we have two pairs of units; in each pair, the two units are in a constituency relationship (CR) to each other:

Word	Symbol
CR	CR
Morpheme	Letter

Obviously, words and morphemes are 'larger' units than symbols and letters, so we might arrange the two pairs vertically as follows, with 'CR' again indicating the constituency relationship:

Word
CR
Morpheme

Symbol
CR
Letter

At this point we need to note that the constituency relationship holds between Morpheme and Symbol just as it does between Word and Morpheme and between Symbol and Letter. In the spelling system of English, *morphemes consist of one or more symbols*:

Morpheme	[un-	[happy]	-ness]	-es]	[cat]	[chat]	[catch]
Symbol	°u n	h a pp y	n e ss	e s	°c a t	°ch a t	°c a tch

As for [caught], I am calling it one 'morpheme of spelling':

°[caught]   (grammatically [catch]PAST]: the spelling system treats it in
°c augh t   the same way as the pronunciation system treats it)

The vast majority of the morphemes of spelling coincide with the morphemes of grammar; here are two such run-of-the-mill morphemes with the same sequence of four letters, °augh, but different symbol segmentations:

Morpheme	[daughter]	[laugh]
Symbol	°d augh t er	°l au gh

So we have a four-tier constituency model:

Word
CR
Morpheme
CR
Symbol
CR
Letter

Every word consists of one or more morphemes, which in turn consist of one or more symbols, which in turn consist of one or more letters.

That is to say, constituency is not merely common to Part I and Part II; it is the link between them and fuses the four units into a continuous hierarchy.

25.4   Nitty gritty

Here are some examples of 'four-tier' segmentation, using words from the Darwin passage (Chapter 17). First, two illustrations of the form of display:

Row	Unit	Segmentation		Segmentation	
1	Word	|v a l l e y|	1W	|r o c k s|	1W
2	Morpheme	|v a l l e y|	1M	|r o c k|s|	2M
3	Symbol	|v|a|l l|e y|	4S	|r|o|c k|s|	4S
4	Letter	|v|a|l|l|e|y|	6L	|r|o|c|k|s|	5L

The essence of this form of display is that once a vertical line begins it continues to the bottom (a word boundary is morpheme boundary is a symbol boundary is a letter boundary). Of course, word boundaries and letter boundaries are given in advance; the interest lies in Rows 2 and 3, where a boundary between morphemes is also a boundary between symbols (not always, but usually – see Section 23.2).

The figures on the right are unit-counts; I shall not include them in the examples which follow. I could add comments to these examples (for instance, at the morpheme level, the division of °phenomena and the non-division of °spent), but it is more important to present the 'gritty' words which follow after these.

W	|o n|	|t h i s|	|t o u r|	|i|	|h a d|	|a|	|s t r i k i n g|
M	|o n|	|t h i s|	|t o u r|	|i|	|h a d|	|a|	|s t r i k|i n g|
S	|o|n|	|t h|i|s|	|t|o u|r|	|i|	|h|a|d|	|a|	|s|t|r|i|k|i|n g|
L	|o|n|	|t|h|i|s|	|t|o|u|r|	|i|	|h|a|d|	|a|	|s|t|r|i|k|i|n|g|

```
W   |how| |easy| |it| |is| |to| |overlook|
M   |how| |easy| |it| |is| |to| |over|look|
S   |h|o w| |e a|s|y| |i|t| |i|s| |t|o| |o|v e r||o o|k|
L   |h|o|w| |e|a|s|y| |i|t| |i|s| |t|o| |o|v|e|r||o|o|k|
```

```
W   |phenomena| |however| |conspicuous|
M   |phen|ome|na| |how|ever| |con|spic|uous|
S   |p h|e|n|o|m|e|n|a| |h o w|e|v|e r| |c|o|n|s p|i|c u|o u|s|
L   |p|h|e|n|o|m|e|n|a| |h|o|w|e|v|e|r| |c|o|n|s|p|i|c|u|o|u|s|
```

```
W   |we| |spent| |many| |hours| |examining|
M   |we| |spent| |many| |hours| |examin|ing|
S   |w|e| |s|p|e|n|t| |m|a|n|y| |h o u r|s| |e|x|a|m|i|n|i|n g|
L   |w|e| |s|p|e|n|t| |m|a|n|y| |h|o|u|r|s| |e|x|a|m|i|n|i|n|g|
```

The 'gritty' words in the Darwin text, or in any text, are words with discontinuous symbols, arising always from Terminal-E – for example:

°t r a c e °h a v e °h ou s e

The grittiness now, however, in Part III, is not in the segmentation of such words (see Part II), but merely in how to treat discontinuous symbols in a four-tier display. Here is one solution:

```
W   |trace|      1        W   |have|      1        W   |house|      1
M   |trace|      1        M   |have|      1        M   |house|      1
S   |t|r|a.e|c|  4        S   |h|a.e|v|   3        S   |h|ou.e|s|   3
L   |t|r|a|c|e|  5        L   |h|a|v|e|   4        L   |h|o|u|s|e|  5
```

Here are two other (rarer) cases: °instance, with two intervening consonant letters between °a and °e, and °moraines with °s following the °e.

```
W   |instance|       1          W   |moraines|       1
M   |in|st|ance|     3          M   |moraine|s|      2
S   |i|n|s|t|a.e|n|c| 7          S   |m|o|r|a i.e|n|s| 6
L   |i|n|s|t|a|n|c|e| 8          L   |m|o|r|a|i|n|e|s| 8
```

Note that there is a morpheme boundary before the °s at the end of °moraines and that the °s is unaffected by the adjustments between Rows 3 and 4, unlike the °s in °house. *Discontinuous symbols are always contained within the morpheme, just like other symbols.*

25.5   Conceptual significance

Most words in a text are unproblematical:

```
W   |u n p r o b l e m a t i c a l|
M   |u n|p r o b l e m|a t i c|a l|
S   |u|n|p|r|o|b|l|e|m|a|t|i|c|a|l|
L   |u|n|p|r|o|b|l|e|m|a|t|i|c|a|l|
```

(see Section 13.3)

The problematical has often in this book occupied more time than the unproblematical. This is in the nature of things (and of people!). Terminal-E is a case in point: most symbols in a text are continuous (solid), not discontinuous. In this section I shall say something more about the significance of different concepts of Terminal-E, and then go on to some general points about the constituency model.

Terminal-E is inescapably a problematical feature of the English spelling system, indeed the most prominent one. It has often been conceived of as a 'silent E', associating it with 'silent vowels' in words like °head and °toe, and with 'silent consonants' in words like °know and °thumb. I am not happy with the concept 'silent letter' unless it is carefully interpreted in terms of constituency.

No symbol is 'silent'. Every symbol in a text has sound value. It is much more important to grasp that point (the essence of the concept of 'symbol' as a constituent in English spelling), than to be left thinking that every letter has sound value – except the ones that don't. A case can be made for the term 'silent letter', characterising certain letters as constituents of certain symbols (for instance, °k in °<u>kn</u>, °b in °<u>mb</u>), but only when the constituency model has been well and truly internalised.

Finally, some general points about this model.

- The four-tier constituency model applies to every word in the language and accounts for every letter.

- It distinguishes the unit levels at which other aspects of spelling analysis apply, in particular junction analysis at morpheme level and correspondence analysis at symbol level.

- It establishes these two inner units as constituent units in the spelling system, mediating between the familiar units of word and letter.

- In so doing, it not only provides a more adequate model than a 'word and letter' model, but assimilates the structure of the spelling system to language structure in general.

26 *Letters and alphabet in SOE*

26.1 Codes, ciphers, cryptographies

```
X   |v o q s p c m f n b u j d b m|
N   |v o|q s p c m f n|b u j d|b m|
T   |v|o|q|s|p|c|m|f|n|b|u|j|d|b|m|
M   |v|o|q|s|p|c|m|f|n|b|u|j|d|b|m|      (tff Tfdujpo 13.3)
```

This version of the four-tier display which appeared at the head of Section 25.5 is in a very simple cipher, given away by, for instance:

$$(tff\ Tfdujpo\ 13.3)$$
$$= (see\ Section\ 13.3)$$

and by

$$
\left.\begin{array}{c} X \\ N \\ T \\ M \end{array}\right\} = \left\{\begin{array}{ll} W & \text{(Word)} \\ M & \text{(Morpheme)} \\ S & \text{(Symbol)} \\ L & \text{(Letter)} \end{array}\right.
$$

This is the starting point of all substitution ciphers for English, the substitution of one letter for another. Ciphers, using substitution and other devices, are big business today, especially with the advent of computers. Less sophisticated ones are still enjoyed by children (and grown-ups) under the name of 'codes'.

   If you want to invent one for English, you can base it on the standard orthography ('SOE'), like the example above, or you can start from scratch, as Isaac Pitman did when he invented his shorthand, designed, of course, not for secrecy but for speed. I shall say more about these different kinds of writing-systems (orthographies, cryptographies, stenographies) in Chapter 27.

In this chapter I want to look at the nature of letters (Section 26.2), at the concept of a writing system (26.3), and at the role of the alphabet (26.4).

26.2   Letters

1   abcdefghijklmnopqrstuvwxyz

2   bcdefghijklmnopqrstuvwxyza

This is the key to the code in the last section: 'for A write B, for B write C' and so on until 'for Z write A'. Easy to write – not so easy to read. (Yet 'tff Tfdujpo 13.3' may already have a certain familiarity to it!)

The first point I want to make is very simple, but at the same time far-reaching. It is this. In line 2 we can shift the alphabet along one place, two places, three ... up to 25 places, and produce up to 25 different substitutes for each letter. We can go further and shuffle the letters in line 2 into I don't know how many million sequences. As long as we have the key (line 1 and the right line 2), then simple substitution, letter by letter, will recover the original spelling. Whatever else has been changed, *the spelling system has not*.

To go further still, we can scrap the Roman-alphabet letter-shapes altogether and replace them by shapes of our own devising (which is quite an entertaining exercise) and, obviously, it's the same story. Any 26 shapes, as long as they are distinct from each other, will do instead of the letters. Provided the same shape always replaces the same letter, the spelling system is unchanged. Every word will be as distinct from every other word as it is now, and every word will carry the same resemblances to other words as it does now. So will the constituents of words, the morphemes: morphemes that are invariable in spelling will remain invariable; morphemes that are variable in spelling will vary in exactly the same way.

To revert to the key above: If E-Deletion becomes F-Deletion, F will be deleted wherever E is now deleted: °come will be 'dpnf', °coming will be 'dpnjoh'.

This is territory worth exploring, but the point I want to make can be made without more ado: no amount of this kind of substitution changes the spelling system. If you do want to change the spelling system, you must either change the number of letters (to more or fewer), or you must change their distribution (for instance spell °come as *cum, or °coming as *comeing), or both. Substituting 26 new 'black marks' for the 26 old 'black marks' we call letters does not change the spelling system – though it can turn an orthographic text, directly accessible to everybody, into a cryptographic text, accessible only via a key.

26.3   Writing-system, spelling system, and script

A substitution cipher, then, will change an orthographic writing-system into a cryptographic writing-system. If it is not the spelling system that has been changed, what is it?

It is the visual shapes – the 'black marks' – in which the spelling system is manifested. The shapes you might substitute might be like Russian cyrillic letters, or Hebrew square ones, or Chinese characters, or they might be geometric lines like Pitman's shorthand, or flowing lines like Arabic script – and I shall in fact call this aspect of the writing-system 'script'. What has been changed in a substitution cipher is *script*, not spelling.

Script is infinitely variable, whether printed or handwritten; in this respect you might possibly compare it to speech and the diversity of community accents and individual voices. But we must concentrate on the concept of 'spelling system'.

A spelling system and a script are the two essential components of a *writing-system*. A writing-system is any one way of writing a particular language.

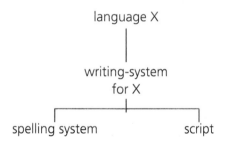

The term 'writing-system' has leaked out from linguistics in recent years. This is a good thing, as it is a scientific term of universal application. But it is a bad thing if it is mistakenly used in the lower-level sense of 'spelling system'.

A spelling system is a *component* of a writing-system, a necessary component: it is the system by which the writing-system of a given language organises the realisation of the morphemes, and thereby of the words, of that language. The other necessary component of a writing-system is a script component, a system of visible signs which manifest the elements of the spelling system.

We saw in the last section that spelling system and script are independent of each other: the script can be varied while the spelling system remains constant. Conversely, the script can be the constant, and the spelling system can be the variable: spelling reform proposals for English often pursue this course, keeping the 26 letters but changing °night into *niet.

My first point, then, is to distinguish 'spelling system' from 'script'; my second point is to distinguish both of these terms from 'writing-system'. *The writing-system is the whole, of which the spelling system and the script are parts.*

26.4   The alphabet

Every established language has its standard orthography. This is a well-codified writing-system which can be used for all the highly varied activities of society, from government to graffiti. A standard orthography is a highly elaborated writing-system, serving many, many purposes, which fall, for the most part, under two main headings – communication, and information storage and retrieval. It's the latter which concerns us in this section.

In a modern society information is stored, ready for retrieval, about anything and everything, including people and words. Most of this information we never see: it's stored in millions of places and accessed, added to, altered and acted on by its various groups of users, large or small, all day and every day. But its storage and retrieval are familiar to us from an early age, for example in the form of the class register with names arranged alphabetically, or the telephone directory (people), the dictionary (words), and the sort of books which have indexes. The essence of an index is alphabetical arrangement (contrast 'Contents'), and one vital and pervasive function of the alphabet is its indexing function.

Every standard orthography must provide its users with an indexing system, and the more easily people can memorise that indexing system the more use they can make of the standard orthography to retrieve, and to store, information in it. The standard orthography is the paramount medium of storage – not of all information, but of written information.

In the next chapter I shall sketch the Standard Orthography of English (SOE), a highly elaborated writing-system more widely used than any other in the world today. In this chapter I have tried to show that our writing-system does not consist only of a spelling system – however interesting that spelling system may be; it includes script, it includes 'the alphabet', and other things too.

27 *A writing-system called SOE*

27.1   The need for a name

Languages are often identified by their standard orthographies; they are also often identified *with* their standard orthographies, especially if they are other peoples' languages. When we think of Russian, it is probably Russian writing that comes to mind, in the Cyrillic alphabet. Greek is recognisable in Greek letters, Chinese in Chinese characters, Hebrew in 'square letters', Arabic in flowing Arabic script (remembering that the last two 'go from right to left'). And Japanese? We 'see' Japanese in Instructions for Use and tourist leaflets, just as we used to 'see' Irish on Irish pennies.

The computer has now made all these fascinating phenomena (and they *are* fascinating) wonderfully available. However, the purpose of this section is conceptual: *a language must not be confused with its writing-system*. The images of languages in the last paragraph are images of standard orthographies, visual images, in fact, of the *scripts* (see Section 26.3) of the orthographies; and language is, first and foremost, speech.

English is just as liable to this misconception as other languages. And unless great care is taken in education it is a misconception which takes root in the minds of those who speak it as their mother tongue. But the conceptual warning applies, critically: *English, the language, must not be identified with SOE, its standard orthography*.

Hence the importance of a name for the writing-system (SOE) as an entity distinct from the language (English).

27.2   The name 'SOE'

We need a handy name for the writing-system because we need to *talk* about it, both now in this chapter and in education and in the community generally.

The maintenance of *orthographic quality* depends on the insight people have into the role and resources of the standard orthography, the skill with which they can use it (both in reading and writing), and the ease with which they can discuss its practical problems.

'SOE' is a handy shortening of the Standard Orthography of English: the language concerned is **English,** the writing-system is an **orthography,** and it the **standard** orthography of the language.

In the two sections which follow I will explain its role as an orthography (Section 27.3) and sketch its resources (Section 27.4).

27.3   The role of SOE

I have referred already (Section 26.1), to different kinds of writing-systems for English (orthographies, cryptographies, stenographies) and to Isaac Pitman's invention of a shorthand for English.

Shorthand (stenography) has a long history in Europe. Shorthands for English have been in continuous development since the end of the 16th century, their popularity interwoven with social, economic and technological changes. Pitman's success in the 19th century was, in addition, conceptually significant: he broke away both from the spelling system and from the script of SOE. In the late 20th century, his system and others – handwritten and machine-written – are in daily use in business, law-courts, the Press, Parliament and so on, although audiotyping has taken over some of the ground. Few of us have first-hand knowledge of stenographic writing-systems for English (or any other language – Pitman's has been widely adapted to other languages), but most of us know of their existence.

The significance of stenographic writing-systems, or stenographies, is that they are special-purpose writing-systems, as are cryptographies (Section 26.1–2). They are designed, in terms of their spelling system, their script and their other features, to serve a particular purpose distinct from that of the standard orthography. Orthographies are not designed for verbatim reporting, to be written at the speed of speech, as stenographies are; nor are they designed to be difficult to read at a glance or impossible to read without a key, as cryptographies are. Orthographies are designed as *general-purpose writing-systems.*

That is the role of a standard orthography – to be an *ordinary* writing-system. In fact, what we may call the orthographic function is so ordinary, so taken for granted, that it has tended to go unnamed. Like the ordinary number system, which we only call 'to the base ten' when we encounter non-ordinary systems with other bases, the ordinary writing-system needs to be seen in contrast to other functional kinds of writing-systems before we recognise positively its own function.

SOE, then, is a standard orthography – not as the result of design or decision like many of the world's officially recognised orthographies, but as the product of centuries of co-development with the language, English. In common with standard orthographies everywhere, as the general-purpose writing-system of the community, it is, like the standard language itself, both taught in the school curriculum and used in the school curriculum as a principal medium of teaching and learning.

27.4   The resources of SOE

SOE is a highly elaborated writing-system. This is because it is, as I have just said, an orthography – a general-purpose writing-system (contrast shorthand) – for a highly developed language. We can explore its resources with the help of the example of printed SOE presented by this book. This will enable me to speak of black marks (ink) and white space (paper); but, of course, neither colours nor material are significant, as long as the writing is visible against a background.

The black marks are significant and fall into four groups:

alphabetic	a	b	c	etc.
punctuational	.	,	;	etc.
numeric	1	2	3	etc.
conventional	&	£	$	etc.

In addition to an inventory of these basic sequential elements for making a linear text, SOE has a number of differentiating resources which apply to stretches of text:

case-contrast	upper case (capitals)/lower case
angle-contrast	roman (upright)/italic (slanting)
weight-contrast	light (normal, non-bold)/bold
font varieties	Courier, Times, Gothic, etc.
size variation	fine, small, large, etc.

SOE also makes use of distinguishing devices (especially capitalisation, as in 'London' 'Bath'), abbreviatory devices ('£1.5m' is a condensed bit of SOE: note that it draws on all four of the black-mark groups above), and other devices called for by orthographies (such as using an asterisk or superscript figures to refer readers to footnotes or to the small print in advertisements and contracts).

In addition to *black marks* and *differentiation resources* out of which text is made (text is *always* differentiated: for example, if it isn't italic (slanting), it's roman), there is the *disposition* of different kinds of text on the page – sectioning, headings, subheadings, titles, captions to diagrams, labels within diagrams, and so on. Everything, from title-page and Contents to Index, displays a deliberate deployment of the disposition resources of SOE – the exploitation, you might say, of the white space.

For the dispositional resources are governed by the axis, direction and lining of the writing-system. SOE is horizontal (unlike the traditional vertical axis of Chinese and Japanese); it goes from left to right (unlike the right to left direction of Arabic and Hebrew); and its lines succeed each other down the page, not up (at which end do you open a Chinese or Japanese book? Which way do the vertical lines succeed each other?).

These features of *orientation* are features of the writing-system, not of the spelling system. In SOE, what's on the left takes precedence over what's on the right, what's above takes precedence over what's below. It could all be the other way round, but this would not affect the spelling system. These features belong to script.

All these resources are visual resources. The spelling system is visual too.

28 *Some junction errors*

28.1 Errors, not slips

It's a long time since I introduced *comming (Chapter 1), *tommorrow (Chapter 2) and *definately (Chapter 3). What can we say about them twenty-five chapters later?

I will look at some 'junction errors' in this chapter and at some 'symbol errors' in the next. I'm talking about *errors*, where the speller's knowledge of the spelling system needs to advance, not about *slips*, which the speller can correct without further learning. We all make slips in writing – and not only in writing, but in reading, as well, and in speaking and hearing/listening too. Language is like that.

I have exaggerated the contrast between the two kinds of error by concentrating on certain consonant errors (double letters) in this chapter and on certain vowel errors (°ie and °ei) in Chapter 29. To counter this, bear in mind that, logically, all errors must be symbol errors; junction errors are a subset that invite a particular kind of attention. In this chapter I have included one example of a junction error involving only vowel-letters: *comeing. A counterbalancing example for the next chapter, of a symbol error involving only consonant-letters would be *skool or *charicature; but do not look for these in Chapter 29 – see rather Section 13.4.

28.2 Junction errors from Part I

comming

The junction analysis of °coming is

$$°come \times ing \rightarrow °coming \qquad \textit{change-junction: E-Deletion}$$

°e here is Terminal-E (it follows a consonant letter, Section 6.2); only E-Deletion can apply. E-Deletion and Consonant-Doubling are mutually exclusive (Sections 1.1, 9.6).

In the misspelling *comming, °e has been deleted – good. But °m has been doubled. Why? This is a common misspelling: why is it so attractive? The attraction lies in the pronunciation of °come: it rhymes with °hum, and °hum fulfils the Terminal-Consonant conditions (Section 6.1):

$$°hum \times ing \rightarrow °humming$$

What is special about the morpheme °come is not its behaviour in inflection but its vowel correspondence:

Where   °hum has the correspondence °u̱ – /u/
         °come has the correspondence °o̱.e – /u/

The primary value of the discontinuous symbol °o̱.e is the long vowel /oe/ as in °home. Spellers are unlikely to make the same mistake with

$$°home \times ing \rightarrow °homing$$

*comeing

This is a better misspelling than *comming: there is nothing to undo, so to speak. All that is required is application of the E-Deletion rule – a generalisation which covers thousands of instances, instances which are continually encountered in reading. For the learner, joining morphemes by a plus-junction is a prudent course: it demonstrates knowledge of the spelling of the morphemes involved, and perhaps caution about applying processes imperfectly grasped. Note that in both *comeing and *comming we must give the speller credit for rightly using an O-symbol: both errors are junction errors.

*accross

I suspect that some learners go from writing °across to writing *accross; they do this under the influence of their advancing vocabulary, as they take on, in reading and writing, words like °according °account °accurate °accuse. (Words beginning with °accr ... are pretty sophisticated: °accredit °accretion °accrue.) If °across has been learnt morphemically, it should be immune to this kind of error:

$$°a + cross \rightarrow °across$$

°across is a Function Word, but it belongs to a very clear pattern which is familiar in our core vocabulary:

aboard	along
across	aloud
afloat	around
ahead	ashore
alight	aside
alike	asleep
alive	aware
alone	away

All these words have the same structure: [a-[NUCLEAR]; and in each case the nuclear morpheme is a free morpheme, in fact a familiar monosyllable. There is much more evidence for the prefix °a- than there is for the prefix °to- that we met in Chapter 2; an ordinary dictionary search will double the list of examples (°ablaze °athwart and so on). It's only got the one form °a-; it can't be °ac-; and °cross can't be °-ccross. So there is always a plus-junction after [a-], as in 'across and along the curriculum' (in Chapter 30).

*tommorow

Is the first error in *tommorow just another double-M by mistake? Perhaps, but it's a very different case from the double-M in *comming. In the word °coming, there's no problem about recognising the morpheme boundary: inflections, in this respect, are easy (starting with °cat/cats).

In °tomorrow, the morpheme boundary may be below consciousness, until, perhaps, we invoke °today and °tonight (as in Chapter 2), and then a pattern can be seen. °to- and °morrow can be recognised as morphemes – °morrow as a nuclear morpheme like °day and °night (only much rarer as a word on its own; for many people °morrow is never a word on its own), and °to- as a prefix. There is no such thing as Consonant-Doubling at prefix/nuclear boundaries, and the prefix °to- is invariant – it could never change to °tom-.

So why write *tommorow? It's a case of doubt about doubles, a doubt which, for plenty of spellers, hangs over many words which contain double consonant letters, for example °beginning °commitment °disappear °occasion °occurrence °profession °accommodation. In all of these examples, clarification comes with recognition of morpheme boundaries and knowledge of junction behaviour at those boundaries.

There may be a tendency to move the double letters leftwards: *tommorow *beggining and *dissapear show this shift, in each case upsetting the plus-junction at the prefix/nuclear boundary:

°to + morrow → °tomorrow.

*beggining

A whole chapter was devoted to the verb 'to begin' in Part I; but there is always more to add and new angles to approach from (especially when there are new learners to learn from – see Chapter 12). At first sight, this misspelling looks closely parallel to the misspelling *tommorow: if in doubt, double the earlier consonant and single the later one (compensatorily, perhaps).

But that is reckoning without the morphemes; it is failing to see the structure under the surface (see Chapter 10). The morphemic structures of the two words are not the same:

1 [be[gin]ing]   2 [to[morrow]]

In number 1 we have to ask the learner how they would spell 'begin'; in number 2 we cannot ask them how they would spell 'tomorr-', because 'tomorr-' is not a constituent: it's neither one morpheme nor two morphemes. We have to ask them how they would spell 'morrow', because that is one of the two constituent morphemes of the word °tomorrow.

Where °tomorrow has two constituents, °beginning has three; and the first one to strip away is the inflection °-ing. With that out of the way, we can see how the learner spells the word °begin, the base form of the verb. If they spell it °begin, then explicating the standard spelling can start with the change-junction

°begin × ing → °beginning

if they spell it *beggin, then the explication must start with the plus-junction

°be + gin → °begin   (see Chapter 12)

The change-junction needs to be followed up by the plus-junction, and vice versa: the account is not complete until °-gin- is recognised as a nuclear morpheme.

28.3   More junction errors

*committment

This is a misspelling which finds its way into high circles. I have even heard it defended. Yet it violates the conditions of Consonant-Doubling, while the standard spelling obeys them in the form of a plus-junction:

°commit + ment → °commitment

Remember, a plus-junction is the simplest kind of junction you can possibly have.

The condition which is violated is the right-hand condition. A Terminal-Consonant is doubled before a vowel suffix, but not before a consonant suffix; °-ment is a suffix beginning with °m; °m is a consonant letter. Therefore °t cannot double.

This is such a knockdown argument that we don't need to look into °commit at all. But it would be good practice (in both senses!) to do so.

°commit is not like °summit or °grommet. These are each one morpheme: [summit], [grommet]. And they are stressed on the first syllable: /⸜ –/. °commit is two morphemes, [com[mit], and is stressed on the second syllable, /– ⸜/. Its morphemic structure is the same as that of °begin, though its junction is different:

$$°con \times mit \rightarrow °commit \qquad \textit{Consonant-Assimilation}$$

The nuclear of °commit is a lame morpheme, [-mit-]. Like that of °begin, it's never found without a prefix, but unlike °-gin- it's found with several different prefixes:

°admit /admission
°commit /commission
°emit /emission
°permit /permission
°remit /remission
°submit /submission
°transmit /transmission

The nucleus of °commit, then, is °-mit-, a stressed nuclear morpheme with the letter-profile °CVC. These are all the conditions required on the left-hand side for Consonant-Doubling to apply if the right-hand condition is satisfied – namely, if there is a vowel-suffix following, as in these inflected forms:

$$°commit \times ing \rightarrow °committing$$
$$°commit \times ed \rightarrow °committed$$

and in the following derived forms:

$$°commit \times al \rightarrow °committal$$
$$°commit \times ee \rightarrow °committee$$

I think it is the last item, °committee, which exerts an influence over °commitment and doubles the °t in the face of a huge regularity in the spelling system – °committee, and the fact that the verbs in °-mit- tend not to take consonant suffixes. There's no °admitment or °transmitment. But there is the S-inflection, and who would write *committs?

*dissapear

There is a prefix °dis-; there is no prefix °diss- (and no Consonant-Doubling at prefix boundaries). The second °s cannot belong to the nuclear morpheme – in fact, the second °s cannot belong anywhere. What we have is a simple plus-junction:

$$°dis + appear → °disappear$$

A speller who knows °appear should not complicate a plus-junction if they are spelling by morphemes. Spelling by syllables may be the source of *diss- in some spellers who are in the habit of stressing first syllables (°disappear is stressed on the last syllable; its rhythmic profile is /– – ⁄/; see Section 14.4).

Equally a speller who knows °appear has no grounds for writing *apear as the nuclear morpheme in the prefixed word °disappear. The same tendency is at work as in *tommorow and *beggining (see Section 28.2).

*occurence

This misspelling results in the same consonant pattern as *tommorow and *dissapear, a 'double and single' pattern; but this time the double is right and the single is wrong. The suffix °-ence forms nouns from verbs, as in

$$°exist + ence → °existence$$

°exist has a stable terminal; hence the plus junction. The verb °occur has a °CVC-Terminal, liable to doubling; °-ence begins with a vowel letter, so we get the change-junction:

$$°occur × ence → °occurrence$$

and also
$$°recur × ence → °recurrence$$
$$°concur × ence → °concurrence$$

These three examples show that the nuclear morpheme is [-cur-]. This is a lame nuclear (Section 4.5), but spelling-wise it behaves just like the free nuclear °fur, as in °fur × y → °furry. (Note that all three verbs have the rhythmic profile /– ⁄/, with stress on the nuclear.)

We can now look into the structure of °occur itself. It has the same morphemic structure as

$$°re + cur → °recur$$
$$°con + cur → °concur$$

but it has a change-junction:

$$°ob × cur → °occur \qquad \textit{Consonant-Assimilation}$$

The same assimilation underlies °occasion, which is a prefixed form with the same nuclear as °casual (see next entry). The °cur-/curr- morpheme is the nuclear of the word °current. °ob- is the prefix in °observe °object °obstruct.

*occassion

I have just mentioned that °occasion has the same nuclear morpheme as °casual. The misspelling *occassion (or, less often, *ocassion) is best looked at in terms of sound/symbol relationships; but both °occasion and °casual are related to °case (think of 'in case'/'should the occasion arise' and 'case history/casualty') and these semantic links may also help the speller at a certain stage.

*writting

The spelling °writing is FRG – Fully Rule-Governed:

$$°write × ing → °writing$$

No problem. The problem is that a lot of people are writing *writting instead! Why?

Junction-wise the error is exactly the same as *comming: E-Deletion must take place; and Consonant-Doubling cannot take place as well. There is an important difference, however. The vowel sound in °come is short; the vowel sound in °write is long. The inflection '-ing' is the most stable and regular of all the inflections: and, like the other inflections, it never affects the pronunciation of the nuclear. Hence everybody pronounces °writing with /ie/ just as they pronounce °write with /ie/. Symbol-wise this is incompatible with the misspelling *writting.

So what is at work? The answer may be that °written is learnt successfully and is allowed to influence °writing. It shouldn't get a chance to, because °writing is as regular as can be: full absorption of the E-Deletion rule should block both *comming and *writting.

But the next question to ask is 'Why is °t doubled in °written?' The first answer to this relates to sound/symbol regularities: the vowel-sound is short so the pattern is that of °bite/bitten °hide/hidden. This interdependency between a single-letter vowel symbol and two consonant letters (especially double ones) immediately following it is well known – it's what makes *writting impossible for a word with /ie/ as its stressed vowel sound. The second answer is hinted at by °bitten and °hidden which are formed from their past tenses:

$$°bit \times en \rightarrow °bitten$$
$$°hid \times en \rightarrow °hidden$$

An old past tense of °write was °writ, which gives:

$$°writ \times en \rightarrow °written$$

but the past tense was standardised as °wrote and, as a verb form, °writ became a dialect (and poetic) form.

28.4   *keeness and *testube

Despite its pronunciation (see Section 10.4), °keenness gets misspelt, along with °greenness. 'N-deletion', if it existed, would be a complication of the spelling system, which is in fact as simple as can be:

$$°keen + ness \rightarrow °keenness$$

A factor here is the presence of three sets of double letters in a word only eight letters long (though I have seen the same error with °meanness).

Leaving pronunciation aside, the error is the same as in *testube. Plus-junctions are all cases of abutment, and this produces 'doubles by abutment' (Section 10.4) wherever the letter on the left-hand side of the junction is the same as the letter on the right-hand side. In °keenness we have a nuclear/suffix boundary; in °testtube we have a nuclear/nuclear boundary; and both are plus-junctions.

Plus-junctions are virtually universal in nuclear/nuclear words like °football (see Section 9.2). °testtube, however, is not quite like °football, because it is often written open, as two words: test tube.

There are three 'degrees of aggregation' possible with an item like this, as the following structured classification shows:

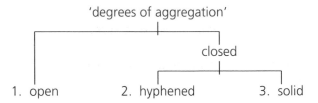

Any of these three is acceptable with 'test tube' in SOE (for SOE, see Chapter 27, especially 27.4). What is not acceptable is 'T-Deletion' – though we all say 'testube' with only one /t/ in the middle, just as we all say 'lampost' with only one /p/. *lampost is a parallel error to *testube:

°test + tube→ °testtube

°lamp + post → °lamppost

28.5   *critisise

There's one letter wrong in the misspelling *critisise. At the letter level you simply correct letter °s to °c: °criticise. At the symbol level you can say that both symbol °s̲ and symbol °c̲ can correspond to the sound /s/ and that in °criticise we have the less common of the two, °c̲. At the morpheme level you can explain why we have °c̲ – and the explanation can give considerable insight into the spelling system.

The suffix °-ise serves to form verbs, usually from adjectives, as in

°national + ise → °nationalise

Though °critic is a noun, °criticise belongs to this pattern:

°critic + ise → °criticise

°public + ise → °publicise

°italic + ise → °italicise

°anglic + ise → °anglicise

In these four words °c̲ at the end of the stem has the value /k/ in the stem on its own, and the value /s/ in the derived form: thus °critic, which we can treat as a nuclear morpheme, maintains its shape in spelling but changes its shape in pronunciation.

As a noun, °critic forms its adjective, as °nation does, with the suffix °-al.

The dual value of °c̲ enables the spelling junctions to be the simplest possible, namely plus-junctions:

$$°\text{critic} + \text{al} \rightarrow °\text{critical}$$
$$°\text{critic} + \text{ise} \rightarrow °\text{criticise}$$

With the dual value of °c̲ in °critic/criticise compare the dual-value role of the vowel symbol °a̲ in

$$°\text{nation} + \text{al} \rightarrow °\text{national}$$

where we also have plus-junction ('no change') in the spelling accompanying change in the pronunciation.

There is more to say about °c̲. The two values involved are /k/ and /s/, and the two correspondences are well known under the names:

'Hard C'	°c̲ – /k/
'Soft C'	°c̲ – /s/

Hard C is always given precedence over Soft C. Why? It is not just on grounds of frequency; it is because Hard C is the norm, and Soft C is the special case. This can be expressed more precisely in the form of a rule. °c̲ only has the value /s/ before the three vowel letters °e °i and °y; otherwise it has the value /k/. 'Otherwise' embraces all other environments, which are of three kinds immediately following °c̲:

• the other three vowel letters, °a °o and °u

• any consonant letter

• no letter at all (that is, where °c̲ is word-final).

More concisely: °c̲ – /s/ before °e °i °y
            °c̲ – /k/ elsewhere.

/k/ is the norm; it is the default value of °c̲. With all such rules and regularities, you have to decide whether to put the norm (the general pattern) before the exceptions, or the exceptions before the norm, according to the demands of the situation. As with plus-junctions and change-junctions, the exceptions must not be allowed to overshadow the norm.

The default rule we have here is an interdependency rule: there is an interdependency between adjacent letters, but it must be carefully studied. Miscellaneous 'spelling rules' have often been expressed in terms of interdependencies between letters: 'QU' is an example of this, where the absence of the concept of one-letter symbols has created misunderstanding (see

Section 18.6). In the case of Hard C and Soft C we must remember that the entity on the left of the correspondence is a symbol, not just a letter.

A question to ask about any apparent pattern or regularity is whether it is found anywhere else in the system. This one, which certainly exists for °c̲, is also found, though less conspicuously, with °g̲ (as mentioned in Section 15.3). Instances of the dual value of °g are fewer, less visible and less familiar than in the case of °c̲: for example, °purge/purgation °rigid/rigour °turgid/turgor. Not only that: counter-instances lurk in the heart of our vocabulary: °girl °get °begin (to which one might compare, for their everydayness, counter-examples of another kind – °great °break °steak, which really belong in the next chapter, but I would refer you instead to the matrix for °e̲a̲ in Chapter 22).

These three words, °girl °get °begin, are near the starting-line of literacy, but it need not be too long before the special role of the symbol °g in the last two, in °get/got and °begin/began/begun, is noticed and explained; it need not be never, as at present. The default rule, parallel to that for °c̲, still captures 99% of the data: Soft G (a correspondence, *not* a letter, *not* a symbol – see Section 15.3) before °e °i and °y; Hard G everywhere else. This is the pattern to be found in the thousands of words containing °g (not quite all of them, because °g, like °c̲, enters into a third correspondence – see Table 20.2 and Chapter 23).

This account of Hard/Soft correspondences suggests the following hypothesis for exploration. If a correspondence, or even a symbol, is 'functional somewhere' in the system, then it is available, without that function, throughout the system. For example, the dual-value function of °c̲, as in °critic/criticise, makes the Hard C/Soft C regularity available in °cat and °city and thousands of other words.

In this book I have played down quantitative aspects of the spelling system in favour of conceptual aspects. The insight of the title is that spelling and grammar, spelling and vocabulary interlock. In exploring their interconnectedness, different entities need to be distinguished (as in the first paragraph of this section) and need to be named. In this way what is the same can be distinguished from what is different, and what changes can be distinguished from what doesn't change. Neither languages nor writing-systems are subject to laws like the laws of physics, but both are structured. In the study of their structure, rules and exceptions are mutually defining: the rule provides the exception; and because it is an exception, the exception proves the rule.

To return to the misspelling *critisise. The only error is located in the first °s – in the nuclear morpheme [critic] or the suffix °-ic if we split down further into [crit]ic]. There is no error in the verb suffix °-ise: this morpheme has two standard spellings, °...ise and °...ize. Penalising (or penalizing) one or the other does *not* give much insight into the spelling system – though orthographic quality in SOE rightly expects consistency.

28.6 Errors and selectivity

In attending to spelling errors we have to be selective. We may help the learner best by zero-selection, or by 100%-selection, or by something in-between. Something in-between means a judicious focusing on those features of the spelling system which the learner can profit from most at their present stage of learning and in the immediate situation.

If learners can be helped to control junctions, not only are they eliminating an important class of errors but they are increasing their control over the spelling system as a system and making other kinds of error more obvious and correctable – even more avoidable.

29 *Some symbol errors*

29.1 An error and its ERF

In Chapter 28 I concentrated on a particular group of consonant errors in order to illustrate how some errors can be analysed in terms of spelling junctions. Two things to note are:

1 that such analysis of errors presupposes analysis of the standard spelling – that is to say, spelling analysis must precede error analysis

2 that getting junction errors out of the way makes the diagnosis, and possibly the cure, of symbol errors more practicable: they can be located within their morphemes.

We're talking all along about a certain persistent level of imperfect control, not about gross misspellings where control itself is in doubt. In junction errors one of the most stubborn is *committment (Section 28.3); equally stubborn, amongst symbol errors, is *existance. This error is located in an unstressed suffix with a minimal vowel sound. Common knowledge should tell us that, in the adjective °existential, the suffix in question carries the stress and so the vowel sound in it is maximised. The vowel sound is /e/ and the correspondence is straightforward °e – /e/. Knowledge of the existence of °existential is all that is needed, and that is widespread in the echelons where this suffix error thrives. (°existential, with its rhythmic profile /– – ⌐ –/, is an example of an ERF – see Section 18.7.)

In the four sections which follow, I deal with a clutch of errors in more everyday words – errors in vowel symbols located in nuclear morphemes and in function words. Errors in consonant symbols are also widespread, but this chapter balances Chapter 28 – see reference in 28.1 to *skool and *charicature.

29.2   *freind for °friend

°friend is a free nuclear morpheme. It's important to put it like that for two reasons.

First, because if there's only one morpheme, there's no problem locating which morpheme the error is in: it's in [friend]. If there is an error at all, it must be a symbol error, and in fact the error in *freind is located in the vowel symbol: °ei has been written for °ie.

Very understandably, too. The vowel sound is /e/, as in °end °Fred °fend; so an E-symbol would be normal. But what we have is an I-symbol: °i as leading letter, with °e as trailing letter, giving the correspondence:

$$°ie - /e/$$

What everyone should know about this correspondence is that it is unique – unique to the morpheme [friend].

It's tempting to say 'unique to the word °friend', because 'word' is so much more familiar. But if we say 'word', the claim ceases to be true – and that is the second reason for speaking of the *morpheme* [friend]. Remember, the inflected forms are distinct words: besides °friend there is also °friends – that's two distinct words for a start (°friend is one morpheme, °friends is two – they must be different. See Sections 4.4, 6.2–3 and 16.3). Two words is enough, but to drive the point home, look at the derived forms as well – that is, at all the words which have [friend] as their nuclear morpheme:

°friend	°unfriendly
°friends	°unfriendliness
°friendly	°befriend
°friendlier	°befriends
°friendliest	°befriending
°friendliness	°befriended
°friendless	
°friendship	
°friendships	

Fifteen words (and you may find more). Here, then, is a practical reason for stating that the correspondence °ie – /e/ is unique to the *morpheme* [friend]: it enables us to state the facts very economically.

This correspondence, so distinctive of °friend, is truly 'one of those funny things you get in English spelling', in the words of the girl in Chapter 12. Long familiarity with the word leaves us incurious about it. This incuriosity does not help the learner, but *knowledge* about the word may well do so –

especially if it is common knowledge. Everyone should know what is special about this word.

°friend epitomises the old familiar faces of English spelling. We may be fond of them, but if we fail to analyse them we are doing a disservice to the learners to whom we introduce them. We are also being less than professional if we pass on unanalysed material; analysis might just be the key to passing it on more successfully.

As with most free nuclear morphemes, the spelling of [friend] is completely stable. It doesn't change under derivation: its evocative value is drawn on in recent coinages such as °user-friendly and °reader-friendly.

One last point about the misspelling *freind. Learners should be given credit for putting °i in. They have got four-fifths of the word right (all the consonant symbols); they know that the vowel symbol is a 2-letter symbol, and that the two letters are °e and °i; they have, as I said above, understandably chosen °e as the leading letter. What they don't know is what the common knowledge of the community can easily tell them *at the right time*.

Common knowledge doesn't change the spelling system, but it can make it more learner-friendly.

29.3   *thier for °their

Of course, the commonest misspelling of the Function Word °their is the other Function Word °there, which is either a slip (quite common) or evidence of a confusion more serious than just getting the wrong symbol. I mention it here because both of these Function Words (which are totally distinct grammatically) have unusual symbols for the vowel sound they share.

In RefP (the reference pronunciation) they both rhyme with °share, and the usual symbols for this vowel sound are A-symbols, as in °hair and °hare. But here we are up against E-symbols instead:

°there	°ere – /aer/	in °there/where
°their	°eir – /aer/	in °their/theirs

Note now, about the misspelling *thier, that although there is a symbol °ier as in °pier, it never has the value /aer/. There is no correspondence °ier – /aer/: *thier is therefore an impossible spelling for this word.

But we can be much more positive than that. °their is a Function Word: more specifically it is a possessive adjective; more specifically still it is the possessive adjective of the third person plural pronoun °they. We can treat °their as a single spelling-morpheme, but we can also treat it as derived from

°they. Already the first three letters are seen to be identical, and that's all that's needed as a guide to spelling:

°they
°their

Where does the °r come from? It's the same morphemic °r as we get in

°you + r → °your

which is grammatically an exact parallel to °they/their. Only, in °their we have a change-junction (°eyr is not a symbol we find outside proper names):

°they × r → °their

°y has been replaced by °i, a familiar process. The circumstances are unusual, but there are one or two other similar cases:

°pay × ed → °paid
°lay × ed → °laid
°say × ed → °said

Why not *thay in the first place (as young children cheerfully write)? Whatever the historical reason for the standardised form °they, we can find a grammar-related reason within the spelling system as it is today. °they is the subject form of the third person plural pronoun; the object form is °them, the spelling of which is straightforward and provides a starting point for the spelling of the three related forms:

°them		°they
they	or	them
their		their

The first three letters are seen to be identical. Enough said.

29.4   *recieve for °receive

I met this misspelling most recently in print on an Income Tax form. What may have escaped official vigilance is the relation between °receive and °reception. This is a morphemic relation, and the evidence for the relation between [-ceive-] and [-cept-] is not just in °receive/reception but in the following derivation set:

°conceive/conception
deceive/deception
perceive/perception
receive/reception

The regularity in sound change, /ee/ to /e/, is matched by a regularity of change in the spelling: Symbol °ei.e changing to Symbol °e. In keeping with Chapter 11, /ee/ has a long symbol, and /e/ has a short symbol.

There are many such derivational pairs and sets of derivational pairs in English, in which the change in morphemic shape is not worth describing in terms of elaborate spelling junctions. (Focusing more closely on [-cept-], we can see in it two morphemes: [cep]t]; more evidence for this comes from °concept °conceit °deceit °receipt and °except/exception, and from recognition of °-ion as a morpheme, see Section 18.5.) What we need to look for are more general patterns in the spelling system into which these pairs fall.

One general pattern is the long and short E-sounds, in pronunciation, already mentioned, which is reflected by the two E-symbols. The discontinuous symbol °ei.e is related, as in °receive/receiving, to °ei by E-Deletion (a morphemic relationship which holds systematically between discontinuous symbols and their continuous counterparts), and it is the loss of °i that is of real interest. Trailing °i is lost in a small number of diverse derivational pairs, such as:

E-symbols	°vein/venous	(°intravenous)
	reign/regnal	('regnal years')
	veil/revelation	(also °reveal)
	heir/inherit	(°heritage)
A-symbols	°grain/granary	
	vain/vanity	
	prevail/prevalent	
O-symbols	°voice/vocal	
	choir/choral	
U-symbols	°fruit/fructify	

The derivational set based on °-ceive/-ception is in fact the most telling example of this deletion of internal °i, and that is all one needs in order to establish a regularity. As for the °ei sequence in °receive itself, all one needs as guidance is the pair °receive/reception.

29.5 *beleive for °believe

The derivational pair °receive/reception, from the last section, is really our anchor in this section. In °receive/reception the two E-symbols match the two E-sounds:

long symbol °ei.e to long sound /ee/ in the morpheme [-ceive-]
short symbol °e to short sound /e/ in the morpheme [-cept-].

Both symbols are E-symbols corresponding to E-sounds – reflected in the convergence between symbol and sound notation. That convergence represents the norm in sound/symbol relationships.

°belief/believe, by contrast, represents divergence. In this pair we have only one E-sound to deal with, the long sound /ee/. We expect the symbols for this sound to be long symbols, and they are – two letters and three letters respectively:

°ie	– /ee/	in °belief	NOUN
°ie.e	– /ee/	in °believe	VERB

What is unexpected is that the symbols for this sound should be, not E-symbols, but I-symbols. °belief/believe represents a counter-pattern to the general pattern of sound/symbol convergence: the I-symbols in the nuclear morpheme diverge from the norm, in exactly the same way as the I-symbol in °friend does (Section 29.2).

This pattern is repeated in three other noun/verb pairs:

°grief/ grieve
thief/ thieve
belief/believe
relief/ relieve

to which we can add two more nouns and three more verbs:

°brief/
chief/
/ achieve
/reprieve
/ retrieve

I have set these words out in a vertical alignment which makes the identical letter endings obvious. In the four pairs, we are dealing with free nuclear morphemes (the nouns) together with the verbs derived from them by a morphological change. In pronunciation the change is from a voiceless to a voiced final consonant sound: /f/ → /v/ (see Section 20.3). This is reflected in the spelling by the change from °f to °v, accompanied by an extension of the vowel symbol (°ie/ie.e).

Morphemes are important in this description; symbols are important in this description: the two together are responsible for the letter patterns we see. And those letter patterns may be the memory aid that works for some learners, for some of whom it will be °. . .ef at the end of nouns that is visually memorable, while for others it will be °. . .eve at the end of verbs.

Bringing out the contrast between °belief/believe (noun/verb) on the one hand and °receive/reception (verb/noun) on the other can help the learner merely by the attention it gives to the spelling. But there is much more to learn than just the spelling. For instance, the voiceless/voiced (Table 20.4) contrast between noun and verb that we found in the °belief/believe pattern is part of a larger pattern that, grammatically, also runs through some singular/plural pairs (°leaf/leaves), and, phonologically, through other pairs of consonant sounds (/th/ → /dh/ in °breath/breathe °youth/youths; /s/ → /z/ in °choice/choose °use/use °advice/advise).

29.6   Common knowledge

The uniqueness of °ie – /e/ in °friend, the triplet °they/them/their, and the pair °receive/reception in contrast to the pair °belief/believe, can all be part of the common knowledge imparted to everybody over the years of formal education. Perhaps °they/them/their belongs to the concentration on Function Words appropriate to Infant School; sorting out symbols and correspondences, which ones are unusual, or even unique, belongs to Junior School (but °friend need not wait that long!); and drawing up and comparing derivation sets belongs to Secondary School. These are broad suggestions about the weight of attention at different stages.

What really matters is to build up a stock of common knowledge shared by the whole community and contributing to intelligent talk about spelling. With that in mind, think over the last four Sections and compare them with the jingle about the letters °i and °e (and °c) which I am spared from printing because all my readers know it. That jingle, alas, represents the common knowledge about English spelling current in the community today.

Education, education, education

30.1 Introduction

I said earlier that this is not a textbook. It's not a book about education either. It's not even a book about the teaching of spelling or about the skill of spelling. It's a book about the spelling system of English. Why, I haven't even mentioned the National Curriculum! Nonetheless, I think people will discern the educational concern – and the educational hope – which lies behind the book.

30.2 Professionalism

> Anyone who trains as a reading teacher comes across the terms *consonant blend* and *consonant digraph*. After a few years of teaching, though, a person is likely to have forgotten the difference between them. Knowing the difference between a blend and a digraph is probably not necessary to successful reading instruction. But digraphs do present serious challenges to young spellers.[1]

This quotation comes from the USA. My guess is that any teacher who has forgotten the difference between a blend and a digraph did not have a very

[1] Charles Temple *et al. The Beginnings of Writing* (Boston: Allyn & Bacon, 1988) p. 60.

good grasp of it in the first place. And not only in the USA. In the UK I've certainly met experienced teachers of reading who have been engagingly embarrassed at the thought of having to describe blends and digraphs and the difference between them. The two terms are 'training' terms rather than 'classroom' terms; but if they become lapsed training terms it does not say much for the training.

For the child, 'the classroom' lasts ten years or more, and consists of many classrooms, in which English is the language of the curriculum, and SOE is the writing-system which makes it available for reading and writing – that is, for literacy. The heart of SOE (the Standard Orthography of English) is its spelling system: it is this which makes the words visible, for teachers and learners alike – both across the curriculum and all along it. And in the world outside/beyond the curriculum.

Talk about spelling (one of the themes of this book) can take place anywhere – at home, at work, at play, out travelling, out shopping. . . . But the talkers in the community will look to the teachers to provide the professional input, from Year 1 to Year 11 and beyond. And the professionals, in an education system, need to be professionally equipped, in this aspect of the curriculum as in all others, if they are to play their special part in the talking.

I do not think our teachers have been professionally equipped in the second half of the twentieth century for this part, the teaching-of-spelling part, of their job. And I am thinking of the job that *all* teachers do: educate – educate in a curriculum conducted in English.

30.3   Spelling analysis

The structure of this book should illustrate what I mean. We have just had two chapters in which I have analysed a score and a half of misspellings of a score of words. That's only a teacupful of the words around us and only a thimbleful of the possible misspellings. Those two chapters (28 and 29) followed twenty-seven chapters about the structure of the spelling system. This illustrates a very simple moral: *spelling analysis* must precede spelling error analysis.

With a misspelled word we expect a teacher to answer the question 'What's wrong with this word?' (and to get it right!). But with a word written as it should be in SOE, the teacher is never asked the question 'How do you analyse the spelling of this word?' Yet it is agreed analyses of standard spellings which can lead to agreed strategies and to agreed policies of teaching the spelling system. In fact, *disagreed* analyses are far, far better than no analyses at all: they generate *talk* – and that way lies the path to greater understanding.

30.4 Orthographic quality

That question, 'How do you analyse the spelling of this word?', is the seed question from which the concept of spelling analysis grows. But standard spelling is only part of SOE – the spelling system is only part of the standard writing-system. It is SOE, the whole writing-system (see Chapter 27), which provides the framework of layout, elaboration, punctuation, spelling, script (the handwriting of letters *and* of figures) to which all teachers work.

Orthographic quality, like any other quality that is subject to decay, is maintained by continuous effort. That's how the reliable orthographic quality of most of the print you read – books, forms, advertisements, magazines, maps, bus-tickets, notices, even newspapers – is maintained.

The single greatest force in that maintenance is the education system, which at one and the same time operates with SOE and initiates children into SOE.

30.5 Literacy

In 1970 *Breakthrough to Literacy*[2] insisted on the full stop right from the start for the sentences children composed. This symbolises the fact that all writing uses a writing-system embodying grammatical units, not just a spelling system embodying isolated words. My own feeling is that going for orthographic quality as a whole takes spelling along with it: that you can afford at intervals to let spelling develop on its own, as long as you are monitoring it and as long as you are fostering growing control of SOE overall.

Breakthrough to Literacy was well-named. In the 1960s, if you looked up 'Literacy' in an index, you found a cross-reference (if you found an entry at all): 'Literacy – see Illiteracy'. That began to change in the 1970s. One catalyst was the positive 'adult literacy' campaign. Another was the success in schools of *Breakthrough* itself: 'beginning reading' began to be subsumed, together with 'beginning writing', under the more general term 'initial literacy'.

All I want to say now about this fundamental linguistic concept 'literacy' is to repeat what I said in Part I: whether reading or writing, we are using the spelling system. To associate spelling with writing and not with reading is to teach literacy with one arm tied behind your back – and to tie the learner up in the same way.

[2] David Mackay *et al. Breakthrough to Literacy (Teachers Manual)*, London: Longman, 1970 (reissued 1995).

30.6   Across the curriculum

Some of the best teaching I have ever seen was in PE. The organisation, the instruction, the motivation was all done by voice (and the presence that goes with voice face-to-face). The language was English. The language in which the class was learning (and they knew they were getting good value!) was the language the teacher was using – standard English, pretty colloquial at times, but still the English of the curriculum, not one of the plentiful dialect varieties of English in the world today.

Do children write about PE? Do they read about PE? Think of all that vocabulary that goes with PE, some of it common stock (°one °two °three . . . °up!), some of it special to PE (°gym – a CVC word: I've heard students claim it as a word 'with no vowel' . . .), some of it bestriding the curriculum, like °vault, with one foot, so to speak, in the gym and the other in engineering. And speaking of common-stock vocabulary, I'm reminded of the maths student familiar with the term 'differential' but who wrote *differant consistently for °different.

There is continuity across the curriculum as well as along it, and it can be harnessed to progression.

30.7   Along the curriculum

There is no way of telling 'by ear' whether to write °different or *differant, so an ERF like °differential, whether you actively use the word or not, is invaluable (compare °existential in Section 29.1). As we can see from the maths student, guidance is needed. It was needed over the spelling *definately in Chapter 3. This is a misspelling which you can expect at some point in a learner's progress; it's not serious. But guidance is needed, at the right time – certainly in time to prevent the learner from writing *defination for °definition, a word which comes into vocabulary later than °definite/definitely.

This guidance can come, and should come, from the teaching staff as a whole. SOE, spelling system and all, is the common property of the curriculum. This is the spelling system which has organised the morphemes of the language into written form, and once its morphemic nature has been understood learners can be guided through it. It has structure and is as susceptible to analysis as any other aspect of the world we live in.

As we have seen many times in this book, vocabulary and spelling interlock; each can be a limiting factor on the other, each can be a liberating factor for the other. We undermine the rationality of our curriculum if we allow spelling to breed irrational attitudes at its core. To be struggling at sixteen with elementary problems you first encountered at six is not the way to gain confidence through education or in education.

30.8   Beyond the curriculum

The three educations in the title of this chapter can be linked to these three sections, 30.6, 30.7 and 30.8.

Education of the teachers: Across the curriculum

The children are experiencing the whole of the curriculum. Teachers must cater for that experience as a whole. In SOE they have a framework which the children need and which the teachers across the curriculum can all supply as they use it. Where the spelling system is concerned, they have hugely extensive and highly accessible data, both in reading and writing, to which a model structure can be applied; they can be exploring and learning that structure for themselves at the same time as they facilitate (and explore) children's learning of it. This is the axis of the curriculum on which the teachers' own literacy learning can concentrate.

Education of the children: Along the curriculum

The children experience the whole of the curriculum as they move progressively through it week by week and year by year. This movement is the children's, not the teachers'. Eleven years is a long time: over that time the concept of spelling and the control of spelling can develop at a leisurely pace, if guided by teachers professionally equipped for the job. This axis of the curriculum is unique to children, and too precious to waste.

Education of the community: Beyond the curriculum

Most people are not in school, either as children or as teachers. But we all have schooling and SOE and its spelling system in common. School is not the only place to talk about spelling: talk can go on all the time, within the generations and between the generations, if the necessary concepts and language (terminology/notation) are there. And they can be acquired at any stage in life, at any age – and still give the same sense of discovery, including self-discovery.

30.9 Last scene of all

An echo, in this title, of old age. But though the spelling system awaits discovery for some people in retirement, I want to end back in the early years of literacy. Marian wrote last Christmas:

> thankyou for the lovely
> birth of Jesus seen

The grammatical structure of this is complicated: the phrase 'birth of Jesus' which itself contains a prepositional phrase 'of Jesus' is used as an adjectival phrase on a par with the adjective 'lovely' (but you can't swap places and say the 'birth of Jesus lovely scene'); and this whole complicated noun phrase 'the lovely birth of Jesus scene' is itself dependent on a preposition 'for', making a prepositional phrase which in turn is dependent on 'thankyou'. °thankyou is correctly spelled (though it needn't be written solid), the three Function Words, °for °the °of, are correctly spelled, the proper name (capitalised) and the two Content Words are correctly spelled, including the discontinuous symbol and the plus-junction in °lovely (same correspondence as in °come).

What price *seen? Marian is nine. There is plenty of time for her to discover the difference between the morpheme °seen (or is it two morphemes?) and the morpheme °scene. She may discover it in her *reading*. I hope she will have someone to *talk* to about it: once she has learnt to notice these things, she will learn rapidly.